from Sound to Symbol

Fundamentals of Music

SECOND EDITION

MÍCHEÁL HOULAHAN
Millersville University of Pennsylvania

PHILIP TACKA
Millersville University of Pennsylvania

D0103344

New York   Oxford

OXFORD UNIVERSITY PRESS

Oxford University Press, Inc., publishes works that further Oxford University's
objective of excellence in research, scholarship, and education.

Oxford New York
Auckland Cape Town Dar es Salaam Hong Kong Karachi
Kuala Lumpur Madrid Melbourne Mexico City Nairobi
New Delhi Shanghai Taipei Toronto

With offices in
Argentina Austria Brazil Chile Czech Republic France Greece
Guatemala Hungary Italy Japan Poland Portugal Singapore
South Korea Switzerland Thailand Turkey Ukraine Vietnam

For titles covered by Section 112 of the US Higher Education Opportunity Act, please
visit www.oup.com/us/he for the latest information about pricing and alternate formats.

Published by Oxford University Press, Inc.
198 Madison Avenue, New York, New York 10016
http://www.oup.com

Oxford is a registered trademark of Oxford University Press

Library of Congress Cataloging-in-Publication Data

Houlahan, Mícheál.
    From sound to symbol : fundamentals of music / Mícheál Houlahan, Philip Tacka. -- 2nd ed.
       p. cm.
    ISBN 978-0-19-975191-4 (pbk.)
 1. Music theory--Textbooks. I. Tacka, Philip. II. Title.
    MT6.H598 2011
    781.2—dc22
                                            2010049220

Printing number: 9 8 7 6 5 4 3 2

Printed in the United States of America
on acid-free paper

To all those from whom we continue to learn

Contents

Preface

We perceive the world without labels, and we can label it only when we have decided how its features should be organized.

Israel Rosenfield

Part of the musicianship of many (but not all) musical practices worldwide is knowledge about notation and knowledge of how to decode and encode musical sound patterns in staff notation, graphic notation, hand signs, or rhythmic syllables. But "music literacy," or the ability to decode and encode a system of musical notation, is not equivalent to musicianship. It is only part of the formal and procedural dimensions of musicianship. Moreover, literacy should be taught and learned parenthetically and contextually—as a coding problem to be gradually reduced within the larger process of musical problem solving through active music making.

David Elliott[1]

During the past decade, much has been written about teaching music fundamentals. Although music theorists believe that music performance, music theory, sight singing, and dictation skills should have equal importance in the fundamentals curriculum, fundamentals textbooks do not reflect this conviction. A review of these texts reveals that most are formulaic in structure and follow a traditional presentation of symbol to sound. Although this model of teaching certainly promotes theoretical understanding of the fundamentals of music theory, its effectiveness for developing sight singing and aural skills is questionable in light of current research in the field of music perception and cognition. We have used traditional theory books in our teaching, and these works have influenced our own research and approach. We are grateful to Michael R. Rogers (*Teaching Approaches in Music Theory*), Thomas Manoff (*The Music Kit*), William Duckworth (*A Creative Approach to Music Fundamentals*), José Rodríguez Alvira (*Music Teoria*), and the Associated Board of the Royal Schools of Music for their pedagogical insights as well as selection of musical materials.

---

[1]David J. Elliott, *Music Matters: A New Philosophy of Music Education* (New York: Oxford University Press, 1995), 61.

OUR APPROACH

This fundamentals text-workbook develops students' knowledge of music theory by first building a deep understanding of the rhythmic and melodic building blocks of music. Although some of the routines we suggest may seem repetitive to the instructor, they ultimately ensure students' grasp of music fundamentals that are common to a variety of musical styles. In the first section of each chapter, we guide students in listening to, memorizing, singing, and analyzing by ear short musical examples that demonstrate musical concepts and elements. Next, we show students how to describe a piece of music with rhythm or solfège syllables before showing them how to notate the piece of music on the staff. This is the essence of our sound-to-symbol approach: students learn first how to listen and then how to notate, internalizing basic musical concepts in the process. The first section of each chapter concludes with key terms and concepts, suggestions for practice, suggestions for incorporating the in-text Skills CD into a practice schedule, and a guide to reading a particular musical score. In the second section of each chapter, we provide students with a variety of music theory exercises to practice music notation.

Our approach to teaching reverses the pedagogical process normally associated with a traditional theory classroom—one where symbols are presented before being linked to sounds. Some research suggests that this "subject-logic" approach often leads to a superficial development of aural and sight singing skills and to subsequent problems in understanding music theory concepts.[2] We believe that helping students understand musical sounds first and *then* linking this knowledge to an understanding of musical symbols is the most efficient and effective approach to developing music literacy skills. As the noted educator David J. Hargreaves points out, "The intuitive experience and enjoyment of music should come first, such that the latter acquisition of formal musical skills occurs inductively . . . A good deal of traditional music education has worked deductively: the formal rules have been taught in the abstract, for example, through verbal description or written notation, rather than in the practical context of making the sounds themselves."[3]

Discovery learning and collaborative learning are at the center of the learning process, and we have used these techniques throughout the text. We have also relied on the most compelling research findings from the fields of Kodály studies as well as music perception and cognition to guide our presentation.

In our approach, theoretical explanations are the final stage of musical learning. Musical concepts and elements are derived from major, minor, and modal folk songs and art music examples. Beginning with folk music and art music with a limited range of notes allows each rhythmic and melodic element to be introduced sequentially, using the three phases of instruction and learning: cognitive (preparation), associative (presentation), and assimilative (practice). As a result, students develop a strong association between the sounds and the symbols of music. We are convinced that these phases of instruction and learning are of prime importance in the development of musical memory, sight singing, ear training, and dictation skills. In the context of this sequence, musical elements are not abstracted from a musical example but are presented in relation to a complete musical composition.

---

[2]Michael R. Rogers, *Teaching Approaches in Music Theory* (Carbondale, IL: Southern Illinois University Press, 2004).

[3]D. J. Hargreaves, *The Developmental Psychology of Music* (London: Cambridge University Press, 1986), 215.

Although our pedagogical approach is the reverse of the traditional symbol-to-sound approach, the text introduces the essentials of music fundamentals in the same order as other fundamentals theory texts. The main difference between our text and others is that we initially explore all theoretical information *perceptually* through instructor-guided activities. Only after students have experienced the musical elements and concepts presented do we explain them in detail. By exploring rhythmic and melodic patterns through kinesthetic, aural, and visual activities before learning the traditional names and terms, students internalize musical knowledge rapidly—and we've found that it sticks with them.

We are convinced that all students benefit from a perceptual orientation to music instruction and learning that allows them to simultaneously develop both theoretical and musicianship skills. This text offers a comprehensive approach to teaching music fundamentals that positions music listening, performance, critical thinking, and creativity as the basis for a music education. We hope that you'll find it useful, and if we can answer questions, please don't hesitate to contact us at micheal.houlahan@millersville.edu and philip.tacka@millersville.edu.

New to the Second Edition

- Chapters start with **helpful overviews** and are now divided into two sections: an introduction to basic concepts followed by written music theory exercises.
- All chapters include **more written exercises**, grouped together in tear-out sections, and the in-text Skills CD includes more dictation exercises for each chapter.
- **"How to Read a Musical Score"** sections in Chapters 1–9 ask students to identify newly learned musical elements in more complex musical works.
- **"How to Practice"** sections in Chapters 1–11 guide students in developing greater mastery of the chapter material.
- The *la* **minor and** *do* **minor approaches** to pedagogy are now clearly distinguished and separated in Chapters 8 and 9.
- **All forms of the minor scale are included in one chapter** (Chapter 9) instead of two.
- **Chapters 10 and 11 on triads and harmony have been reorganized** to reflect a traditional sequence for presentation of this material but through a sound-to-symbol approach.
- A **new chapter, "Composing a Song"** (Chapter 12), provides students with the opportunity to apply their cumulative knowledge to writing songs and music compositions, reinforcing concepts presented throughout the book.
- **Pages have been redesigned for clarity**, with two marginal icons—one referencing the in-text Audio CD (with track numbers) and one referencing longer pieces available on iTunes or YouTube for further study. Pages are also perforated and three-hole-punched for convenience.
- **Key Terms and Concepts** are included after the first sections of Chapters 1–11.
- A new **Glossary of Musical Terms** is included at the back of the text.
- A **Companion Website at www.oup.com/us/houlahan** offers both students and instructors extensive additional resources. Students will find supplementary musicianship exercises to develop their singing, memory, audiation, sight singing, and keyboard skills. Instructors will find video clips of the authors teaching, sample lesson plans and teaching strategies, and sample tests and assessment rubrics.

Distinctive Features

- This fundamentals text-workbook takes a sound-to-symbol approach—that is, it explores concepts initially through the sound of music before moving to an explanation of how symbols are used to represent the sound—to cover all the traditional topics of music fundamentals.
- We use examples from both folk songs and classical music that are simple, memorable, and easy to sing or play, allowing students to actively engage in the learning process and easily internalize concepts. These easily learned musical examples provide the scaffolding for future learning in each succeeding chapter. Their simplicity and familiarity make them excellent tools for guiding students through layers of increasing detail. Students learn to combine and manipulate these concepts to read, write, improvise, and compose increasingly complex music.
- "Sing, Memorize, and Analyze" sections ask students to listen to a melody from the in-text Audio CD and then construct a representation from memory without using standard music notation.
- Once students can aurally and visually discern the attributes of a particular melodic or rhythmic pattern, "Music Theory" sections explain how to describe as well as notate these sounds.
- The in-text Audio CD includes all essential melodies from the book, examples of chord functions and harmonic progressions, and several exercises to develop singing skills.
- "Listening" sections suggest longer pieces available on iTunes or YouTube for further study.
- The in-text Skills CD, created in collaboration with José Rodríguez Alvira of the Conservatory of Music of Puerto Rico, provides tutorials for chapter review, theory exercise drills, and dictation exercises. "Using the Musical Skills CD" sections offer suggestions for incorporating the in-text Skills CD into practice sessions.
- Because music performance is at the heart of learning, we focus on active music-making, supported by activities. We use kinesthetic, aural, and visual modes of learning as means of helping students understand the fundamentals of music.
- Exercises at the end of each chapter and online at **www.oup.com/us/houlahan** develop both theoretical understanding and musicianship skills at progressive levels of difficulty.
- A fold-out, laminated keyboard is included at the back of the text.

ACKNOWLEDGMENTS

Many individuals have provided us with invaluable advice and assistance in both scholarly and practical matters in the production of this book. At Oxford University Press, we thank Janet M. Beatty, executive editor, and Lauren Mine, associate editor, for their encouragement and critical guidance. Many thanks, too, to Jennifer Bossert, senior production editor, for expertly shepherding the manuscript through copyediting and typesetting. Our students at Georgetown University, Washington, D.C.; Millersville University of Pennsylvania; Texas State University, San Marcos, Texas; Belmont University in Nashville, Tennessee; and The Eastman School of Music in Rochester, New York, have all helped us shape the approach of instruction and learning that is presented herein. José

Rodríguez Alvira (*Music Teoria*) is due a great debt of gratitude for his help in creating the Skills CD that accompanies *From Sound to Symbol*. We also thank our recording artists, Ashley J. Walker, voice, and Tyler Riegel, piano. We thank Dr. Jennifer Jester for her guidance and assistance with the audio recording. We thank our students Seth Moyer and Tyler Hart for their assistance in creating a number of the musical examples found throughout the book and on the website. We thank the following reviewers of this edition for their comments and suggestions: Margaret Angelini, Stonehill College; Mark Carlson, Richland College; Jeff Donovick, St. Petersburg College; Ann Fairbanks, University of St. Thomas; Laura Kelly, University of Texas at San Antonio; Stephen Moro, University of Toledo; Ron Newman, Michigan State University; Michael Pisani, Vassar College; Teresa Reed, University of Tulsa; Jennifer Russell, Northern Arizona University; and Mark Zanter, Marshall University. Special thanks are due to Nico Schüler of Texas State University for his critical reading of the manuscript and his insightful suggestions.

Introduction

Even if you have no formal training in music, you already have a considerable intuitive knowledge of music. You know what music you like, as well as what performers you like to listen to. The primary goal of this book is to simultaneously develop your musical thought, your knowledge of music fundamentals, and your musicianship skills.

In order to help you grow as a musician, each chapter of the book has been designed to show you how to apply your new knowledge in creative ways. Learning about music fundamentals will undoubtedly add to your enjoyment of music, both as a listener and as a performer.

The Six Basic Elements of Music

The basic elements of music are found in all styles of music. These elements include:

Rhythm
Melody
Texture
Form
Harmony
Timbre

Rhythm can be defined as "the perceptible organization of musical events in time."[1] If you sing a melody with text and clap the words, then you are clapping the

---

[1] Definitions in quotation marks are from *The Oxford Dictionary of Musical Terms*.

rhythm of a melody. You will be working with rhythm throughout this text, but we will devote Chapter 1, Chapter 3, and Chapter 10 to a more in-depth study of it.

Melody is composed of musical sounds, and they may be high or low. *Pitch* is the highness or lowness of a musical sound. Another name for a *high note* is a *high pitch*, and another name for a *low note* is a *low pitch*. *Melody* may also be defined as "a succession of notes of varying pitch with an organized and recognized shape." "Pitch" is a basic dimension of musical sounds, in which they are heard to be high or low. Melody is the result of the interaction of rhythm and pitch. We will devote Chapters 2, 4, 5, 6, 7, 8, and 9 to the study of melody and pitch.

Texture refers to how the individual instrumental or vocal parts in a piece of music are combined. The texture of the melodies in this text is *monophonic*, meaning that they contain one line of music. When a melody has an accompaniment, we refer to this music as *homophonic*. When a piece of music is composed of several lines of music, or *voices*, and each voice part is of equal importance, we refer to this music as *polyphonic*. In this book we will sing a number of homophonic and polyphonic examples.

Form describes the structure, architecture, or organization of a piece of music. Each phrase of music is labeled with a letter. The first phrase is always labeled "A." If the second phrase is the same as the first, we repeat the letter "A"; if it is different, we use the letter "B". If the phrase is similar, we can use A1, meaning *A prime*, or *Av*, meaning *variation*. Throughout the text, we will examine the form of musical examples as well as use this element as a guide to composing and improvising music. Sometimes musicians prefer to use lowercase letters for describing the form of shorter music examples such as folk songs.

Harmony is the simultaneous sounding of notes. When three or more pitches are produced at the same time, the resulting sound is called a *chord*. Chords are the building blocks of harmony. A series of chords is referred to as *harmony*. We will study the basics of harmony in Chapters 11 and 12.

Timbre refers to the tone quality of sound. The properties of sound are most clearly evidenced through a brief review of musical instruments. Musical instruments produce different timbres. For example, a piano that plays the note middle C produces a pitch that vibrates at about 260 vibrations per second (vps); a violin can produce that same number of vibrations per second, but the sound quality (timbre) is distinctively different. So is that of a clarinet playing the same pitch. Timbre enables us to distinguish and classify musical instruments according to various families. The following are the musical instruments found in Western and American art music:

Strings

String instruments produce sound by plucking the string or drawing a bow across it, producing vibration. Members of the string family include violin, viola, cello, double bass, guitar, banjo, harp, and lute, among others.

Woodwind

Sound is generated in wind instruments by the vibration of air through a tube or pipe. Covering the finger holes in woodwind instruments changes the length of the vibrating column of air, producing different pitches. Members of the woodwind family include piccolo, flute, clarinet, oboe, bassoon, English horn, and saxophone.

Brass

The varying length of tubing produces the fundamental pitch, and different air speeds produce the notes of the overtone series. Members of the brass family include trumpet, trombone, French horn, tuba, euphonium, and cornet.

Percussion

Percussion instruments produce sound by being struck. Percussion instruments include timpani, snare drum, castanets, chimes, cymbals, and triangle. Pitched percussion, such as xylophone, marimba, and vibraphone, are barred instruments that are struck with mallets.

Keyboard Instruments

Members of the keyboard family include, piano, harpsichord, and organ.

The Multiple Dimensions of Musicianship

All musicians, no matter what style of music they perform, share the following: performance ability, critical-thinking skills, creativity, informed listening, and stewardship of musical repertoire. Therefore, when developing musicianship skills, we need to address the different facets of what it means to be a musical human being. These facets are encompassed in the design of each chapter. All musicians practice, and your task will be to develop your own practice strategies that will allow you to become skilled in the multiple dimensions of musicianship.

A. Musicians as Performers: Singing, Playing Instruments, and Conducting

Music performance is at the core of this text. Through performance you will engage in singing, playing instruments, and conducting. We have recorded melodies that we will use to abstract knowledge of music fundamentals. Please put these melodies on your iPod and listen to them frequently until you can sing them from memory. All of these melodies are performed without accompaniment so that you can listen more carefully to the rhythms and melodies. Most of the material we have chosen is easy to sing and memorize. You will find yourself humming these melodies; this is really the first step in developing your musicianship skills as well as playing an instrument. Remember that we are going to teach you how to internalize the sounds of music before we show you how to notate these melodies. Once you have mastered singing and notating simple melodies, you will be able to tackle more complicated ones.

B. Musicians as Stewards of Musical Repertoire

All great performers, including jazz, popular, and classical musicians, have a detailed knowledge and understanding of the repertoire they perform. In this book we want to provide you with an understanding of several types of repertoire. One type, folk music, comes from an oral tradition, meaning music that has been passed on from one generation of musicians to another without being learned through notation. This is quite similar to some jazz musicians, who learn their repertoire by ear and not from notation. We will also study classical melodies that we will learn through notation for teaching music fundamentals. Each chapter includes melodies, sometimes referred to as *focus songs*. These melodies have been recorded on the accompanying CD. This material is suited to the development of your knowledge of fundamentals of music. Through their tradition of oral transmission, folk songs have long been considered ideal for developing ear training and musical memory. Each chapter will show you how to aurally analyze these melodies before we show you how to notate them. In this way, you will be developing the same skills used by musicians of both the oral and classical music traditions. Your instructor will be able to demonstrate lots of other examples drawn from different styles of music.

C. Musicians as Critical Thinkers: Music Literacy

Folk music has existed for centuries without a notation system, but other styles of music, such as European and American art music (composed by Mozart, Beethoven, Gershwin, and Ellington), were notated, and we need to be able to read this music to perform it. But no matter what style of music, all musicians are critical thinkers. They understand the basic building blocks of the music they perform either aurally or visually. In each chapter you will learn how to aurally analyze these building blocks of music and how to read and write musical notation. To accommodate the teaching of rhythmic and melodic elements, we use teaching tools to facilitate instruction and learning; they assist your musical skill development as well as your musicality. We will use the moveable *do* system of solmization, and rhythmic syllables. The moveable do or tonic sol-fa system can be traced to the eleventh century, when Guido d'Arezzo (991/992–after 1033) used a form of it for musical instruction. This system was adapted by Sarah Glover (1785–1867), an English music teacher; her system was later adapted by John Curwen (1816–1880).

The following chart shows the solfège syllables for the natural, raised, and lowered steps of the major scale. Solfège syllables are always written in lowercase letters. We will use the abbreviated form of the solfège syllable, first syllable only in *lowercase*, throughout the book. We prefer to use the syllables *ma*, *lo*, and *ta* to achieve a darker-sounding note. But other instructors prefer to use *me*, *le*, and *te*.

raised scale steps		di	ri	*		fi	si	li	*	
natural scale steps	do	re	mi	fa	so	la	ti	do		
			ma			lo	ta			
lowered scale			or			or	or			
steps	*	ra	me	*	sa	le	te			

* = not used

The upper octave is indicated by a superscript prime placed on the syllable, e.g., example *d′*.

The lower octave is indicated by a subscript prime on the syllable, e.g., *d′*.

Letter Names

Letter names become significant to students when they are applied to an instrument, because a letter name has both an absolute position on the staff and a fingering on an instrument. The German letter names can be used for singing because they may be sung with one syllable and therefore will not compromise the rhythmic integrity of the musical example. For example, instead of singing *F-sharp* (two syllables), students sing *fis*. Letter names are always written with uppercase, e.g., F, G, D.

The German system of letter names:

sharps	ais	bis	cis	dis	eis	fis	gis
natural	A	B	C	D	E	F	G
flats	ass	bes	ces	des	ees	fes	ges

Rhythm Syllables

We use rhythm syllables and counting with numbers to help read and write music. Rhythm syllables will help you associate a syllable with the number of sounds you hear on particular beats. This is the first step in understanding music notation. Once you can notate music, you can use rhythm syllables or numbers to help you count music and perform it correctly. The French pedagogue Emile-Joseph Chevé (1804–1864) developed rhythm syllables in the nineteenth century. There are many rhythmic reading systems available. We use the Takadimi system.[2] These rhythm syllables are not related to the notation of music but rather to the number of sounds occurring on the beat.

D. Students as Creative Human Beings: Music Composition and Improvisation

Music improvisation, the art of composing extemporaneously, and composition, the art of formulating and writing music, are indispensable components of a music education. We use improvisation and composition activities so that you will develop the ability to understand the creative process in music as well as the stylistic elements of a piece. Students who are able to improvise and compose music based on the typical forms, melodic patterns, and rhythmic patterns of folk songs and art music have developed a greater feeling and understanding for musical style. Improvisation will enable you to create your own music compositions.

E. Students as Informed Audience Members

Although we begin each chapter with simple folk melodies, we will try to show you how a particular concept can be found not just in a simple folk song but also in an example of jazz or classical music.

Music listening is an important component of each chapter. No matter what music activity you will be engaged in, you will be provided with opportunities to listen when you perform, create, and develop your critical-thinking skills.

---

[2]Richard Hoffman, William Pelto, and John W. White, "Takadimi: A Beat-Oriented System of Rhythm Pedagogy," *Journal of Music Theory Pedagogy* 10 (1996): 7–30. Throughout this text, we cite this approach to teaching rhythm. From our own work with university as well as elementary-school students, we are strongly convinced that it is a superior system for rhythmic reading and hearing.

Chapter 1

Basic Rhythms in Simple Meter

CHAPTER OVERVIEW

In this chapter you will be studying one of the basic elements of music—rhythm. Before you begin to learn any music theory concept, you will have the chance to learn a short musical example found on the audio CD. As you sing each example, pay particular attention to the phrasing; this corresponds to punctuation in language. The chapter begins with a discussion of phrasing and the construction of simple melodies. Becoming musically engaged with the material before you start learning about music theory concepts will ultimately make those concepts clearer in your mind.

The goal of this chapter is to focus your listening skills so you will be able to aurally identify aspects of rhythm. We will instruct you in how to aurally identify basic rhythms as well as how to notate them. You will also learn how to read and perform basic rhythm patterns plus compose and improvise using basic rhythm patterns. Start by locating a recording or YouTube performance of Steve Reich's (1936–) *Clapping Music*, composed in 1972. Although quite complex, this piece of music is composed of the basic rhythms you will study in this chapter.

1.1 Phrase, Beat, and Tempo

Phrase

Listen to "Are You Sleeping" on Track 1. Memorize the song.

Sing "Are You Sleeping" and determine the number of breaths you take when singing the whole song. Each time you take a breath, this indicates a phrase of music.

Phrases indicate breathing points in the music. A **phrase** is a musical unit defined by the interrelation of melody, rhythm, and harmony that ends with a **cadence** (a point of rest) of some kind. The length of phrases varies, and a phrase is often followed by an answering phrase of the same length. A **phrase mark** (the arched line above each line of music) suggests a musical idea.

As you sing "Are You Sleeping," trace phrase marks on the paper.

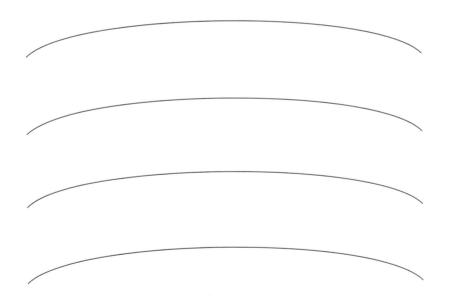

Form

Form describes the structure, architecture, or organization of a piece of music. Form is indicated with letters. Each phrase of music is labeled with a letter. The first phrase is always labeled *a*. If the second phrase is the same as the first, we repeat the letter *a*; if it is different, we use a different letter. If the phrase is similar, we can use *a′* meaning a variation (a prime or superscript). "Are You Sleeping" has four phrases, and they are labeled *a b c d*. These letters indicate the form of the composition. We use lowercase letters for small music compositions and uppercase letters to indicate the form for larger compositions.

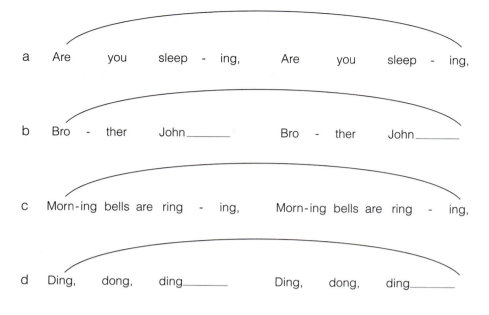

a Are   you   sleep - ing,   Are   you   sleep - ing,

b Bro - ther   John_____   Bro - ther   John_____

c Morn-ing bells are ring - ing,   Morn-ing bells are ring - ing,

d Ding,   dong,   ding_____   Ding,   dong,   ding_____

Dynamics

Dynamics refers to the varying and contrasting degrees of loudness or sound intensity of a composition. Scientists use the term *amplitude*. Although amplitude is measured in decibels, dynamics are often indicated with Italian, French, German, or English words. In music we use the letter *f* (*forte* in Italian) to indicate loud and *p* (*piano* in Italian) to indicate soft.

Consider the text and determine which phrases should be sung *forte* (loud) and which phrases should be sung *piano* (soft). Once you determine the form of a composition, decide appropriate dynamics for the performance. There are many solutions for the performance of this and all songs.

Beat and Pulsation

Music takes place over a period of time and therefore can be called a temporal art. When you clap the words of a song, you are clapping the rhythm. **Duration** is the length of time a sound lasts. Patterns of duration or beats are called **rhythm**. The basis for rhythm is **beat**, a regular series of **pulsations** that divides a period of time into equal parts. As you listen to the songs on the CD, you will notice that they are accompanied by the beat.

In general, music has a steady beat. When we tap our foot during the performance of a composition, we are responding to the pulse of the music. Listeners may feel different levels of pulsation in music, each of which may be referred to as the beat. Beat is used to describe how time in music is broken into repeating units. The duration of all notes or silences can be measured by the beat in music. We can demonstrate the beat through clapping, marching, tapping our feet, or even dancing. We can use *blocks* to represent the beat, as we will do throughout this text.

Beat Blocks

Notation

Notation is a representation of the musical sounds we hear. We use music symbols to notate music. The beat can be represented by the following types of notes. (There are other note values that will be introduced in the text.)

Beats can be represented by **quarter notes**.

A quarter note is made up of a **note head** and a **stem**. Note heads are oval. A stem can go up or down from a note head.

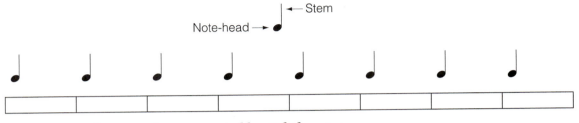

Beats can be represented by **eighth notes**.
An eighth note is made up of note head, a stem, and a **flag**.

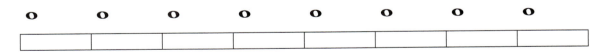

When the stem is pointing up, it is always placed on the right side of the note head. When the stem is pointing down, it is always placed on the left side of the note head. The flag is always placed to the right of the stem.

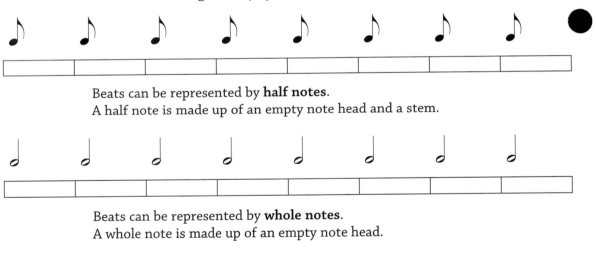

Beats can be represented by **half notes**.
A half note is made up of an empty note head and a stem.

Beats can be represented by **whole notes**.
A whole note is made up of an empty note head.

Tempo

Tempo refers to the speed of the beat. The tempo can be fast or slow and therefore has an impact on the speed of the piece. We use a metronome marking to indicate the tempo. The metronome was a machine for establishing an regulating the speed of a performance, specifically the clockwork-driven machine introduced by Johann Nepomuk Maelzel in 1815. Some composers indicate the intended speed of a piece by giving the metronome marking: MM (Metronome Maelzel) = beats per minute.

Tempo markings indicate the appropriate tempo.

Some common tempo indications:

Name	Approximate Speed	Approximate Beats per Minute
Adagio	slow	50
Andante	somewhat slow	72
Moderato	moderate speed	96
Allegro	fast	120
Presto	very fast	152

Listening

All listening suggestions can be downloaded from iTunes or viewed on YouTube. Your instructor will also share examples with you of music that includes particular concepts and elements that you are learning about in each chapter. It is also important for you to listen to your own music and try to identify some of the elements of music that you are studying in each chapter.

Listen to the following examples. Can you determine the tempo and the beat?

"March" from *The Nutcracker Suite* by Peter Ilich Tchaikovsky (1840–1893).

"Hornpipe" from *Water Music* by George Frideric Handel (1685–1759).

"Spring" from *The Four Seasons* by Antonio Vivaldi (1678–1741).

"The Ball" from *Children's Games* by Georges Bizet (1838–1875).

Louis Armstrong (1901–1971) playing "12th Street Rag".

1.2 Introduction to Meter

Sing, Memorize, and Analyze

2

Internalizing Music

1. Listen to "Rocky Mountain" on Track 2. Memorize the song.
2. Sing "Rocky Mountain" and tap the pulse.

Analyzing What You Hear

1. Sing "Rocky Mountain" and determine the number of phrases in the song.
2. How many beats are in each phrase of "Rocky Mountain"?
3. Which beats of "Rocky Mountain" seem stronger?

Constructing a Rhythmic Representation from Memory

1. As you sing "Rocky Mountain", draw a representation indicating the number of phrases you sing in the song and the number of beats you tap in each phrase.
2. Once you have counted the phrases and the beats in each phrase, determine which beats seem stronger.

Meter

Meter is the regular grouping of beats that occur in patterns of strong (accented) and weak (unaccented) beats.

As you listen to music, you will notice that some beats are stronger than others. The strong beats are called *primary beats* (or *accented beats*) and are followed by weak beats. These weak beats are called *secondary beats* or *unaccented beats*. This grouping of strong and weak beats forms a recurring pattern known as the *meter*.

The most common meters are duple, triple, and quadruple. We can use the sign > to indicate an accent. Please note that the tempo, how quickly or slowly you keep a beat, does not change the meter.

Listen to "Rocky Mountain" again. It is an example of **duple meter**.

In duple meter, a primary beat (accented) is followed by a secondary beat (unaccented).

"America (My Country 'Tis of Thee)" is an example of **triple meter**.

In triple meter, a primary beat is followed by two secondary beats. The first beat is the *downbeat* and is stronger than beats two and three. The third beat is sometimes experienced as an *upbeat* leading to the downbeat. Consider the first phrase of "America." It is written in triple meter.

"Are You Sleeping" is an example of **quadruple meter**.

In quadruple meter, a primary beat is followed by three secondary beats. Consider the first phrase of "Are You Sleeping." It is written in quadruple meter.

All of these meters are **simple meters** because the basic pulse can be divided into two equal parts, as you will discover in the next section.

Measures

Measures mark each pattern of strong and weak beats. Each measure is indicated by vertical lines called **bar lines**. There is always a bar line in front of a strong beat. (There is no bar line at the beginning of a composition.)

Double Bar Line

A **double bar line** indicates the end of a piece of music or the end of a section. Two bar lines of equal width indicate the end of a large section of a piece, and one thin bar line followed by one thick bar line indicates the end of a piece of music. As with strong and weak beats, measures can also form strong and weak combinations. For example, "America" is in triple meter; the measures of this melody also group into a strong-and-weak pattern. This pattern is referred to as a *duple hypermeter*.

bar line ↑   bar lines of equal width ↑   double bar line ↑

Conducting Patterns

To keep the beat, a conductor uses the following patterns. **Conducting patterns** help indicate the primary and secondary beats. Perform conducting patterns with the right hand. The first beat of each pattern is called the downbeat. To begin conducting, remember to give an upbeat; this is always the beat before the first beat of the piece.

The conducting pattern for duple meter is:

1   2

The conducting pattern for triple meter is:

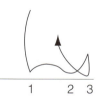

1   2 3

The conducting pattern for quadruple meter is:

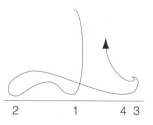

2   1   4 3

Listening   🎧   It is important for you to listen to your own music and try to identify the meter of some of your favorite pieces.

Listen to the following compositions and conduct.

Listening examples in duple meter:

"Bourée" from *Royal Fireworks Music* by George Frideric Handel (1685–1759).

"Romance" from *Eine Kleine Nachtmusik* by Wolfgang Amadeus Mozart (1756–1791).

Listening examples in triple meter:

Young Person's Guide to the Orchestra by Benjamin Britten (1913–1976).

Listening examples in quadruple meter:

"March" from *The Nutcracker* by Peter Ilich Tchaikovsky (1840–1893).
"Allegro" from *Eine Kleine Nachtmusik* by Wolfgang Amadeus Mozart (1756–1791).

Time Signatures in Simple Meter

Meter is the pattern of regular pulses (and the arrangement of their constituent parts) by which a piece of music is organized. One complete pattern is called a *measure*. The prevailing meter is identified at the beginning of a piece (and during it whenever it changes) by a time signature.

In a **time signature,** or meter signature, the top number indicates the number of beats in each measure, or the meter of the piece; the lower number indicates the note value to be used for describing the duration of the beat. In $\frac{4}{4}$ meter, there are four beats in each measure, and each beat is a quarter note in duration.

The number of beats in the measure ⟶ **4**

The note value that represents the beat ⟶ **4**

Duple-Meter Time Signatures

$\frac{2}{4}$ is often used as a duple-meter time signature. It indicates that each beat is given the value of a quarter note and there are two quarter-note beats per measure.

$\frac{2}{2}$ meter is used as a duple-meter time signature. It indicates that each beat is given the value of a half note and there are two half-note beats per measure. ₵ is often used to indicate meter and is referred to as *cut time*.

$\frac{2}{8}$ is often used as a simple duple-meter time signature. It indicates that each beat is given the value of an eighth note and there are two eighth notes per measure.

Triple-Meter Time Signatures

$\frac{3}{4}$ is often used as a triple-meter time signature. It indicates that each beat is given the value of a quarter note and there are three quarter-note beats per measure.

$\frac{3}{2}$ meter is often used as a triple-meter time signature. It indicates that each beat is given the value of a half note and there are three half-note beats per measure.

$\frac{3}{8}$ is often used as a simple triple-meter time signature. It indicates that each beat is given the value of an eighth note and there are three eighth notes per measure.

Quadruple-Meter Time Signatures

$\frac{4}{4}$ or **C** is often used as a quadruple-meter time signature. It indicates that each beat is given the value of a quarter note and there are four quarter-note beats per measure.

$\frac{4}{2}$ meter is often used as a quadruple-meter time signature. It indicates that each beat is given the value of a half note and there are four half-note beats per measure. In $\frac{4}{2}$ meter the music may require the use of a double whole note. A double whole note, ‖o‖ , is equal to four half notes.

$\frac{4}{8}$ is often used as a quadruple-meter time signature. It indicates that each beat is given the value of an eighth note and there are four eighth notes per measure.

Listening 🎧

Determine the meter of the following pieces of music and conduct each composition:

"Allegro assi," *Brandenburg Concerto No. 2*, by Johann Sebastian Bach (1685–1750).

"Adagio movement," Clarinet Concerto K. 622, by Wolfgang Amadeus Mozart (1756–1791).

"Elephant" from *Carnival of the Animals* by Camille Saint-Saëns (1835–1921).

"March movement" from *The Love of Three Oranges* by Sergei Prokofiev (1891–1953).

1.3 Basic Rhythm Patterns in Simple Meter

Sing, Memorize, and Analyze 💿

3

Internalizing Music

1. Listen to the theme of the Beethoven Violin Concerto on Track 3. Memorize the example.
2. Sing the theme of the Beethoven Violin Concerto on "loo" and keep the beat.
3. Sing the theme of the Beethoven Violin Concerto on "loo" and clap the rhythm.
4. Sing the theme of the Beethoven Violin Concerto while you tap the beat with your left hand and tap the rhythm with your right hand.

Analyzing What You Hear

Now we're going to ask you to think about what you've heard. We're asking you to draw on your musical memory without looking at any notation.

1. As you sing the theme of the Beethoven Violin Concerto, determine the number of beats within each phrase.
2. Which beats have one sound?
3. Which beats have two sounds?
4. Which beats have sounds that last longer than one beat?
5. Determine the number of sounds on each beat in each phrase of the theme of the Beethoven Violin Concerto.

Constructing a Rhythmic Representation from Memory

In-class or individual work:

1. As you sing the theme of the Beethoven Violin Concerto, draw a representation indicating the number of sounds you hear in each beat. Do not use traditional music notation.

Music Theory

Describing What You Hear with Rhythm Syllables

Rhythm syllables are one way for figuring out the rhythm of music that we hear. There are many rhythmic reading systems available; we use the *Takadimi* system, with slight modifications. It is important to remember that these rhythm syllables are related to the number of sounds occurring on the beat.

When we hear *one sound on the beat*, we can label it with the rhythm syllable *ta*. When we hear *two even sounds on the beat*, we can label them with the rhythm syllables *ta di*. The rhythm syllable *ta* is always assigned to the beat note. When we hear one sound over two beats, we label it with the rhythm syllable *ta–ah*, or *ta* (and hold it for two beats). When we hear one sound over four beats, we label it with the rhythm syllable *ta–ah–ah–ah*, or *ta* (and hold it for four beats).

Rhythm syllables for the theme from Beethoven's Violin Concerto

ta	ta	ta	ta	di	ta_____	ah_____	ta_____	ah_____

ta	ta	ta	ta	di	ta_____	ah_____	ta_____	ah_____

ta	ta	ta	ta	di	ta_____	ah_____	ta_____	ah_____

ta	ta	ta	ta	ta_____	ah_____	ah_____	ah_____

Notating What You Hear

Rhythm notation is a method for representing the number of actions in time. It indicates the number of actions as related to the pulsation we call *beat*. Rhythmic sounds are represented by symbols referred to as *notes*.

When the beat is assigned the value of a quarter note, one sound on a beat is a **quarter note**, two even sounds on a beat can be represented by two **eighth notes**, and one sound that lasts for two beats is called a **half note**. A note that is sustained for four beats is called a **whole note**.

Two half notes equal one whole note in duration when the beat is a quarter note in duration.

A whole note is equal to four quarter notes or two half notes when the beat is a quarter note in duration.

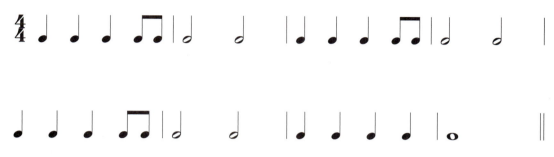

Here is the rhythmic notation for the theme from Beethoven's Violin Concerto.

Beams in Simple Meter

Notes are normally grouped, or **beamed,** according to the duration of the beat to facilitate the reading of rhythms. In $\frac{2}{4}$, $\frac{3}{4}$, and $\frac{4}{4}$ meter, since the beat is one quarter note long, two eighth notes are beamed as follows so that the number of beats can be seen more easily:

In $\frac{4}{4}$ meter, note that in the second measure the eighth notes on beats two and three are not connected.

In $\frac{3}{4}$ meter, if the measure is made up of all eighth notes, they may be joined together.

In some vocal music, eighth notes are sometimes written individually to facilitate the reading of a text.

Rock - y   moun - tain   rock - y   moun - tain

Counting with Numbers in Simple Meter
Counting with Numbers in Duple Meter

We can also use numbers as a method of counting music and figuring out the rhythm. In duple meter, we can count one note on a beat by calling it "one" on a strong beat and "two" on a weak beat.

counting in duple meter

1   2   1   2   1   2   1   2

Counting with Numbers in Triple Meter

In triple meter, we can count one note on a beat by calling it "one" on a strong beat, "two" on the second beat of the measure, and "three" on the third beat of the measure.

counting in triple meter

1   2   3   1   2   3

Counting with Numbers in Quadruple Meter

In quadruple meter, we can count one note on a beat by calling it "one" on a strong beat and "two" on the second beat of the measure, "three" on the third beat of the measure and "four" on the fourth beat of the measure.

counting in quadruple meter

1   2   3   4   1   2   3   4

Division of the Beat

When music contains beats that are divided, musicians mentally count the beats within each measure and think "and" (&) on the second half of the beat to help perform the rhythm accurately.

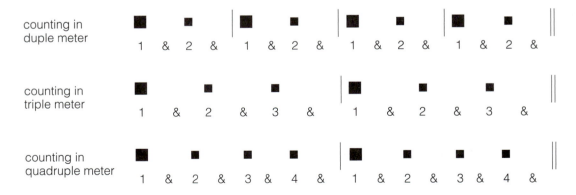

counting in duple meter

1 & 2 &   1 & 2 &   1 & 2 &   1 & 2 &

counting in triple meter

1 & 2 & 3 &   1 & 2 & 3 &

counting in quadruple meter

1 & 2 & 3 & 4 &   1 & 2 & 3 & 4 &

We can count the theme of the Beethoven Violin Concerto with numbers.

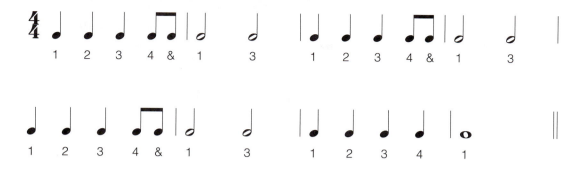

Listening 🎧   Listen to each example. Can you identify patterns of four and eight beats using rhythm syllables?

"Allegretto" from *Symphony No. 94* ("The Surprise Symphony") by Joseph Haydn (1732–1809).

"Allegretto" from *Symphony No. 7 in A, op. 92*, by Beethoven (1770–1827).

"In the Hall of the Mountain King" from the *Peer Gynt Suite No. 1* by Edvard Grieg (1843–1907).

1.4 Basic Rhythm Patterns That Include Rests in Simple Meter

Rests are symbols that represent the absence of sounds. Rests may be counted silently using the rhythm syllables of the corresponding notes.

Sing, Memorize, and Analyze 💿 2

Internalizing Music

1. Listen to "Rocky Mountain" on Track 2. Memorize the song.
2. Sing "Rocky Mountain" and keep the beat. (Watch out for the beat that has no sound!)
3. Sing "Rocky Mountain" and clap the rhythm.
4. Sing "Rocky Mountain" while you tap the beat with your left hand and tap the rhythm with your right hand.

Analyzing What You Hear

1. As you sing "Rocky Mountain," determine which beats in each phrase have no sound.
2. Determine the number of sounds on each beat in each phrase of "Rocky Mountain."

Constructing a Rhythmic Representation from Memory

1. As you sing "Rocky Mountain," draw a representation indicating the number of sounds you hear in each beat; try to indicate the duration of each sound.
2. As you point to your representation, sing "Rocky Mountain" with rhythm syllables.

Music Theory

Describing What You Hear with Rhythm Syllables

As we learned with the Beethoven Violin Concerto example, when we hear one sound on the beat, we can label it with the rhythm syllable *ta*. When we hear two sounds on the beat, we can label them with the rhythm syllable *ta di*. A rest is a place in the music with no sound. Rests may be counted silently using the rhythm syllables. We can sing "Rocky Mountain" with rhythm syllables as follows:

ta di ta di ta di ta di ta di ta di ta

ta di ta di ta di ta di ta di ta di ta

ta ta ta ta ta di ta di ta

ta ta ta ta ta di ta di ta

Notating What You Hear

Rests are symbols that show durations of silence. Each note value has its own rest.

Quarter-Note Rest

When the beat is assigned the value of a quarter note and there is a silence for one beat, we use a **quarter-note rest** to represent this silence.

A quarter note rest: 𝄽

Eighth-Note Rest

When the beat is assigned the value of a quarter note, two even sounds on a beat are called **eighth notes**. If there is a silence for one of these eighth notes, we use an **eighth-note rest**.

An eighth note rest: 𝄾

Half-Note Rest

When the beat is assigned the value of a quarter note and there is a silence for two beats, we use a **half-note rest**.

A half-note rest is written on the third line of the staff, as follows:

Whole-Note Rest

When the beat is assigned the value of a quarter note and there is a silence for four beats, we use a **whole-note rest**.

A whole rest is written on the fourth line of the staff as follows:

Notice that it hangs from the fourth line. This rest must be used to indicate a measure rest in any meter, even if the values of the beats in the measure are not worth a whole note.

Double-Whole-Note Rest

A double-whole-note rest is equal to four half-note rests.

We can write the rhythm of "Rocky Mountain" in simple duple meter as follows when the beat is assigned the value of a quarter note.

Rocky Mountain

We can also write "Rocky Mountain" in a different way while keeping exactly the same relationships between the notes. If each beat is equal to a half note, then two sounds on a beat will be written with two quarter notes. We can indicate this information by using a $\frac{2}{2}$ time signature. You will use the exact same rhythm syllables as used when singing in $\frac{2}{4}$.

Rocky Mountain in $\frac{2}{2}$

Summary of Traditional Notation Symbols and Corresponding Rests

The following table is a summary of notes and their corresponding rests.

Note Name	Traditional Notation Symbol	Corresponding Rest
Quarter note	♩	𝄽
Eighth note	♪	𝄾
Half note	𝅗𝅥	▬
Whole note	𝅝	▬

Hierarchy of Durations

In the following diagram, you can observe that the note values are proportionately related to each other. The tempo of a piece of music does not change this relationship. Each line of music lasts four beats.

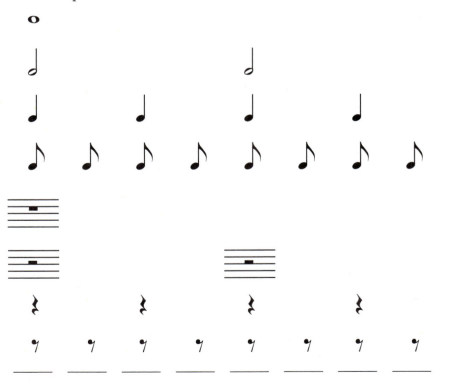

Ties

A **tie** is a curved line used to join two successive notes of the same pitch, showing that they should form one sound lasting for the duration of their combined values.

In the above chart, we can tie two quarter notes together that will form one sound lasting two beats. We can tie two half notes together that will form one sound lasting for the duration of four beats or a whole note.

A tie is also used to join notes on either side of a bar line or to make up a total note value that is not available in single notes. The tied note in the following example is equal to three quarter notes.

The whole note tied to a half note in the following example is equal to six quarter notes.

Listening 🎧

Listen to each example. Can you identify patterns of four and eight beats using rhythm syllables? Can you write the rhythm patterns of some of these examples using quarter and eighth notes?

"Children's Song," *For Children* Vol. 1, by Béla Bartók (1882–1945) (London, New York, and Berlin: Boosey & Hawkes, 2003). Recording: Jenö Jandó. Bartók: *For Children*. Naxos, 2005.

"In the Hall of the Mountain King," Movement 4 from the *Peer Gynt Suite* No. 1, 46, by Edvard Grieg (1843–1907).

Movement 2 from Symphony No. 7 by Ludwig van Beethoven (1770–1827).

> Listen to Sarah Brightman on the album *La Luna* singing "Figlio Perduto." It uses a theme from Symphony No. 7 Movement 2, by Ludwig van Beethoven (1770–1827).

1.5   Repeat Signs

A **repeat sign** (‖: :‖) appears at the beginning and end of a section of music that needs to be repeated. If the first measure of music is to be included in a repeat, the repeat sign is omitted from the beginning of the composition.

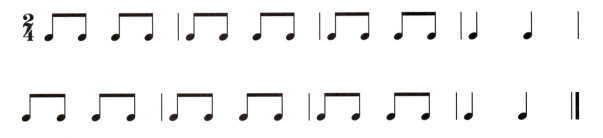

In the above example, two phrases of music have the same rhythm. Another way of writing this example is below. Perform the measures inside the repeat signs twice.

First and Second Endings

Great Big House

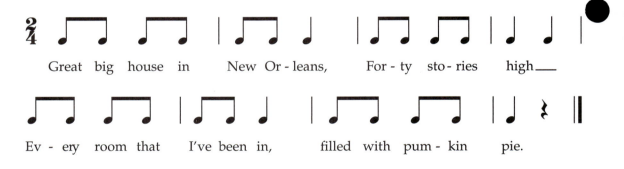

Great   big   house   in   New Or-leans,   For-ty   sto-ries   high____

Ev-ery   room   that   I've been in,   filled   with   pum-kin   pie.

Another way of writing the above example is as follows:

Perform measures one through three, then the measure bracketed with a *1* and a repeat sign at the end. Return to the beginning and perform measures one through three, skip the bracketed measure, and go to the measure marked with a *2*.

    D.C. al fine is another repetition direction. It stands for *da capo al fine*, Italian for "from the head to the end." This is an instruction provided at the end of the notation to go back to the beginning of a piece and play to the word *fine* (end).

    D.S. al fine is also a repetition direction. It stands for *dal segno al fine*, Italian for "from the sign to the end." A passage is repeated not from the beginning of the composition but from the place marked by a *dal segno* sign. Return to the *dal segno* sign (𝄋) and perform to the end of the piece.

Key Terms and Concepts

Phrase
Cadence
Phrase Mark
Form
Dynamics
Duration
Rhythm
Beat
Pulsation
Notation
Quarter Note
Note Head
Stem

Eighth Note
Flag
Half Note
Whole Note
Tempo
Meter
Duple Meter
Triple Meter
Quadruple Meter
Simple Meters
Measure
Bar Lines
Double Bar Line

Conducting Patterns
Time Signatures
Rhythm Syllables
Beam
Rests
Quarter-Note Rest
Eighth-Note Rest
Half-Note Rest
Whole-Note Rest
Ties
Repeat Sign
First and Second
    Endings

How to Practice

The mastery of reading and writing music takes many hours of practice. But we can make this practice more efficient by using a variety of practice techniques. For every chapter, we will provide you with a list of practice techniques for the new material.

Here are some general practice tips:

- Set goals for your practice. At the beginning of each practice session, write down what you want to achieve. Once you have completed your practice session, review what you achieved and what you have to work on in later practice sessions. Keep a journal of what you have accomplished.
- It is important to practice the material in a logical way. Always begin your practice with a review of the focus songs, found on the CD, for a particular unit or chapter. It is important to begin with singing the materials.
- Practicing in small groups with your peers will be invaluable to your development, as it will provide you with peer assessment and will sharpen your listening skills. This will also let you become more secure when called on by your instructor in class.

Here are some useful suggestions for practicing rhythms in a variety of ways:

Performing	Sing all of the melodies with rhythm syllables.
	Establish a tempo for "Rocky Mountain." Sing silently in your head and conduct.
	Establish a tempo for "Are You Sleeping." Sing silently in your head and conduct the song.
	Establish a tempo for "America." Sing silently in your head and conduct.
	Sing the theme of the Beethoven Violin Concerto on "loo" while quietly tapping a beat.
	Sing the theme of the Beethoven Violin Concerto with rhythm syllables while quietly tapping a beat.
	Sing the theme of the Beethoven Violin Concerto with rhythm syllables while conducting.
	Sing "Rocky Mountain" with words while keeping a beat.
	Sing "Rocky Mountain" with rhythm syllables while tapping the beat.
	Sing "Rocky Mountain" with rhythm syllables while conducting the beat.
Performing the Rhythm and the Beat at the Same Time	Divide into two groups: one group performs the rhythm of the focus song; the other keeps the beat. Practice this activity in different combinations: • Instructor/class • Class/instructor • Divided class • Two individual students Individually, keep the beat with one hand and tap the rhythm with the other hand.
Standard Practice	Sing or speak the rhythm patterns of focus songs while tapping the beat. Count with numbers as you keep the beat.
Echo Clapping	Practice with a classmate or in class. One of you will clap the rhythm of a melody or a rhythmic pattern. The other will "echo" what was clapped with rhythm syllables.
Conducting	Sing and conduct at the same time.
Aural Analysis	Identify which beat or beats contain specified rhythmic patterns.
Notating Your Rhythm	Practice with a classmate or in class. One of you will clap the rhythm of a melody or a rhythmic pattern. The other will "echo" what was clapped with rhythm syllables and then notate the pattern in a given meter.
Error Dictation	One student plays the melody, deliberately making a mistake. Another student follows the score and locates the error.
Memory	Memorize an entire rhythmic exercise from Chapter 1 and notate it without referring to the notation. First analyze the form by looking for repeated and similar parts. This will simplify the task.
Improvisation/ Composition	First select a meter and length for the composition, then decide what rhythmic form to use (for example, abba). Create an improvisation or composition using only known rhythms.
Performing a Rhythmic Canon	Say the rhythm names while clapping the rhythm of the melody. Think the rhythm names and clap the rhythm. Think and clap the rhythm while another person claps the melody starting after 4 beats. Perform the canon by yourself. Tap one part with one hand and use a pencil to tap the other part with the other hand.

Using the Musical Skills CD

Access Chapter 1 on the skills CD to reinforce some of the important rhythmic concepts introduced in this chapter through tutorials and dictations. Use the arrows on the top right of the page to move from one page to another.

In the Tutorial section, you can review the following information:

1. Duple, triple, and quadruple time signatures
2. Whole- , half- , quarter-, and eighth-note values
3. Whole- , half- , quarter- , and eighth-note rest values

In the Dictation section, you will have the opportunity to practice writing simple rhythm patterns that are two measures in length. There are two types of rhythmic dictations:

1. Rhythmic dictations including whole, half, quarter, and eighth notes with no rests
2. Rhythmic dictations including whole, half, quarter, and eighth notes with rests

Before attempting to write the dictations, listen to each example several times and try to clap and say the rhythm syllables. You might want to notate your example on staff paper before doing so on the computer.

How to Read a Musical Score

Throughout the text we will introduce you to some useful ideas for how to read a musical score. In each chapter, you will begin to recognize some of the basic elements of music.

Look at Minuet by Johann Sebastian Bach on the following page and answer the following questions.

Rhythm

Identify the time signature. Identify the quarter notes, half notes, whole notes, and eighth notes. Identify the tempo of the piece.

Melody

Identify the dynamic markings and define them.

Texture

What is the texture of the piece?

Form

What is the form?

Minuet

Johann Sebastian Bach (1685–1750)

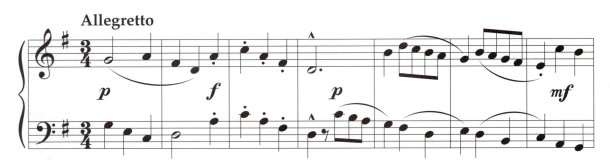

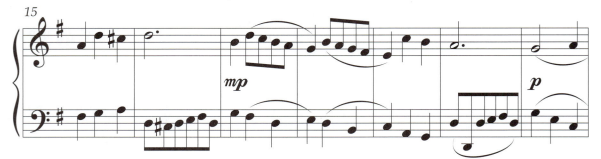

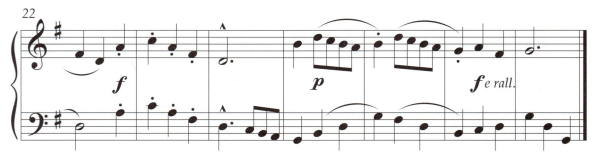

Look at the Minuet in G Major by Johann Sebastian Bach below.

Rhythm

Identify the time signature. Identify quarter notes, half notes, whole notes, and eighth notes. Identify the tempo of the piece.

Melody

Identify the phrases. Identify the dynamic markings and define them.

Form

What is the form?

Minuet in G Major

Johann Sebastian Bach (1685–1750)

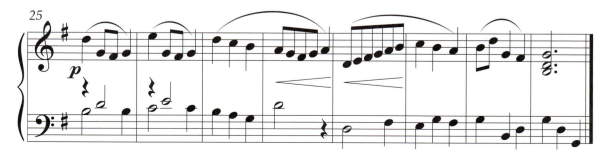

MUSIC THEORY EXERCISES

1.1   Exercises: Beat

Exercise 1.1

1. Sing "Are You Sleeping" and draw the phrase marks as you sing.
2. Indicate the form of "Are You Sleeping" on the left side of each phrase.

Are	you	sleep-	ing,	Are	you	sleep-	ing
Bro-	ther	John		Bro-	ther	John	
Morn-ing	bells are	ring-	ing,	Morn-ing	bells are	ring-	ing
Ding,	dong,	ding——		Ding,	dong,	ding——	

Exercise 1.2

1. Listen to "Row, Row, Row Your Boat."
2. Sing and draw the phrase marks as you sing over the words provided for you below.
3. Indicate the form of "Row, Row, Row Your Boat" on the left side of each phrase.
4. Add appropriate dynamic marks to each phrase.

Row,	row,	row, your	boat
Gen-tly	down the	stream—	
Mer-ri-ly,	mer-ri-ly,	mer-ri-ly,	mer-ri-ly,
Life is	but a	dream—	

Exercise 1.3

1. Fill in the missing text above the appropriate beat blocks.

Are You Sleeping

Are	you	sleep	- ing,	Are	you	sleep	- ing,

2. Fill in the missing text above the appropriate beat blocks.

Row, Row, Row Your Boat

Row,	row,	row, your	boat

Chapter 2

The Keyboard and Notation of Pitch

CHAPTER OVERVIEW

Melody is composed of musical sounds, which may be high or low according to vibrations of **pitch**—the "highness" or "lowness" of a musical sound. A high note can be called a high pitch, and a low note a low pitch. In this chapter you will be introduced to the basics of pitch. All melodies in this chapter contain the rhythms that were introduced in Chapter 1. You will be introduced to the musical staff (the plural is *staves*) that is used to notate pitch. The staff consists of a number of horizontal lines on and between which musical notes are placed. In addition, you will learn how to play melodies with your right and left hand on the piano. Understanding how to play a keyboard reinforces your ability to understand music fundamentals as well as helping you to create music. There is a folded, laminated keyboard at the back of the text for you to use. You should always have the keyboard open as you are studying music so that you can refer to it to help with your understanding of music theory concepts.

2.1 The Keyboard and Basic Concepts Associated with Pitch

Keyboards are useful aids in studying music fundamentals. They allow us to hear and visualize concepts in theory. The goal of this chapter is to introduce you to the general layout of a keyboard and to teach you to play simple melodies using the rhythms in Chapter 1.

Orientation to the Keyboard

Look at the piano keyboard. The notes are lower as you move to the left and higher as you move to the right.

Low Notes   High Notes

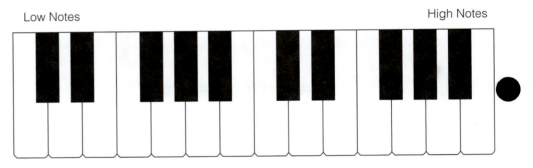

Keyboard Design

The piano keyboard has white keys and black keys. A standard keyboard has 88 keys: 52 are white and 36 are black. All the black and white keys are identified with letter names.

Naming White Keys

The first seven **letters** of the alphabet are used to identify keys: A–B–C–D–E–F–G. Notice that after the note G we start the alphabet again with A–B–C–D–E–F–G.

The relationship between two notes that have the same name is called an **octave**. For example, from C to the next C is called an octave: CDEFGABC. The second C is an octave higher than the first. We say the second C is in a higher register.

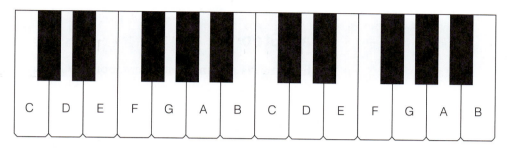

Key patterns of the keyboard are consistent.

You can find a C on the piano just to the left of any group of two black keys.

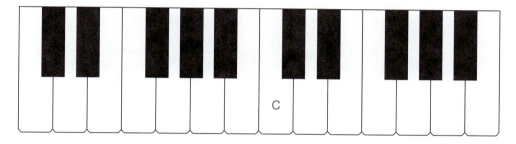

Naming Black Keys

Notice the way the black keys are grouped on the keyboard. From the left side of the keyboard, only the first group has one black key. The others have two black keys or three black keys.

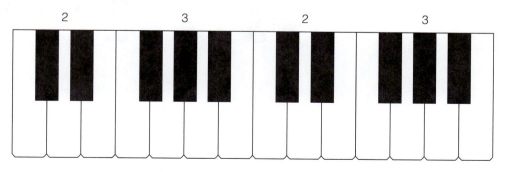

2.2   Whole-Step and Half-Step Intervals at the Keyboard

Interval

An **interval** is the musical distance between two pitches.

Half Step

A **half step** is the smallest interval on the keyboard. It is the distance between two adjacent keys, regardless of color. The half step usually occurs between white keys and neighboring black keys. The half step occurs only in two places between white keys—between the notes E and F, and between the notes B and C.

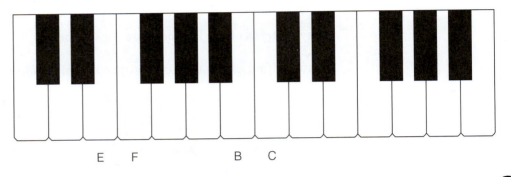

Whole Step

A **whole step** is the distance of two half steps on the keyboard. Whole steps can occur from white key to white key; from black key to black key; from white key to black key; and from black key to white key. From C to D is a whole step, and from E to F♯ is a whole step.

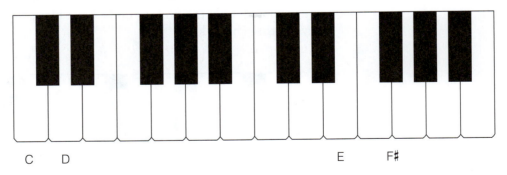

Accidentals

All the black and white keys are identified with letter names from the musical alphabet. All keys can be identified by more than one name through the use of sharps and flats.

Sharp

A **sharp sign** (♯) is the musical symbol that indicates that the note has been raised a half step in pitch to the next white or black key. The black key immediately to the right and above the white key is named by adding a sharp to the white-key name. Once a sharp is indicated within a measure, it remains in effect for the remainder of the measure.

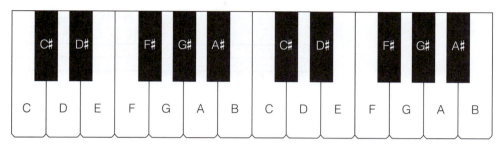

Flat

A **flat sign** (♭) is the musical symbol that indicates the note has been lowered a half step in pitch to the next white or black key. The black key immediately to the left and below a white key is named by adding a flat to the white-key name. Once a flat is indicated within a measure, it remains in effect for the remainder of the measure.

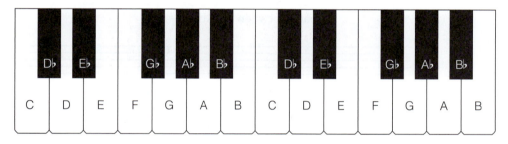

Enharmonic Pitches

Notating the same pitch with a different note name is called an **enharmonic spelling** of the pitch.

Black keys and white keys have at least two possible names. For example, an F♯ (F-sharp) can also be notated as G♭ (G-flat). The note F can also be notated as E-sharp (E♯). Remember that the same notes notated differently sound the same. Note that there isn't a black key between B and C or between E and F. Enharmonic spelling of B can be C-flat, C is B-sharp, E is F-flat, and F is E-sharp.

2.3   **Treble Clef and Introduction to the Notation of Pitch**

Music Notation

Pitch is indicated with notes on the **staff**. The staff is made up of five lines and four spaces. The lines and spaces are always numbered from the bottom to the top.

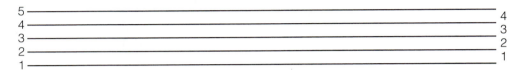

Notes represent musical pitches on the staff. Notes are written on lines or in spaces on the staff.

The following staff contains notes on lines. Notice that the lines go through the middle of the note heads.

Staff with notes on lines.

The next staff contains notes in spaces. Notice that the note heads sit in the space between the lines.

In the next staff, you can see that notes can be placed on a staff on lines or in spaces. Lower pitches are placed lower on the staff; higher pitches are placed higher.

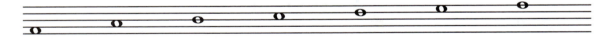

The Treble Clef, or G Clef

The **treble clef**, or **G clef**, identifies the second line on the staff as G, five notes above middle C. Your instructor will show you where middle C is located on the piano. The treble clef normally indicates playing the keyboard with the right hand. Notice how the treble clef sign circles around the second line, G.

Once G is established on the staff, the remaining pitches can be determined.

Notating White Keys in the Treble Clef

Consecutive letter names that move up or down the keyboard alternate between lines and spaces.

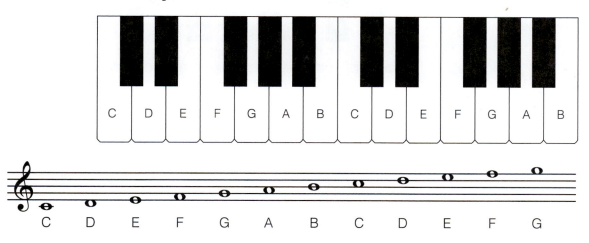

All letter names are arranged according to the alphabetical sequence of letters. Once a pitch has been identified on the staff, the other pitches follow in sequence. Note the repetition of letter names and the placement of note heads on the staff. Note heads are placed around a line or in a space to indicate different musical notes.

The following hints will help in memorizing the names of the lines and spaces in the treble clef. Remember to start on the first line or space (bottom) of each clef.

Treble lines: E, G, B, D, F; Every Good Boy Does Fine.
Treble spaces: F-A-C-E spells "face."

2.4 Bass Clef, Ledger Lines, and Octave Sign

The Bass Clef, or F Clef

The **bass clef**, or **F clef**, identifies the fourth line as F. Notice that the two dots surround the F line.

A note written on this bass clef F line is positioned five notes below middle C on the piano. Other pitches may be derived from the F clef. The bass clef normally indicates playing the keyboard with the left hand.

Notating White Keys in the Bass Clef

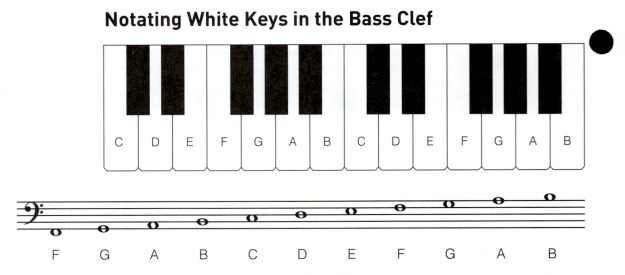

When naming notes, remember that all letter names are arranged according to the alphabetical sequence.

The following will help in memorizing the names of the lines and spaces of the notes in the bass clef.

Bass line notes: G, B, D, F, A; Good Boys Do Fine Always.
Bass space notes: A, C, E, G; All Cows Eat Grass.

Ledger Lines

Notes are sometimes higher or lower than the notes that can be written on the staff. We use ledger lines to show these notes. **Ledger lines** are short lines used to extend the staff above or below the five lines. The sequence of the line and space note-names continues.

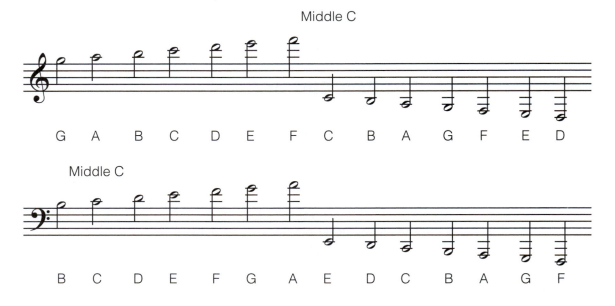

The spacing between ledger lines should be equal to the space between staff lines. Notes written as ledger lines in one clef can appear as notes on the staff in another clef. For example, the following notes have the same number of vibrations per second; however, they are written in two different clefs; In other words, the notes written in the treble staff are exactly the same as those underneath them written in the bass staff.

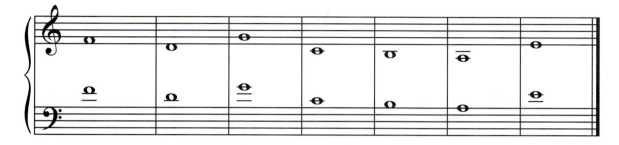

The Octave Sign

An **octave sign** above a group of notes indicates that the notes are to be played one octave higher: (*8va*....). Consistent use of ledger lines makes music difficult to read. To make the reading easier, an octave sign is used.

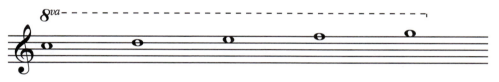

is the same as:

An octave sign (*8va*...) below a group of notes indicates that the notes are to be played one octave lower.

The above example will sound the same as the one below.

The Grand Staff

A **grand staff** is the combination of the treble staff and the bass staff grouped together by a vertical line and a brace. Music for the piano is written on the grand staff. Middle C appears on a ledger line in the treble clef as well as in the bass clef.

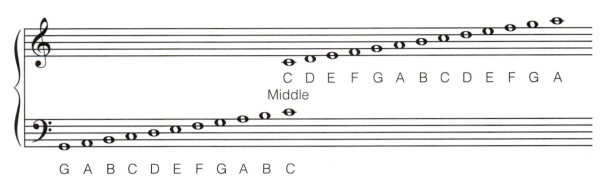

Octave Identification

We can use numbers to identify pitches in a particular octave. Middle C is always C4; the C an octave above middle C is C5; the C an octave below middle C is C3.

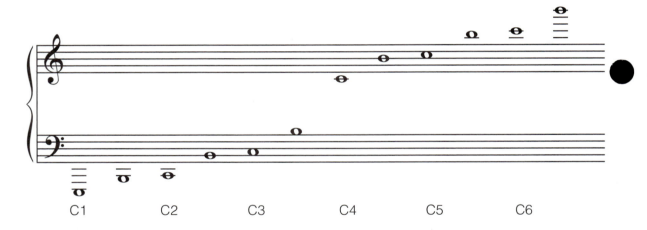

2.5 Notating Sharps and Flats on the Staff

Notating Sharps on the Staff

Sharps on the staff are placed before the notes to which they refer. Even though we say F-sharp, the sharp sign needs to precede the note to which it refers. The sharp symbol must enclose the line or space of the note that is raised. There are two steps in writing sharps:

1. Draw two vertical parallel lines before the note.
2. Complete the sharp sign by drawing two diagonal lines, making sure that the accidental is on the same line or space as the note it belongs to.

In the following song, observe that every F is sharped. Once a sharp is indicated within a measure, it remains in effect for the remainder of the measure.

Who's That Tapping at the Window   **American Folk Song**

Notating Flats on the Staff

Like sharps, flats must be placed before the note even though we say B-flat; the flat sign (♭) needs to precede the note to which it refers. It is important to enclose the line or space of the note that is lowered. There are two steps in writing flats.

1. Draw a vertical line before the note.
2. Complete the flat sign as indicated below.

In the following song, observe that every B is a B-flat. Remember, once a flat is indicated within a measure, it remains in effect for the remainder of the measure.

Who's That Tapping at the Window   **American Folk Song**

Key Signature

Reading a piece of music becomes much easier when we know which accidentals are to be played throughout. The **key signature**, a sharp or group of sharps or a flat or group of flats at the beginning of a piece of music, tells us what accidentals are to be played throughout the piece. For example, the one sharp in the key signature of "Aunt Rhody" in the example below tells us that F-sharp is to be played every time we see an F written on the staff. You will learn more about key signatures in Chapter 5.

Aunt Rhody

Natural (♮)

The function of a **natural sign** (♮) is to cancel the preceding sharp or flat. It remains in effect in the part where it is placed for the duration of the measure.

As with the sharp and flat signs, the natural sign (♮) must be placed before the note to which it refers. Just as with sharps and flats, we enclose the line or space of the note with the square section of the natural sign.

Accidentals Within a Measure of Music

We know that when a note has been altered by an accidental, that note will remain altered for the duration of the measure. Accidentals in a treble clef do not apply to the same note in the bass part or vice versa. If we do not want the note to be altered for the duration of the measure, we add in a natural sign to the next appearance of the note.

will be played as follows:

Chromatic Half Step

A **chromatic half step** is two pitches that use the same letter name but are a half step apart.

G   G♯

G to G♯ is referred to as a chromatic half step. B to B-flat and C to C-flat are other examples of chromatic half steps.

Diatonic Half Step

The distance between G and A♭ is a half step. A **diatonic half step** uses two different letter names; G to A♭ is referred to as a diatonic half step. Chromatic half steps use the same letter names for notes that are a half step apart, and diatonic half steps use adjacent letter names.

G   A♭

half-step interval

Double Sharp

A **double sharp** (𝄪) raises a pitch by two half steps.
In the following example, F-double-sharp is an enharmonic spelling of G; therefore, it is notated differently but sounds the same.

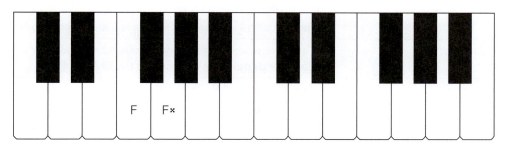

Double Flat

A **double flat** (♭♭) lowers the pitch by two half steps. In the following figure, G♭♭ is an enharmonic spelling of F. It is notated differently but sounds the same.

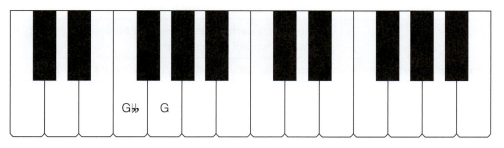

Canceling Part of a Double Flat or Double Sharp

If you have a C-double-sharp and you want to replace it with a C-sharp in the same measure, you must put a sharp sign in front of the second C.

Key Terms and Concepts

Pitch	Flat Sign	Grand Staff
Letter Names	Enharmonic Spelling	Key Signature
Octave	Staff	Natural Sign
Interval	Treble Clef, or G Clef	Chromatic Half Step
Half Step	Bass Clef, or F Clef	Diatonic Half Step
Whole Step	Ledger Lines	Double Sharp
Sharp Sign	Octave Sign	Double Flat

How to Practice

Mastery of playing the piano takes many hours of practice. But we can make practice more efficient by using a variety of practice techniques. If possible, practice with another student who has taken piano lessons, as this will be invaluable to your development and it will provide you with the opportunity of peer assessment.

Here are some useful suggestions for practicing a simple piano piece:

Performing the Rhythm and the Beat at the Same Time	Divide into two groups: one group performs the rhythm of the piece; the other keeps the beat. Practice this activity in different combinations: • Instructor/class • Class/instructor • Divided class • Two individual students Individually, keep the beat with one hand and tap the rhythm with the other hand.
Counting	Sing or speak the rhythm syllables of the piano piece while tapping the beat. Count with numbers as you keep the beat.
Melody	Identify all the notes in the piece of music from the lowest to highest. Play the notes on the piano from lowest to highest. Sing these notes with letter names. Try to sing the melodies with letter names. Try to hum the melodies as you conduct. Identify the phrases and the form of the melodies.
Performing	Clap the rhythm of the piano piece as you say the rhythm syllables. Say the rhythm syllables as you move the fingers you are going to play with in the air. Sing the letter names as you move the fingers you are going to play with in the air. Play the example on the piano.
Memory	Memorize each piano piece. First analyze the form by looking for repeated and similar parts. This will simplify the task.
Improvisation/Composition	Improvise a variation. Maybe compose a new ♭ section to a piece of music.

Using the Musical Skills CD

Access Chapter 2 on the skills CD to reinforce some of the important concepts introduced in this chapter through tutorials and dictations.

In the Tutorial section, you can review information concerning the layout of the keyboard.

How to Read a Musical Score

Examine the following piece by Johann Sebastian Bach.

Rhythm

Identify the time signature, quarter notes, half notes, whole notes, and eighth notes. Identify the tempo of the piece.

Melody

Identify the dynamic markings. Identify all flats. Identify the treble clef. Identify the bass clef. Identify ledger lines. Identify the grand staff. Identify the key signature. Identify the natural signs.

Song   *Johann Sebastian Bach (1685–1750)*

2.5 Exercises: Notating Sharps and Flats on the Staff

Exercise 2.20

Write the possible enharmonic equivalents for the following notes and name the notes.

Exercise 2.21

Identify the following notes on the keyboard and write them on the staff provided. The first note on the keyboard is middle C.

1. G-double-sharp; A-double-flat; B-sharp

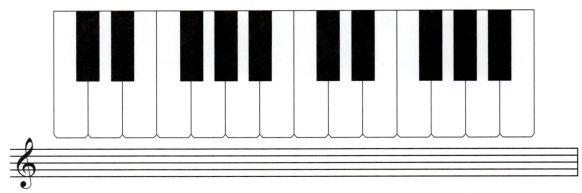

2. G-double-flat; A-double-sharp; C

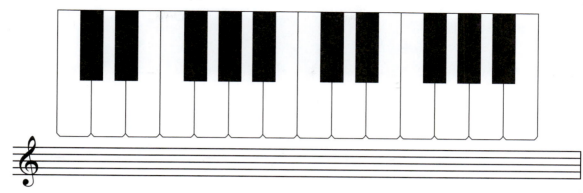

3. F-double-sharp; D; C

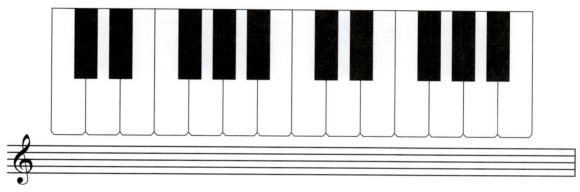

4. D-sharp; G-flat; E-sharp

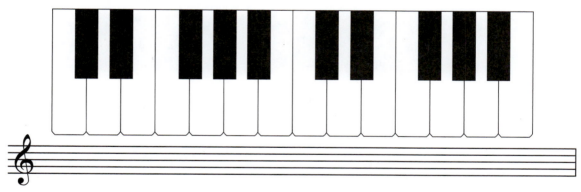

Chapter 3

More-Advanced Rhythms in Simple Meter

CHAPTER OVERVIEW

In the first part of this chapter you will learn that the basic beat can be divided into four equal parts, creating a variety of interesting rhythm patterns. You will be introduced to the concept of syncopation: the displacement of the accent from the strong beat to the weak beat. Syncopation is found in many styles of music, including classical, jazz, and popular. Additionally, you will learn about dotted notes. Dots are used to increase the duration of a note. You will learn how to notate melodies containing the above-mentioned rhythms in different meters. In addition to developing your notation skills you will learn how to count these more-advanced rhythms using rhythm syllables and numbers.

3.1 ♪♪♪♪ Sixteenth Notes

Sing, Memorize, and Analyze

Internalizing Music

1. Listen to "Dinah" on Track 4. Memorize the song.
2. Sing "Dinah" and keep the beat.
3. Sing "Dinah" and clap the rhythm.
4. Work with another student in the class. One of you performs the beat while the other performs the rhythm of "Dinah." Switch parts.
5. Sing "Dinah" while you tap the beat with your left hand and tap the rhythm with your right hand.

Analyzing What You Hear

1. As you sing "Dinah," determine the number of beats within each phrase.
2. On which beats do you hear more than two sounds?
3. Determine the number of sounds on each beat in each phrase of "Dinah."

Constructing a Rhythmic Representation from Memory

1. As you sing "Dinah," draw a representation indicating the number of sounds you hear in each beat; try to indicate the duration of each sound.

Music Theory

Describing What You Hear with Syllables

When we hear four sounds on a beat, we can label it with the rhythm syllables **ta ka di mi**. The rhythm syllables for "Dinah" are written above the beat blocks.

Dinah

takadimi	*ta*	*di*	*ta*	*di*	*ta*	*di*	*takadimi*	*ta*	*di*	*ta*	*di*	*ta*

takadimi	*ta*	*di*	*ta*	*di*	*ta*	*di*	*takadimi*	*ta*	*di*	*ta*

Notating What You Hear

As you have discovered in "Dinah," four even sounds occur on beats one and five of phrases one and two. When the beat is a quarter note in length, four even sounds on a beat can be represented by four sixteenth notes (semiquavers, in England). A sixteenth note is made up of a note head, a stem, and a double flag. The flag is on the right of the stem. Normally, four sixteenth notes are joined together by a double beam. Down stems are placed on the left side of a note head and up stems on the right.

In some vocal music where it is important to align rhythms with text, the beam is not used.

We can write the rhythm of "Dinah" as follows in simple duple meter when the beat is equal to a quarter note.

Dinah

If we write the rhythm of "Dinah" as it is sometimes written in vocal music, we could write it using flagged notes instead of beamed notes. The following is an example of writing with flagged notes.

No one in the house but Din-ah, Din-ah   No one in the house but me I know.

No one in the house but   Din-ah, Din-ah   strum-in' on the old ban - jo.

For the sake of simplicity and clarity, from this point forward in the text we will use beamed notes in our notation.

Reading with Rhythm Syllables

The following figure illustrates how we can use rhythm syllables to read "Dinah."

ta ka di mi ta di   ta   di   ta   di   ta ka di mi ta di   ta di ta

ta ka di mi ta di   ta   di   ta   di   ta ka di mi ta di   ta

Counting with Numbers

The numbers for counting four sixteenth notes are determined by the beat you are on. For example, if the sixteenth notes occur on beat three, count "3-e-&-ah." The numbers in the following example refer only to the top line of music. (You can use "a" instead of "ah," if you choose.)

The numbers below the rhythm of "Dinah" indicate how to count the rhythm.

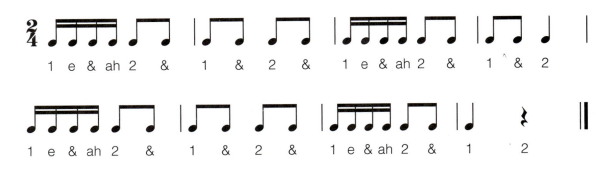

3.2   Notating a Melody in Different Meters

Once you can aurally describe the rhythm of a melody with rhythm syllables, you can notate these patterns in different meters. Composers use this technique to avoid using a lot of smaller note values. The following chart will enable you to notate second division patterns in $\frac{2}{4}$ or $\frac{2}{2}$ or $\frac{2}{8}$ meter. The same principle applies to triple and quadruple meter.

When the beat is equal to a half note, four sounds on a beat can be represented by using four eighth notes.

When the beat is an eighth note long, four even sounds on a beat can be represented by thirty-second notes (demisemiquavers, in England). A thirty-second note is made up of a note head, a stem, and a triple flag. Four thirty-second notes are joined together by a triple beam.

The following chart illustrates how one and two sounds on a beat can be represented in different meters.

Rhythm Syllable	$\frac{2}{4}$ Meter	$\frac{2}{8}$ Meter	$\frac{2}{2}$ Meter
Ta	♩	♪	𝅗𝅥
Ta di	♪ ♪	♪ ♪	♩ ♩
Ta ka di mi	♬♬	♬♬	♫♫

For example, if you want to convert the following rhythm syllables into notation:

ta   ta ka di mi   ta di   ta

it would look like the following in the different simple duple meters we have studied. The note value of the beat changes, as well as the rhythm. What is the note value for the beat in each of the examples? Why can you read each pattern with the same rhythm syllables?

[handwritten: each pattern was ajusted to match the tempo of the others]

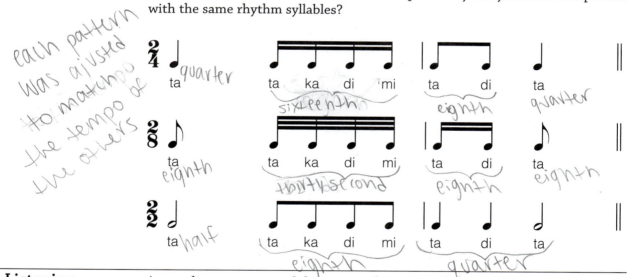

[handwritten annotations under the staves: quarter, sixteenth, eighth, quarter; eighth, thirtysecond, eighth, eighth; half, eighth, quarter]

Listening 🎧

As you listen to some of these examples, try to identify rhythm patterns using rhythm syllables. Notate the rhythm patterns that you recognize.

"Allegro" from Symphony No. 1 by Wolfgang Amadeus Mozart (1756–1791).
"Solfeggietto" by Carl Philipp Emanuel Bach (1714–1788).
"Solfeggietto" by Carl Philipp Emanuel Bach (1714–1788) sung by The Swingle Singers, from the album *Anyone for Mozart, Bach, Handel, Vivaldi?* Philis recording
"Solfeggietto" by Carl Philipp Emanuel Bach (1714–1788), Vernizzi Jazz Quartet and Corrado Giuffredi. Arts Crossing, 2006.
Prelude in C Minor from Book 1 of the *Well-Tempered Clavier* by Johann Sebastian Bach (1685–1750).
"Andante" (Variation 3) from Symphony No. 94 by Joseph Haydn (1732–1809).
Rondo "Alla Turca" for piano by Wolfgang Amadeus Mozart, Theme 1 and Theme 2.

3.3 ♩ ♫ ♫ ♪ Eighth-Note and Sixteenth-Note Combinations

Sing, Memorize, and Analyze

Internalizing Music

1. Listen to "Ida Red" on Track 5. Memorize the song.
2. Sing "Ida Red" and keep the beat.
3. Sing "Ida Red" and clap the rhythm.
4. Work with another student in the class. One of you performs the beat while the other performs the rhythm of "Ida Red." Switch parts.
5. Sing "Ida Red" while you tap the beat with your left hand and tap the rhythm with your right hand.

Analyzing What You Hear

1. Identify whether the meter is duple, triple, or quadruple.
2. As you sing "Ida Red," determine the number of beats within each phrase.
3. Sing phrase one. Determine the number of sounds you hear on each beat. Describe the sounds you hear on beat two with the words "long" and "short."
4. Sing phrase two. Determine the number of sounds on each beat. How many sounds did you sing on beats one and two? Describe these sounds with the words "long" and "short."
5. Determine the number of sounds you hear on each beat of phrases three and four.

Constructing a Rhythmic Representation from Memory

As you sing "Ida Red," indicate the number of sounds you hear in each beat; try to indicate the duration of each sound.

Music Theory

Describing What You Hear with Syllables

When the beat is equal to a quarter note and we hear three uneven sounds (one long sound followed by two short sounds), we use the rhythm syllables *ta di mi*. When we hear three uneven sounds on a beat (two short sounds followed by one long sound), we can use the syllables *ta ka di*. The following are the rhythm syllables for "Ida Red":

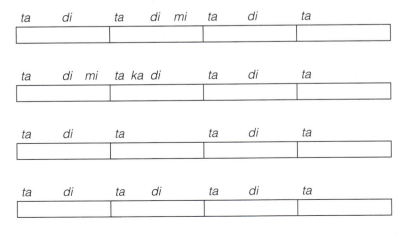

Notating What You Hear

Ida Red

When the beat is a quarter note, we can write the rhythm of "Ida Red" as follows:

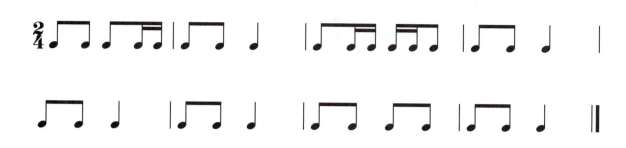

Reading with Rhythm Syllables

We can read the rhythm of "Ida Red" with rhythm syllables.

Counting with Numbers

One eighth note followed by two sixteenth notes can be counted as "1 & ah." Two sixteenth notes followed by an eighth note can be counted as "1 e &."

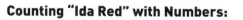

Counting "Ida Red" with Numbers:

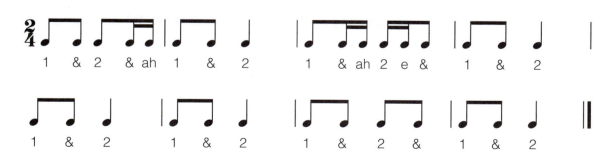

Listening 🎧
As you listen to some of these examples try to identify rhythm patterns using rhythm syllables. Notate the rhythm patterns that you recognize.

"Badinerie" from French Suite No. 2 in B Minor by Johann Sebastian Bach (1685–1750).

"Badinerie" found in *Suite Dreams: The Music of Johann Sebastian Bach for Flute and Jazz Orchestra*, I-Chee Lee/Union Square Group.

Mikrokosmos Vol. 3, No. 77, by Béla Bartók (1882–1945).

"Bagpipes," No. 36 in *44 Duets for Two Violins* by Béla Bartók (1882–1945).

"Russian Dance" from *The Nutcracker Suite*, Op. 71a, by Peter Ilich Tchaikovsky (1840–1893).

Rosamunde Ballet Music by Franz Schubert (1797–1828).

Musette in D by Johann Sebastian Bach (1685–1750).

3.4 ♪. ♬ Dotted Eighth Note Followed by a Sixteenth Note

Sing, Memorize, and Analyze 💿
6

Internalizing Music

1. Listen to "London Bridge" on Track 6. Memorize the song.
2. Sing "London Bridge" and keep the beat.
3. Sing "London Bridge" and clap the rhythm.
4. Work with another student in the class. One of you performs the beat while the other performs the rhythm of "London Bridge." Switch parts.
5. Sing "London Bridge" while you tap the beat with your left hand and tap the rhythm with your right hand.

Analyzing What You Hear

1. Determine the number of phrases in "London Bridge" and the form.
2. Identify whether the meter is duple, triple, or quadruple.
3. Conduct "London Bridge" while you sing.
4. As you sing "London Bridge," determine the number of sounds on each beat.
5. Which beat in phrase one has two uneven sounds?
6. Which beats in phrase two have two uneven sounds?

Constructing a Rhythmic Representation from Memory

1. As you sing "London Bridge," draw a representation indicating the number of sounds you hear in each beat; try to indicate the duration of each sound.
2. Identify all known rhythms in your representation.

Music Theory

Describing What You Hear with Syllables

When we hear two uneven sounds on a beat, a long sound followed by a short sound, we can call it *ta mi*. When we hear two uneven sounds on a beat, a short sound followed by a long sound, we can call it *ta ka*. The following are the rhythm syllables for "London Bridge" written above the beat blocks.

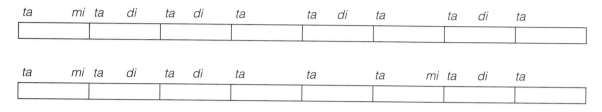

Notating What You Hear

The first beat of phrase one and the first beat of phrase three of "London Bridge" begin with two uneven sounds, the first long and the second short. We can represent this sound with a dotted eighth followed by a sixteenth note when the beat is a quarter note long.

When a note is followed by a dot, it receives the value of the note plus half its value. Therefore, a dotted eighth note receives three-quarters of a quarter-note beat. We can increase the value of a rest with a dot as well.

Reading with Rhythm Syllables

We can read the rhythm of "London Bridge" with rhythm syllables.

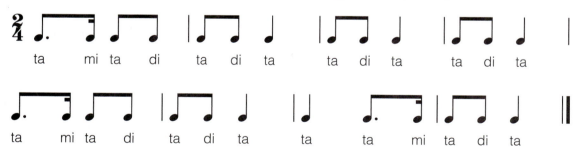

Counting with Numbers

We can use numbers to count sixteenth notes. The numbers for a dotted eighth note followed by one sixteenth note are indicated below. The numbers for counting are determined by the beat you are on. For example, if the dotted eighth note followed by a sixteenth note occurs on beat three in $\frac{4}{4}$ you will count "3–––ah." The numbers refer to the top notes, in the following example.

The numbers below the rhythm of "London Bridge" indicate how to count the rhythm.

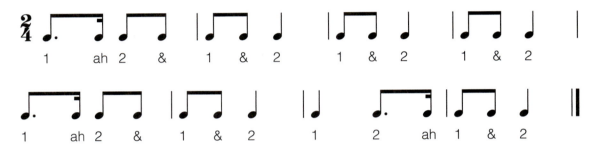

Sixteenth Note Followed by a Dotted Eighth Note

It is possible to have the reverse of a dotted eighth note followed by a sixteenth note. The reverse pattern would be a sixteenth note followed by a dotted eighth note.

This pattern is used in the following song, "Shake Them Simmons Down."

American Folk Song

Cir - cle left,   do - oh, do-oh,   Cir - cle left,   do - oh, do-oh,

Cir - cle left,   do - oh, do-oh,   Shake them 'sim-mons down.

For example, we can sing the seventh bar with rhythm syllables as follows:

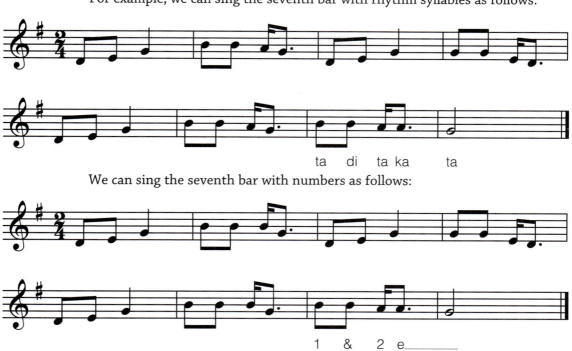

ta   di   ta ka   ta

We can sing the seventh bar with numbers as follows:

1   &   2   e_____

Notating a Melody in Different Meters

The following chart provides a guide for notating a melody into $\frac{2}{4}$ or $\frac{2}{8}$ or $\frac{2}{2}$ meter. The same principle applies for triple and quadruple meters.

Rhythm Syllable	$\frac{2}{4}$ Meter	$\frac{2}{8}$ Meter	$\frac{2}{2}$ Meter
Ta	♩	♪	𝅗𝅥
Ta di	♫	(two beamed sixteenths)	♩ ♩
Ta ka di mi	(four beamed sixteenths)	(four beamed thirty-seconds)	(four beamed eighths)
Ta di mi	(eighth + two sixteenths)	(sixteenth + two thirty-seconds)	♩ (two eighths)
Ta ka di	(two sixteenths + eighth)	(two thirty-seconds + sixteenth)	(two eighths) ♩
Ta mi	(dotted eighth + sixteenth)	(dotted sixteenth + thirty-second)	♩. ♪

Upbeat (Anacrusis)

An **upbeat** or **anacrusis** is an unstressed note or group of notes at the beginning of a phrase of music. This "pickup beat" is borrowed from the last measure of the piece.

"The Three Rogues" is in 𝟦𝟦 time. The final beat of the last measure is accounted for at the beginning of the piece, with the *upbeat*, *pickup*, or *anacrusis*.

The Three Rogues   American Folk Song

| **Listening** 🎧 | As you listen to some of these examples, try to identify rhythm patterns using rhythm syllables. Notate the rhythm patterns that you recognize. |

"London Bridge Is Falling Down" performed by Count Basie (1901–1971) in *The Complete Decca Recordings of Count Basie*.

"London Bridge," in *More Lost Treasures of Ted Heath* vols. 1–2.

"Hommage a Robert Schumann," *Mikrokosmos* Vol. 3, No. 80, by Béla Bartók (1882–1945).

"Andante" from Symphony No. 94 by Joseph Haydn (1732–1809).

"Feierlich und gemessen" from Symphony No. 1 by Gustav Mahler (1860–1911).

"Largo" from Symphony No. 9 by Antonín Dvořák (1841–1904). "Going Home" sung by Kathleen Battle in her recording *So Many Stars* is based on this theme.

Minuet in G by Ludwig van Beethoven (1770–1827).

"Túrót Eszik a Cigány," Andantino. Zoltán Kodály (1882–1967).

3.5 ♩. ♪ Dotted Quarter Note Followed by an Eighth Note

Sing, Memorize, and Analyze

Internalizing Music

1. Listen to "Birch Tree" on Track 7. Memorize the song.
2. Sing "Birch Tree" and keep the beat.
3. Sing "Birch Tree" and clap the rhythm.
4. Work with another student in the class. One of you performs the beat while the other performs the rhythm of "Birch Tree." Switch parts.
5. Sing "Birch Tree" while you tap the beat with your left hand and tap the rhythm with your right hand.

Analyzing What You Hear

1. Perform the beat and rhythm of phrases of "Birch Tree."
2. Which phrases include a sound that lasts longer than a beat?
3. Sing phrase three on "loo" and keep the beat. How many sounds did you sing on beats one and two? Describe these two sounds with long and short.
4. Determine the number of sounds on each of the other beats.

Constructing a Rhythmic Representation from Memory

In-class or individual work:

1. As you sing "Birch Tree," draw a representation indicating the number of sounds you hear in each beat; try to indicate the duration of each sound.

Music Theory

Describing What You Hear with Syllables

When we hear one long and one short sound occurring over two beats, where the first sound is located on the beat and the second sound is located on the second half of the next beat, we can identify them with the rhythm syllables **ta---di.** The dotted line between *ta* and *di* indicates that the rhythm takes place over two beats.

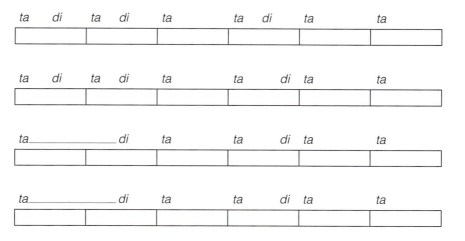

Notating What You Hear

When the beat is a quarter note in duration, two uneven sounds over two beats, when the first beat is three times as long as the second beat, can be represented with a dotted quarter note followed by an eighth note. When a note is followed by a dot, it receives the value of the note plus half its value. Therefore, a dotted quarter note is equal in duration to a quarter note plus an eighth note.

$$\text{♩.} = \text{♩} + \text{♪}$$

The following is the notation of "Birch Tree" when the beat is represented by a quarter note:

Birch Tree

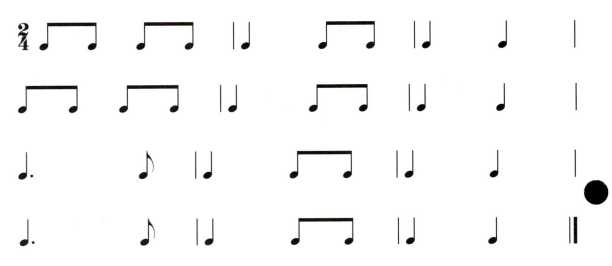

Reading with Rhythm Syllables

We can read the rhythm of "Birch Tree" with rhythm syllables.

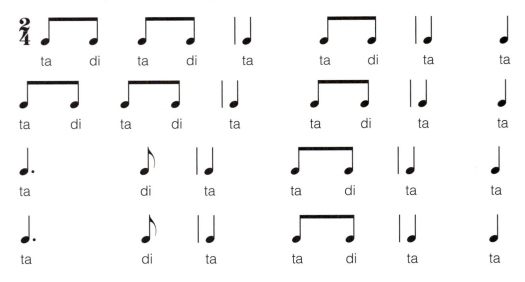

Counting with Numbers

The numbers below the rhythm of "Birch Tree" indicate how to count the rhythm.

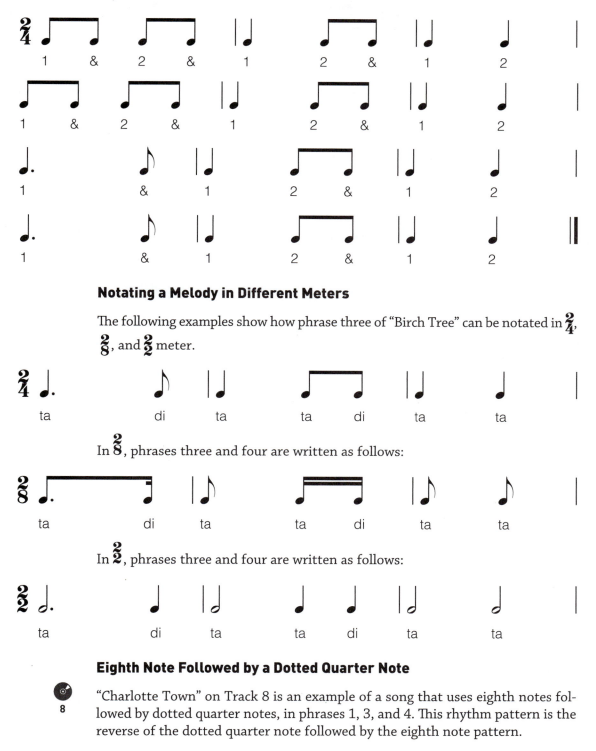

Notating a Melody in Different Meters

The following examples show how phrase three of "Birch Tree" can be notated in $\frac{2}{4}$, $\frac{2}{8}$, and $\frac{2}{2}$ meter.

In $\frac{2}{8}$, phrases three and four are written as follows:

In $\frac{2}{2}$, phrases three and four are written as follows:

Eighth Note Followed by a Dotted Quarter Note

"Charlotte Town" on Track 8 is an example of a song that uses eighth notes followed by dotted quarter notes, in phrases 1, 3, and 4. This rhythm pattern is the reverse of the dotted quarter note followed by the eighth note pattern.

The following is the notation for "Charlotte Town":

Charlotte Town

Char - lotte Town's   burn - ing down,   Good - bye,   good - bye,

Burn - ing down   to   the   ground,   Good-bye, Li - za   Jane.

Ain't   ya might - y   sor - ry?   Good-bye   good-bye,

Ain't   ya might - y   sor - ry?   Good-bye, Li - za   Jane.

Describing What You Hear with Syllables

The rhythm syllables for "Charlotte Town" are written above the beat blocks.

ta   di   ta   ta   di   ta   ta   di_____   ta   di_____

ta   di   ta   ta   di   ta   ta   di   ta   di   ta

ta   mi   ta   di   ta   di_____   ta   di_____   ta   di_____

ta   mi   ta   di   ta   di_____   ta   di   ta   di   ta

Notating What You Hear

We can write the rhythm of "Charlotte Town" as follows:

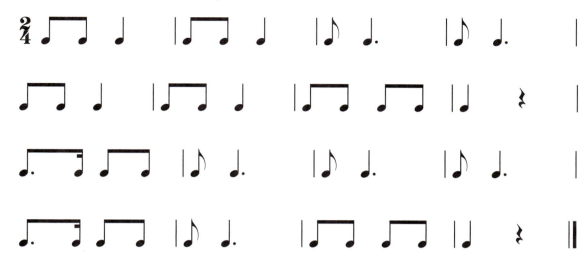

Reading with Rhythm Syllables

We can read the rhythm of "Charlotte Town" with rhythm syllables.

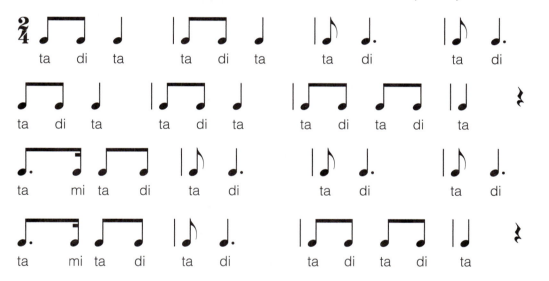

Counting with Numbers

The numbers below the rhythm of "Charlotte Town" indicate how to count the rhythm using numbers.

Listening   🎧   As you listen to some of these examples, try to identify rhythm patterns using rhythm syllables. Notate the rhythm patterns that you recognize.

Dotted Quarter Note Followed by an Eighth Note

"Play Song," *44 Duets*, No. 9, by Béla Bartók (1882–1945).

"To a Wild Rose," from *Ten Woodland Sketches*, Op. 51, by Edward MacDowell (1861–1908).

"The Birch Tree," sung by Slavyanka, Gray Smoke Records, 1991. This theme is used by Peter Tchaikovsky (1840–1893) in Symphony No. 4 in F Minor, Op. 36, movement 4, "Allegro con fuoco."

"Variations on a Shaker Theme" in *Appalachian Spring*, Movement 7, by Aaron Copland (1900–1990).

Finlandia by Jean Sibelius (1865–1957). The Indigo Girls have a version of the hymn tune on their recording *Rarities*.

Eighth Note Followed by a Dotted Quarter Note

"An Evening in the Village" from *Hungarian Sketches*, Theme No. 2, by Béla Bartók (1882–1945).

Mikrokosmos Vol. 3, No. 95 by Béla Bartók (1882–1945).

Mikrokosmos Vol. 5, No. 127, "New Hungarian Folk Song" by Béla Bartók (1882–1945).

"To A Wild Rose," from *Ten Woodland Sketches*, Op. 51 by Edward MacDowell (1861–1908).

3.6 ♪ ♩ ♪ Syncopation

Syncopation is the displacement of the normal musical accent from a strong beat to a weak one. It is used extensively in jazz and rock music. This can be achieved by accents placed over the note.

Syncopation can also occur by holding notes on weak beats over to strong beats or using rests to displace notes on strong beats.

Sing, Memorize, and Analyze

9

Internalizing Music

1. Listen to "Canoe Song" on Track 9. Memorize the song.
2. Sing "Canoe Song" and keep the beat.
3. Sing "Canoe Song" and clap the rhythm.
4. Work with another student in the class. One of you performs the beat while the other performs the rhythm of "Canoe Song." Switch parts.
5. Sing "Canoe Song" while you tap the beat with your left hand and tap the rhythm with your right hand.

Analyzing What You Hear

1. Sing phrase one of "Canoe Song" on "loo" while keeping the beat. How many sounds did you sing on beats one and two? Describe those sounds with the words "long" and "short."
2. Do you sing that same pattern for the beginning of each phrase?

Constructing a Rhythmic Representation from Memory

As you sing "Canoe Song," draw a representation indicating the number of sounds you hear in each beat; try to indicate the duration of each sound.

Music Theory

Describing What You Hear with Syllables

When we hear three sounds unevenly distributed over two beats and the sounds are short, long, short we can call it *ta di----di*. The pattern of three sounds occurring over two beats, spaced with two sounds located on the first beat and one sound located on the second half of the second beat, is an example of a syncopated rhythm. The following are the rhythm syllables for "Canoe Song," written above beat blocks.

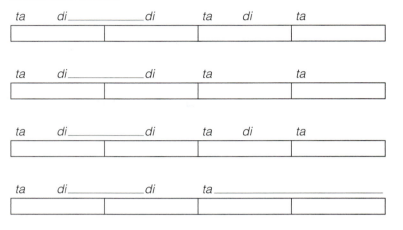

Notating What You Hear

We can write the rhythm of "Canoe Song" as follows when the beat is a quarter note:

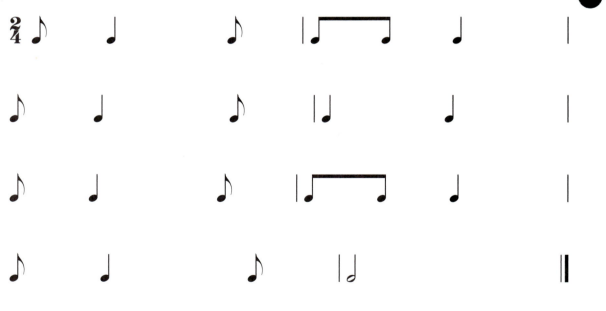

Reading with Rhythm Syllables

We can read the rhythm of "Canoe Song" with rhythm syllables.

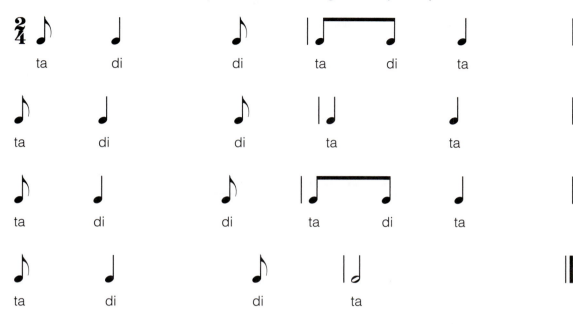

Counting with Numbers

When counting using numbers, we count the beat on which the first sound occurs and the second half of the next beat. The numbers below the rhythm of "Canoe Song" indicate how to count it.

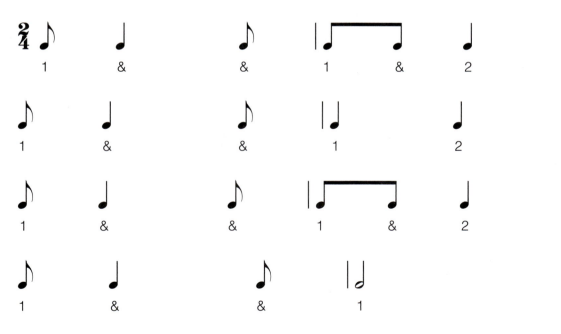

Notating a Syncopated Rhythm Pattern in Different Meters

The following shows how rhythm patterns can be converted from one meter to another.

The first phrase of "Canoe Song" can be converted into $\frac{2}{8}$ and $\frac{2}{2}$ meter.

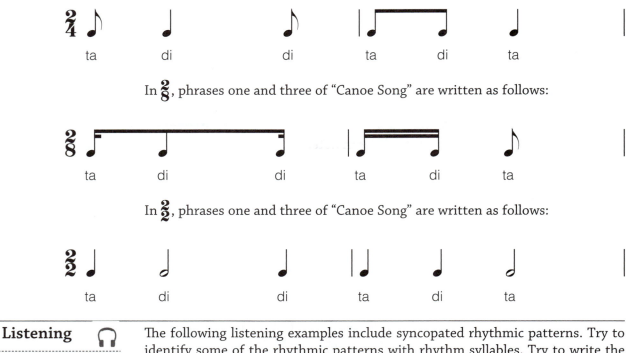

In $\frac{2}{8}$, phrases one and three of "Canoe Song" are written as follows:

In $\frac{2}{2}$, phrases one and three of "Canoe Song" are written as follows:

Listening

The following listening examples include syncopated rhythmic patterns. Try to identify some of the rhythmic patterns with rhythm syllables. Try to write the rhythmic notation of some of these examples.

Three Rondos on Folk Tunes, "Allegro Molto," Movement 3, by Béla Bartók (1882–1945).

Mikrokosmos, Vol. 5, No. 122, "Molto Vivace," by Béla Bartók (1882–1945).

"Jamaican Rumba," by Arthur Benjamin, found on James Galway's *Dances for Flute*.

The Red Poppy, Op. 70: "Russian Sailor's Dance," by Reinhold Glière (1875–1956).

"The Maple Leaf Rag" by Scott Joplin (between July 1867 and January 1868– April 1, 1917).

Key Terms and Concepts

After studying this chapter, you should understand the following terms, concepts, and musical elements.

Rhythm syllables: *ta ka di mi*
The division of the quarter note into four sixteenth notes.
Thirty-second notes and their corresponding rests.

Rhythm syllables; *ta   di mi* and *ta ka   di*
Eighth note followed by two sixteenth notes, and two sixteenth notes followed by an eighth note.

Rhythm syllables *ta mi* and *ta ka*
Dotted eighth note followed by a sixteenth note, and a sixteenth note followed by a dotted eighth note.

Upbeat or Anacrusis
Rhythm syllables *ta----di* and *ta ka---*
Dotted quarter note followed by an eighth note, and an eighth note followed by a dotted quarter note.

Syncopation
Rhythm syllables *ta di-----di*,
The syncopated rhythm pattern of an eighth note followed by a quarter note followed by an eighth note.

Summary of Note Values

The following chart shows the proportionality of note values. Each line of notes has the same duration.

Summary of Note Values and Their Corresponding Rests

Whole note; whole rest

Half note; half rest

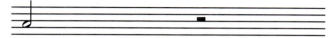

Quarter note; quarter rest

Eighth note; eighth rest

Sixteenth note; sixteenth rest

Thirty-second note; thirty-second rest

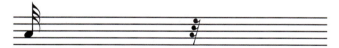

Sixty-fourth note; sixty-fourth rest

How to Practice

The mastery of reading and writing music takes many hours of practice. But we can make practice more efficient by using a variety of practice techniques. Practicing in small groups with your peers will be invaluable to your development as it will provide you with the opportunity of peer assessment and will sharpen your listening skills. This will also let you become more secure when called on by your instructor in the music class. Here are some suggestions for practicing rhythms in a variety of ways.

Performing	Sing all of the melodies with rhythm syllables.
	Sing "Dinah," "Ida Red," "London Bridge," "Birch Tree," "Charlotte Town," and "Canoe Song" with rhythm syllables while tapping the beat.
	Sing "Dinah," "Ida Red," "London Bridge," "Birch Tree," "Charlotte Town," and "Canoe Song" with rhythm syllables while conducting in duple meter.
	Sing "Dinah," "Ida Red," "London Bridge," "Birch Tree," "Charlotte Town," and "Canoe Song" with numbers while conducting in duple meter.
	Work with another student in the class. One of you performs the beat while the other performs the rhythm of Sing "Dinah," "Ida Red," "London Bridge," "Birch Tree," "Charlotte Town," and "Canoe Song." Switch parts.
	Sing "Dinah," "Ida Red," "London Bridge," "Birch Tree," "Charlotte Town," and "Canoe Song" while you tap the beat with your left hand and tap the rhythm with your right hand.
	Go to the Skills CD. Access Chapter 3 and practice the dictation exercises.
Performing the Rhythm and the Beat at the Same Time	Divide into two groups: one group performs the rhythm of the focus song, the other keeps the beat. Practice this activity in different combinations: • Instructor/class • Class/instructor • Divided class • Two individual students Individually, keep the beat with one hand and tap the rhythm with the other hand.
Standard Practice	Sing or speak the rhythm patterns of focus songs while tapping the beat.
Echo Clapping	Practice with a classmate or in class. One of you will clap the rhythm of a melody or a rhythmic pattern. The other will "echo" what was clapped with rhythm syllables.
Conducting	Sing and conduct at the same time.
Aural Analysis	Identify which beat or beats contain specified rhythmic patterns.
Notating Your Rhythm	Practice with a classmate or in class. One of you will clap the rhythm of a melody or a rhythmic pattern. The other will "echo" what was clapped with rhythm syllables and then notate the pattern in a given meter.
Error Dictation	One student plays the melody, deliberately making a mistake. Another student follows the score and locates the error.
Memory	Memorize an entire exercise and notate it without referring to the notation. First analyze the form by looking for repeated and similar parts. This will simplify the task.
Improvisation/ Composition	First select a meter and length for the composition, then decide what rhythmic form to use (for example, abba). Create an improvisation or composition using only known rhythms.
Performing a Rhythmic Canon	Say the rhythm syllables while clapping the rhythm of the melody. Think the rhythm syllables and clap the rhythm. Clap the rhythm while another person claps the melody starting after four beats. Perform the canon by yourself. Tap one part with one hand and use a pencil to tap the other part with the other hand.

Using the Musical Skills CD

Access Chapter 3 on the skills CD, to reinforce more advanced rhythms in simple meter introduced in this chapter through tutorials and dictation. Please use the arrows on the top right of the page to move from one page to another.

In the Tutorial section, you can review the following information:

1. Eighth- and sixteenth-note values, as well as listening to a musical example containing these new rhythms
2. The groupings of eighth- and sixteenth-note values, as well as listening to how these note values sound
3. Eighth- and sixteenth-note values and their corresponding rests, as well as listening to examples containing these new rhythms
4. Dotted notes and ties, as well as listening to a musical example containing these new rhythms

In the Dictation section, you will be provided with the opportunity to practice writing simple rhythm patterns that are two measures in length. There are two types of rhythmic dictations:

1. Rhythmic dictations including whole, half, quarter, eighth, and sixteenth notes with no rests
2. Rhythmic dictations including whole, half, quarter, eighth, and sixteenth notes with rests

Listen to each example several times. Try to clap and say the rhythm syllables before notating each example. You might want to notate your example on staff paper before doing so on the computer.

How to Read a Musical Score

Examine the following chorale by Johann Sebastian Bach.

Rhythm

Identify the time signature. Identify quarter notes, half notes, whole notes, eighth notes and sixteenth notes. Identify the tempo of the piece. Write in the rhythm syllables and numbers for both the treble and the bass clef.

Melody

Identify the dynamic markings. Identify the treble clef. Identify the bass clef. Identify ledger lines. Identify the grand staff. Identify a sharp.

Chorale

Johann Sebastian Bach (1685–1750)

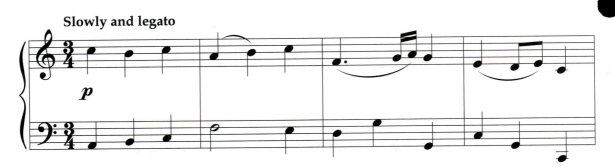

Exercise 3.22

Write the rhythm of "Birch Tree" in $\frac{2}{4}$ meter from memory. Include the time signature, bar lines, and double bar lines. Write the rhythm syllables beneath the rhythm.

_____ _____ _____ _____ _____ _____

_____ _____ _____ _____ _____ _____

_____ _____ _____ _____ _____ _____

_____ _____ _____ _____ _____ _____

Exercise 3.23

Write the rhythm of "Birch Tree" in $\frac{2}{8}$ meter from memory. Include the time signature, bar lines, and double bar lines. Write the rhythm syllables beneath the rhythm.

_____ _____ _____ _____ _____ _____

_____ _____ _____ _____ _____ _____

_____ _____ _____ _____ _____ _____

_____ _____ _____ _____ _____ _____

Exercise 3.24

Write the rhythm of "Birch Tree" in $\frac{2}{2}$ meter from memory. Include the time signature, bar lines, and double bar lines. Write the rhythm syllables beneath the rhythm.

_____ _____ _____ _____ _____ _____

_____ _____ _____ _____ _____ _____

_____ _____ _____ _____ _____ _____

_____ _____ _____ _____ _____ _____

Exercise 3.25

Write the rhythm of "Charlotte Town" in $\frac{2}{8}$ meter from memory. Include the time signature, bar lines, and double bar lines.

Exercise 3.26

Write the rhythm of "Charlotte Town" in $\frac{2}{8}$ meter from memory. Include the time signature, bar lines, and double bar lines.

Exercise 3.27

Write the rhythm of "Charlotte Town" in $\frac{2}{2}$ meter. Include the time signature, bar lines, and double bar lines.

Chapter 4

Orientation to the Major Scale

CHAPTER OVERVIEW

In this chapter we will be studying another basic element of music—melody. A **melody** is a succession of notes of variable sounds (pitches) and recognized shape. Pitches in a melody may move up or down or remain the same. Melodies may move by **skips** or **steps**. This gives a melody its **shape**, or musical **contour**. There are four types of contours:

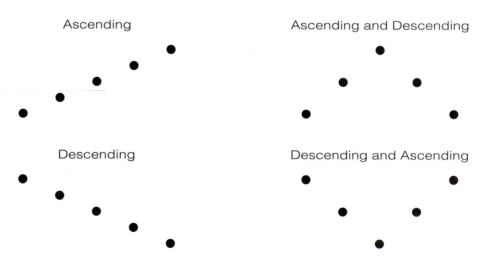

Ascending

Ascending and Descending

Descending

Descending and Ascending

    Pitch is the frequency (high or low) of the individual notes. Pitch is indicated by the placement of notes on a staff. The subjective sense of pitch is closely correlated with frequency. The measurement of frequency is in cycles per second, or hertz (Hz). Frequency is a ratio scale of measurement: each time pitch goes up by an octave, the frequency is doubled. The present international standard pitch A (above middle C) is equal to 440 Hz.

In this chapter you will begin to notate, to read music with solfège syllables, and to compose with the basic building blocks of melody. These basic building blocks form scales. **Scales** are a series of ascending or descending notes that we use to define various pitch collections of notes. These scales are found in all types of Western music. Although the melodies in this book look simple and perhaps not interesting for detailed study, you will discover that they contain the musical principles from which larger, more complex compositions develop. You will learn how the basic building blocks in music, called *motives*, are contained in phrases, and how phrases create large sections in music. These motives can be rhythmic and melodic. This melodic hierarchy is fundamental to music.

4.1 Major Pentachord Scales and Melodies

Much music grows from a system of related collections of pitches called *scales*. A scale is a sequence of notes ascending or descending stepwise. There are a variety of scales used in different cultures. In order to understand these scales, we will be studying repertoire built on smaller scale types: pentachord scales (five-note sections of a diatonic scale) and hexachord scales (six-note sections of a diatonic scale). These scales are tonal, and this means that specific hierarchical pitch relationships are based on a primary note called the **tonic**.

Sing, Memorize, and Analyze

Internalizing Music

1. Listen to "Hungarian Canon No. 1" on Track 10. Memorize the song.
2. Sing "Hungarian Canon No. 1" while you clap the melodic contour. Clapping the melodic contour allows you to internalize the shape and direction of the phrase.
3. Pair off in the class. Facing your partner, sing "Hungarian Canon No. 1" and clap the melodic contour.

Analyzing What You Hear

1. Sing "Hungarian Canon No. 1" with rhythm syllables.
2. Sing the lowest pitch in the song.
3. Sing the highest pitch in the song.
4. Sing the beginning note of the song.
5. Sing the range of notes from the lowest note to the highest note.
6. Sing the range of notes from the highest note to the lowest note.

Constructing a Melodic Representation from Memory

1. As you sing "Hungarian Canon No. 1," draw a representation indicating the pitches in each phrase.
2. As you point to your representation, sing the melody with rhythm syllables.

Music Theory

Describing What You Hear with Solfège Syllables

We can describe the pitches in "Hungarian Canon No. 1" with solfège syllables. **Solfège syllables** are a means for figuring out the relationships between the notes we hear. There are many solfège reading systems. We use the moveable *do* system. It is important to remember that solfège syllables identify the pitches we hear as well as help us to read music.

These are the solfège syllables for "Hungarian Canon No. 1." Notice that the pitches in this melody move mostly by steps. There are only a few skips.

Hungarian Canon No. 1

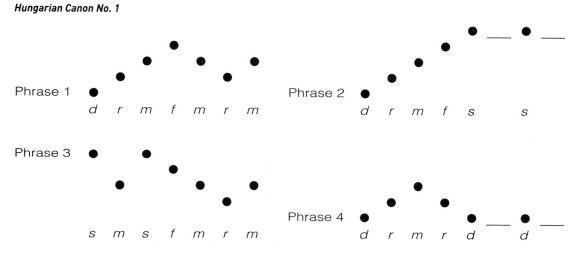

Some musicians have the ability to identify any note heard or to sing any note on demand without a pitch reference; this faculty is known as "perfect pitch." Other musicians have the ability to identify notes heard or to sing any note on demand when given the name of the starting pitch. This is called "relative pitch." Solfège syllables will develop your relative pitch ability. Solfège syllables have been used for centuries by beginners and professionals to teach and to learn to sing and play music.

Solfège Inventory

The **solfège inventory** is a list of the solfège syllables written in ascending order. We can circle or bold the final note of the piece of music. As mentioned earlier, there are many types of scales. A **major pentachord scale** is a series of five adjacent tones (*do–re–mi–fa–so*) with a half step occurring between the third and fourth degrees. The solfège inventory for the *do* pentachord scale is *do–re–mi–fa–so*. We can use an abbreviated form of these written syllables: *d–r–m–f–s*. Such abbreviations make it easier to notate a melody. We will use the full name of the solfège syllable to describe a scale. For example, *do* pentachord scale. Note that solfège syllables will be written in lowercase, while letter names will be written in uppercase.

Notating What You Hear with Solfège Syllables

We can write "Hungarian Canon No. 1" in rhythm notation with solfège syllables.

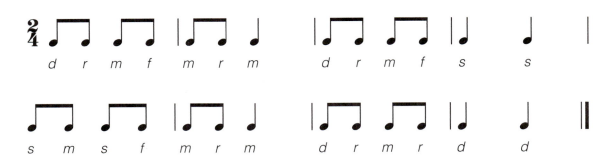

When we write the pitches of "Hungarian Canon No. 1" in ascending order, we discover that there are five adjacent pitches. We can label these pitches with solfège syllables *do–re–mi–fa–so*, or scale degree numbers $\hat{1}$–$\hat{2}$–$\hat{3}$–$\hat{4}$–$\hat{5}$ respectively. These numbers represent the first five pitches of the major pentachord scale. We can call this an ordered collection of pitches.

Solfège Syllable	Scale Degree Number
s	$\hat{5}$
f	$\hat{4}$
m	$\hat{3}$
r	$\hat{2}$
d	$\hat{1}$

Notating What You Hear on the Staff

We can write the "Hungarian Canon No. 1" on the staff beginning on C as follows:

Hungarian Canon No. 1

Listening 🎧   The following listening examples include subsets of the major pentachord scale. Can you sing the theme using solfège syllables? Can you write the themes of some of these examples using staff notation or stick notation with solfège syllables?

Subsets of the Pentachord Scale: *m–r–d*

"Carillon" from *L'Arlésienne Suite* No. 1 by Georges Bizet (1838–1875).

Major Pentachord

Mikrokosmos Vol. 1, Nos. 1, 2, 6, 17, 26; vol. 3, nos. 74 and 86 by Béla Bartók (1882–1945).

"Slovakian Song," Vol. 1, No. 5, from *44 Duets for Two Violins* by Béla Bartók (1882–1945).

"Matchmaking Song," Vol. 1, No. 1, from *44 Duets for Two Violins* by Béla Bartók (1882–1945).

"Play Song," Vol. 1, No. 9, from *44 Duets for Two Violins* by Béla Bartók (1882–1945).

"Pillow Dance," *For Children* Vol. 1, No. 4, by Béla Bartók (1882–1945) (London, New York and Berlin: Boosey & Hawkes 2003).

For Children Vol. 2, No. 1, by Béla Bartók (1882–1945) (London, New York and Berlin: Boosey & Hawkes 2003).

"Round Dance," *For Children* Vol. 2, No. 6, by Béla Bartók (1882–1945) (London, New York and Berlin: Boosey & Hawkes 2003).

"The Five Fingers: Eight Very Easy Melodies on Five Notes" by Igor Stravinsky (1882–1971).

4.2 Determining the Intervals Between Notes of the Pentachord Scale

The distance between one pitch and another is called an **interval**. Intervals are identified by their size and quality. The intervals between *d* and *r*, *r* and *m*, *f* and *s* are whole steps. Since all of these intervals span two notes, we can refer to them as intervals of a *second*; the size of these intervals is a *second*. The quality of these intervals, or the number of half steps they contain, is not the same. There are two half steps between *d* and *r*, *f* and *s*, and *m* to *f* is one half step. We can refer to intervals of a second that contain two half steps as **major seconds (M2)** and intervals of a second that contain one half step as **minor seconds (m2)**.

The following shows the whole- and half-step relationships of the C major pentachord scale on the keyboard. Look at the whole-step (W) and half-step (H) pattern.

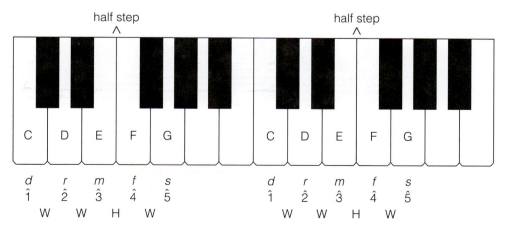

Look at the whole-step (W) and half-step (H) pattern of the C major pentachord scale on the staff.

W   W   H   W   W   H   W   W

The first degree of the scale is called the *tonic* note or *keynote*. There is a half step between the third and fourth degrees of the scale. There is a whole step between all other degrees of the scale (one and two, two and three, four and five).

4.3 Writing a Major Pentachord Scale and Melody Using Accidentals

There are several things to consider when you begin to write pitches on the staff. Consider the placement of stems. Pitches that are written below the third line of the staff have their stems pointing up and to the right of the note head, and pitches written above the third line have their stems pointing down and to the left of the note head.

Stems of notes on the third line can be written either up or down.

Writing a Major Pentachord Scale Using Accidentals

The following is a procedure for writing any major pentachord scale on the staff using accidentals. We will write this example as a D major pentachord scale in the treble clef.

1. Write the solfège syllables *d–r–m–f–s* beneath the staff for the major pentachord scale.

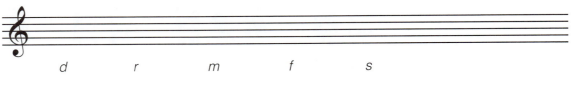

    d   *r*   *m*   *f*   *s*

2. Place a note on the staff above each solfège syllable. For a major pentachord scale we use five adjacent notes; therefore, the pitches should also be adjacent on the staff. The first procedure is to remember the sequential alphabetical spelling of scales and then simply put the notes in order. For example, if the tonic note is C, write C–D–E–F–G, or if the tonic note is D, write D–E–F–G–A. We will write this major pentachord scale beginning on D.

    d   *r*   *m*   *f*   *s*

3. Mark the half step between scale degrees three and four and their corresponding pitches on the staff. Remember the intervals between the other degrees will be whole steps.

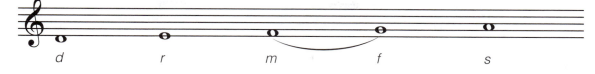

4. Check the intervallic relationship between the solfège syllables and the pitch names to insure the correct intervallic distance between the notes. In this case, we have to raise the F to an F-sharp to make the distance between *r* and *m* a whole step. That's the only alteration we need to make in the D major pentachord scale.

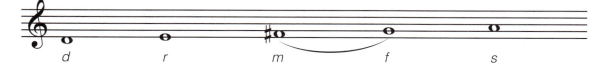

Writing a Major Pentachord Melody Using Accidentals

The following is a procedure for writing any major pentachord melody on the staff using accidentals. For an example, we will write "Lady Come" in the key of D major in treble clef. Music based on a particular scale is said to be in the key of that scale. If music is built on the C major pentachord scale, then the work is in the key of C major and the tonic of the music is C.

"Lady Come" written in rhythm notation with solfège syllables:

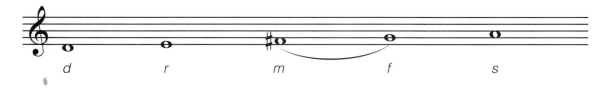

Notice that the second motive (measure two) is a transformation of motive one transposed. We call this a **sequence**. A sequence has the same rhythmic and melodic pattern, but it begins on a different note.

1. Write the D major pentachord scale on the staff using accidentals.

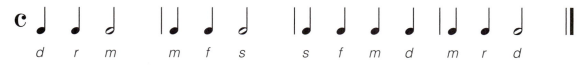

2. Write the solfège syllables below the scale.

3. Write "Lady Come" on the staff by associating the solfège syllables with note names in the D major pentachord.

4.4   Major Hexachord Scales and Melodies

Sing, Memorize, and Analyze

11

Internalizing Music

1. Listen to "Twinkle, Twinkle, Little Star" on Track 11. Memorize the song.
2. Sing "Twinkle, Twinkle, Little Star" while you clap the melodic contour.
3. Stand and face a partner. Sing "Twinkle, Twinkle, Little Star" while you both clap the melodic contour.

Analyzing What You Hear

1. Sing "Twinkle, Twinkle, Little Star" with rhythm syllables.
2. Pair off in the class. Facing your partner, sing "Twinkle, Twinkle, Little Star" and clap the melodic contour.
3. Sing with rhythm names while clapping and showing the melodic contour.
4. Sing the lowest pitches in the song.
5. Sing the highest pitches in the song.
6. Sing the range of notes from the lowest note to the highest note.
7. Sing the range of notes from the highest note to the lowest note.

Constructing a Melodic Representation from Memory

1. As you sing "Twinkle, Twinkle, Little Star," draw a representation of the pitches in each phrase.
2. As you point to your representation, sing the melody with rhythm syllables.

Music Theory

Describing What You Hear with Syllables

We can describe the pitches in "Twinkle, Twinkle, Little Star" with solfège syllables. Notice that the melodic movement of phrases one and five begins with a leap, but the rest of this melody moves mostly in steps.

Twinkle, Twinkle, Little Star

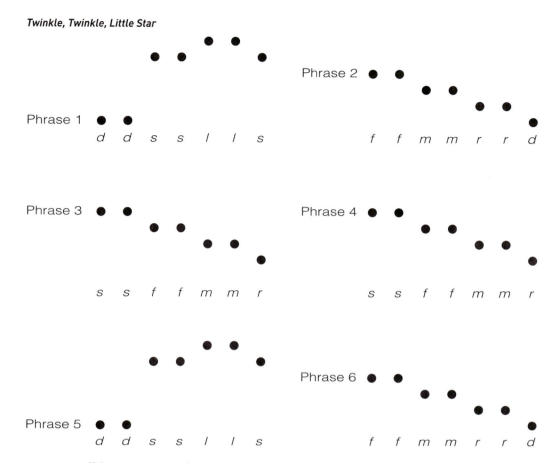

La will be represented by the solfège syllable *l*. When we arrange the pitches of "Twinkle, Twinkle, Little Star" in ascending order, we discover that there are six adjacent pitches or scale degrees. We can label these pitches with solfège syllables *d–r–m–f–s–l* or numbers $\hat{1}$–$\hat{2}$–$\hat{3}$–$\hat{4}$–$\hat{5}$–$\hat{6}$ respectively. We refer to this collection of notes as a **major hexachord scale.** The solfège inventory is *d–r–m–f–s–l*.

Notating What You Hear with Solfège Syllables

We can write "Twinkle, Twinkle, Little Star" in rhythm notation with solfège syllables.

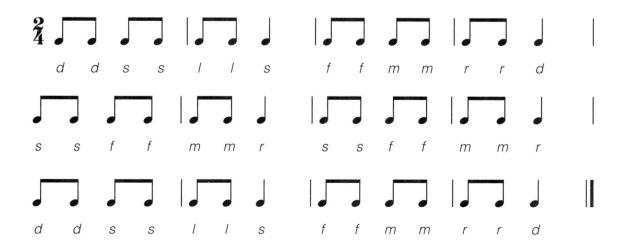

The following figure shows the connection between the solfège syllables and scale degree numbers.

Solfège Syllable	Scale Degree Number
l	$\hat{6}$
s	$\hat{5}$
f	$\hat{4}$
m	$\hat{3}$
r	$\hat{2}$
d	$\hat{1}$

Notating What You Hear on the Staff

We can write "Twinkle, Twinkle, Little Star" on the staff beginning on C as follows:

4.5   Determining the Size and Quality of Intervals Between the Notes of the Major Hexachord Scale

The following shows the whole- and half-step relationships of the C major hexachord scale on the keyboard. Look at the whole-step (W) and half-step (H) pattern.

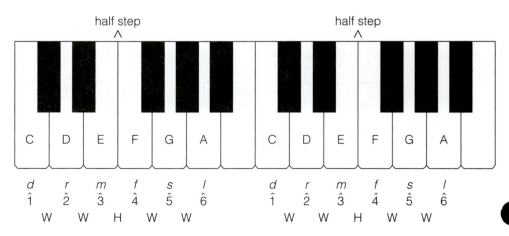

The following shows the whole- and half-step relationships of the C major hexachord scale on the staff. Look at the whole-step (W) and half-step (H) pattern.

The first degree of the scale is called the tonic note or keynote. There is a half step between the third and fourth degree of the scale. There is a whole step between all other degrees of the scale (one and two, two and three, four and five, five and six).

4.6   Writing a Major Hexachord Scale and Melody Using Accidentals

Writing a Major Hexachord Scale Using Accidentals

The following is a procedure for writing any major hexachord scale on the staff using accidentals. We will write this example as a D major hexachord scale in the treble clef.

1. Write the solfège syllables *d–r–m–f–s–l* beneath the staff for the major hexachord scale.

2. Place a note on the staff above each solfège syllable. For a major hexachord scale we use six adjacent notes; therefore, the pitches should also be adjacent on the staff. The first procedure is to remember the sequential alphabetical spelling of scales, then simply put the notes in order. For example, if the tonic note is C, write C–D–E–F–G–A, or if the tonic note is D, write D–E–F–G–A–B. We will write this major hexachord scale beginning on D.

3. Mark the half step between scale degrees three and four and their corresponding pitches on the staff. Remember the intervals between the other degrees will be whole steps.

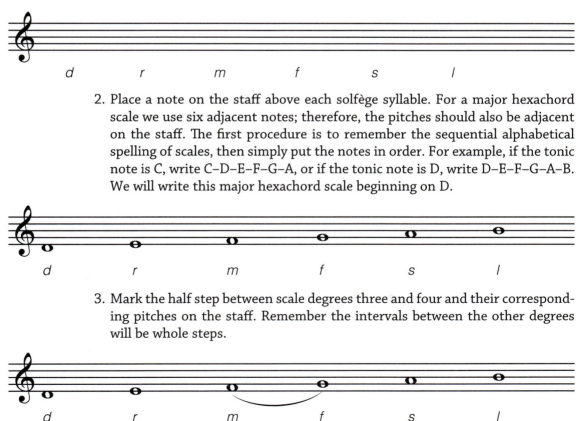

Check the intervallic relationship between the solfège syllables and the pitch names to insure the correct intervallic distance between the notes. In this case, we have to raise the F to an F-sharp to make the distance between *r* and *m* a whole step. That's the only alteration we need to make in the D major hexachord scale.

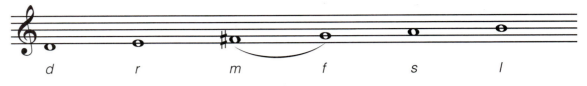

Writing a Major Hexachord Melody Using Accidentals

The following is a procedure for writing any major hexachord melody on the staff using accidentals. For an example we will write "Twinkle, Twinkle, Little Star" in the key of D major hexachord in treble clef using accidentals. Remember, music based on a particular scale is said to be in the key of that scale. If music is built on the C major scale, then the work is in the key of C major and the tonic of the music is C. We will write "Twinkle, Twinkle, Little Star" on the staff in the key of D.

1. Write the D major hexachord scale on the staff using accidentals.

2. Write the solfège syllables below the scale.

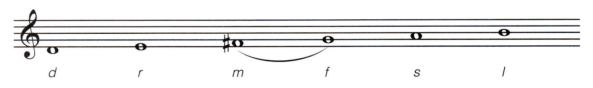

3. Write "Twinkle, Twinkle, Little Star" on the staff by associating the solfège syllables with note names in the key of D major. Note the placement of accidentals.

We can say that "Twinkle, Twinkle, Little Star" is written in the key of D major, as it uses the notes of the D major scale. The tonic of this piece is D.

Listening

Listening 🎧

The following listening examples include subsets of the major pentachord scale. Can you sing the themes using solfège syllables? Can you write the themes of some of these examples using staff notation or stick notation with solfège syllables?

"Ah! Vous dirai-je maman," Variations on "Twinkle, Twinkle, Little Star" K. 265, by Wolfgang Amadeus Mozart (1756–1791).

"Variations on a Nursery Song," Op. 25, by Ernö Dohnányi (1877–1960).

"Maypole Dance," No. 2 from *44 Duets for Two Violins* by Béla Bartók (1882–1945).

"Children at Play," *For Children* Vol. 1, No. 1, by Béla Bartók (1882–1945).

For Children Vol. 2, Nos. 2 and 3, by Béla Bartók (1882–1945).

4.7 Major Pentatonic Scales and Melodies

Sing, Memorize, and Analyze 💿
12

Internalizing Music

1. Listen to "Rocky Mountain" on Track 12. Memorize the song.
2. Sing "Rocky Mountain" while you clap the melodic contour.
3. Stand and face a partner. Sing "Rocky Mountain" while you both clap the melodic contour.

Analyzing What You Hear

1. Sing "Rocky Mountain" with rhythm syllables.
2. Pair off in the class. Facing your partner, sing "Rocky Mountain" and clap the melodic contour. (Imagine that you are pointing to the shape of the melody on the board without looking at it.)
3. Sing with rhythm names while clapping and showing the melodic contour.
4. Sing the lowest pitches in the song.
5. Sing the highest pitches in the song.
6. Sing the range of notes from the lowest note to the highest note.
7. Sing the range of notes from the highest note to the lowest note.

Constructing a Melodic Representation from Memory

1. As you sing "Rocky Mountain," draw a representation of the pitches; try to indicate the duration of each sound.
2. Point to your representation as you sing "Rocky Mountain" with rhythm syllables.

Describing What You Hear with Solfège Syllables

Rocky Mountain

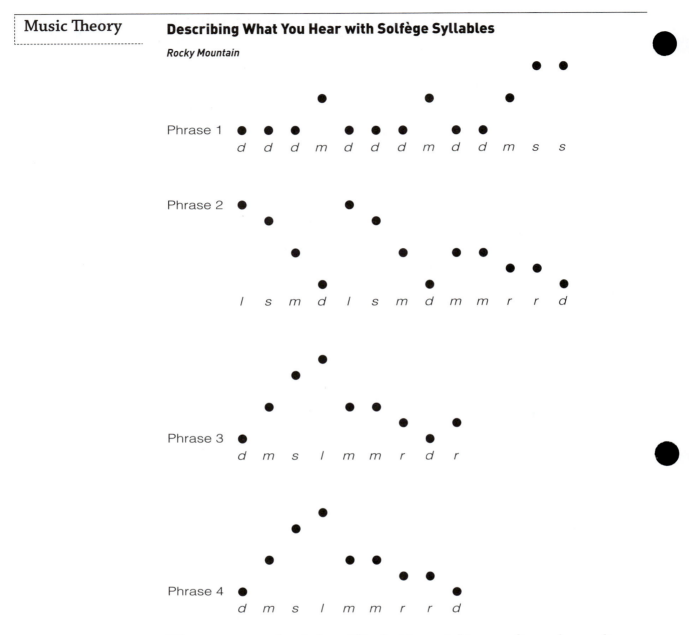

Phrase 1
d d d m d d d m d d m s s

Phrase 2
l s m d l s m d m m r r d

Phrase 3
d m s l m m r d r

Phrase 4
d m s l m m r r d

When we arrange the pitches of "Rocky Mountain" in ascending order, we discover that there are five pitches. The solfège inventory of these pitches is *d–r–m– –s–l*. There is a skip between the third and fourth notes. This skip is made up of three half steps and creates a **minor-third** interval (m3). We refer to this collection of notes as a **major pentatonic scale**.

Notating What You Hear with Solfège Syllables

We can write "Rocky Mountain" in rhythm notation with solfège syllables.

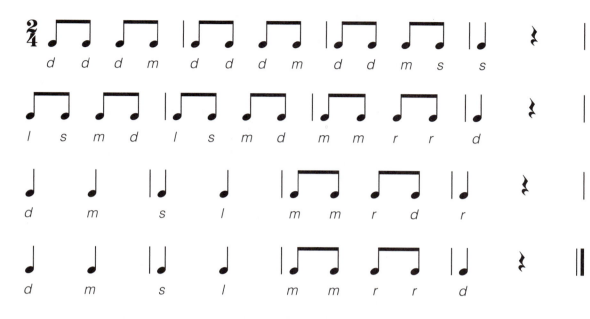

Notating What You Hear on the Staff

We can write "Rocky Mountain" on the staff beginning on C as follows:

4.8 Determining the Size and Quality of Intervals Between the Notes of the Major Pentatonic Scale

The following shows the whole-step and skip relationships of the pentatonic scale on the keyboard beginning on C.

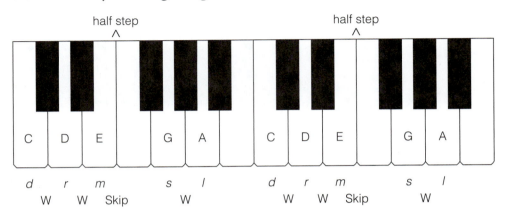

The following shows the relationships of the pentatonic scale on the staff. Look at the whole step (W) and skip (Sk) of the C major pentachord scale.

4.9 Writing a Major Pentatonic Scale and Melody Using Accidentals

Writing a Major Pentatonic Scale on the Staff Using Accidentals

The following is a procedure for writing any major pentatonic scale on the staff using accidentals. We will write this example as a D major pentatonic scale in the treble clef.

1. Write the solfège syllables *d–r–m– –s–l* beneath the staff for the major pentatonic scale.

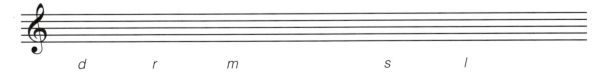

2. Place a note on the staff above each solfège syllable. For a major pentatonic scale we use five notes. There is no half step. The easiest way to think about the major pentatonic scale is to simply omit the f from the major hexachord scale. The first procedure is to put the five notes *d–r–m––s–l* on the staff. For example, if the tonic note is C, write C–D–E––G–A, or if the tonic note is D, write D–E–F–––A–B. We will write this major pentatonic scale beginning on D.

3. There is no half step in the major pentatonic scale. The easiest way to write a pentatonic scale is to think *d–r–m–f–s–l* and omit the *f*. The distance between the intervals *m* and *s* is a minor third.

4. Check the intervallic relationship between the solfège syllables and the pitch names to insure the correct intervallic distance between the notes. In this case, we have to raise the F to an F-sharp to make the distance between *r* and *m* a whole step. That's the only alteration we need to make in the D major pentatonic scale.

Writing a Major Pentatonic Melody Using Accidentals

The following is a procedure for writing a major pentatonic melody on the staff using accidentals. For an example, we will write "Rocky Mountain" in the D major pentatonic scale in treble clef using accidentals.

1. Write the D major pentatonic scale on the staff using accidentals.

2. Write the solfège syllables below the scale.

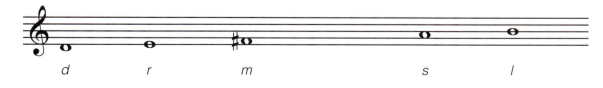

3. Write "Rocky Mountain" on the staff by associating the solfège syllables with note names in the key of D major.

- We can say that "Rocky Mountain" is written in the key of D major pentatonic, as it uses the notes of the D major pentatonic scale. The tonic of this piece is D.

Key Terms and Concepts

Melody	Tonic Note	Sequence
Step	Solfège Syllables	Major Hexachord Scale
Skip	Solfège Inventory	Minor Third (m3)
Shape	Major Pentachord Scale	Major Pentatonic Scale
Contour	Interval	
Pitch	Major Seconds (M2)	
Scale	Minor Seconds (m2)	

How to Practice

Here are some suggestions for practicing pentachord, hexachord, and pentatonic melodies in a variety of ways. Remember to keep practicing in small groups with your peers.

Performing	Sing all of the melodies with rhythm syllables.
	Sing the "Hungarian Canon No. 1" with rhythm syllables and conduct as you sing. Sing the "Hungarian Canon No. 1" with solfège syllables and conduct as you sing. Sing the "Hungarian Canon No. 1" with scale degree numbers and conduct as you sing.
	Sing "Twinkle, Twinkle, Little Star" with rhythm syllables and conduct as you sing. Sing "Twinkle, Twinkle, Little Star" with solfège syllables and conduct as you sing. Sing "Twinkle, Twinkle, Little Star" with scale degree numbers and conduct as you sing.
	Sing "Rocky Mountain" with rhythm syllables and conduct as you sing. Sing "Rocky Mountain" with solfège syllables and conduct as you sing. Sing "Rocky Mountain" with scale degree numbers and conduct as you sing.
Singing Scales	Sing pentachord scales with solfège and letter names. Sing hexachord scales with solfège and letter names. Sing pentatonic scales with solfège and letter names.
Playing on the Piano	Play pentachord scales on the piano and sing with solfège and letter names. Play hexachord scales on the piano and sing with solfège and letter names. Play pentatonic scales on the piano and sing with solfège and letter names.
Sight Singing	Look at the meter. Choose a suitable tempo and speak the rhythm patterns of focus songs while tapping the beat. Identify the scale of the example. Sing the scale with solfège syllables. Sing the music example.
Echo Singing	Practice with a classmate or in class. One of you will hum or play on the piano an eight-beat melody. The other will "echo" what was played with solfège syllables.
Conducting	Sing and conduct at the same time.
Memorizing by Ear	The instructor or another student plays a melody on the piano or hums a melody. • Identify the meter. • Sing the example with rhythm names. • Identify the ending and starting pitches with solfège syllables. • Sing the example with solfège syllables.
Notating the Melody	Practice with a classmate or in class. One of you will sing a known melody with neutral syllables or play on the piano a melody from the chapter. The other will "echo" what was sung or played with solfège syllables and then notate the melody in a given meter and key.
Error Dictation	One student plays the melody, deliberately making a mistake. Another student follows the score and locates the error.
Dictation	Instructor hums or plays typical patterns from the dictation melody and students must sing back with rhythm and solfège syllables. Instructor plays melody and students determine beginning and final note. Students sing the melody with rhythm and solfège syllables. Students notate melody in a key and meter provided by instructor.
Memorizing from a Score	Memorize an entire melody and notate it without referring to the notation. First analyze the form by looking for repeated and similar parts. This will simplify the task.
Improvisation/ Composition	First select a meter and length for the composition, then decide what form to use (for example, ABBA). Create an improvisation or composition using only known rhythms and scales.
Performing a Canon	As you sing the melody, clap the rhythm in canon after two or four beats.

Using the Musical Skills CD

Access Chapter 4 on the skills CD to reinforce the notation of major pentachord and hexachord melodies.

You will be provided with the opportunity to practice the notation of penta-chord and hexachord melodies that include half, quarter, and eighth notes and their corresponding rests on the staff.

Listen to each example several times. Try to clap, say the rhythm, and sing with solfège syllables before notating each example. If you cannot memorize the complete example, try memorizing four measures. Once you can easily memorize four measures, then try to memorize eight measures. You might want to notate your example on staff paper before doing so on the computer. Try writing the example using rhythmic notation and solfège syllables before writing on the staff. You might also want to sing each example and point to the notes on the staff before attempting to notate it.

How to Read a Musical Score

Examine the Musette by Johann Sebastian Bach.

Rhythm

Identify the meter. Identify the sixteenth notes, and sixteenth-note combina-tions. What is the tempo of the Musette? Clap the rhythm of the treble clef while saying rhythm syllables. Clap the rhythm while counting with numbers. Write in the rhythm syllables for the right hand.

Melody

Identify the phrase marks. Identify the dynamic markings. Identify the key sig-nature.

What scale pattern do you find in the first four measures of the treble clef? Sing the first four measures with solfège syllables.

Form

What is the form of the Musette?

Musette

Johann Sebastian Bach (1685–1750)

Giocoso

MUSIC THEORY EXERCISES

4.1   Exercises: Major Pentachord Scales and Melodies

Exercise 4.1

Circle the half steps and put a bracket around the whole steps in "Hungarian Canon No. 1."

Hungarian Canon No. 1

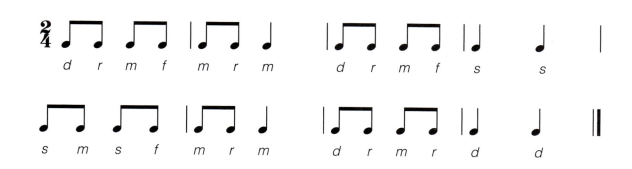

d   r   m   f   m   r   m   d   r   m   f   s   s

s   m   s   f   m   r   m   d   r   m   r   d   d

Exercise 4.2

Fill in the following chart for the major pentachord scale.

Solfège Syllable	Scale Degree Number
d	$\hat{1}$
r	
m	
f	
s	

4.2   Exercise: Determining the Intervals Between Notes of the Pentachord Scale

Exercise 4.3

Consider the whole steps (M2) and half steps (m2) in the major pentachord scale. Complete the following chart using solfège syllables.

Whole Steps Major 2	Half Steps Minor 2
d–r	

4.3   Exercises: Writing a Major Pentachord Scale and Melodies Using Accidentals

Exercise 4.4

Write each of the following major pentachord scales in treble and bass clef using whole notes and accidentals ascending and descending. Include the solfège syllables and scale degree numbers, mark the half steps, and determine the accidentals.

1. G major

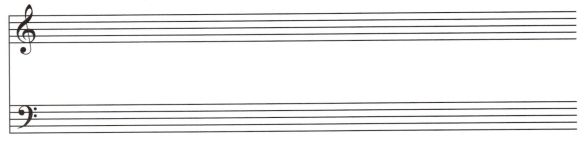

2. D major

3. A major

4. E major

5. B major

6. F-sharp major

7. C-sharp major

8. F major

9. B-flat major

10. E-flat major

11. A-flat major

Exercise 4.5

Write "Hungarian Canon No. 1" beginning on the following notes. Include a time signature, bar lines, and accidentals.

1. Begin on B-flat

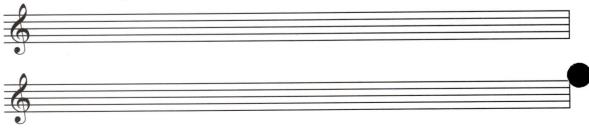

2. Begin on D

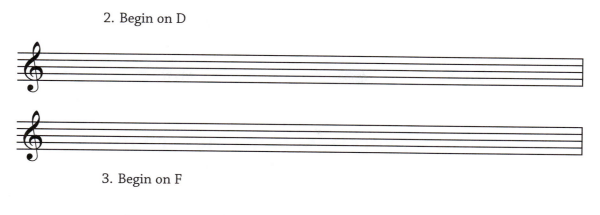

3. Begin on F

Exercise 4.6

To write a major pentachord melody on the staff for a given tonic note:

1. Determine the scale of the melody.
2. Associate the scale degrees of the tone set with absolute pitch names on the staff.
3. Remember to place an accidental in front of every altered note on the staff.

Lady Come

La - dy, come.   Can't you see?   John fell off the   white oak tree.

1. Write "Lady Come" beginning on D. Include the time signature, bar lines, and accidentals.

2. Write "Lady Come" beginning on F. Include the time signature, bar lines, and accidentals.

3. Write "Lady Come" beginning on G. Include the time signature, bar lines, and accidentals.

4. Write "Lady Come" beginning on B-flat. Include the time signature, bar lines, and accidentals.

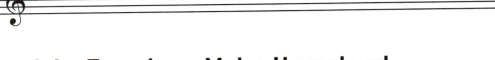

4.4   Exercises: Major Hexachord Scales and Melodies

Exercise 4.7

Circle the half steps (m2) and put a bracket around the whole steps (M2) in "Twinkle, Twinkle, Little Star."

Twinkle, Twinkle, Little Star

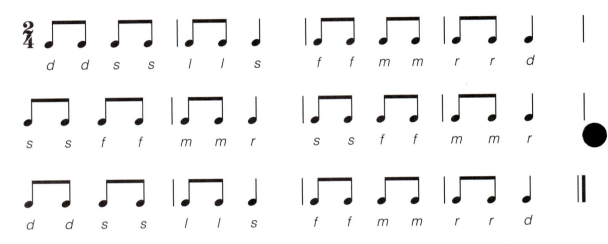

Music Theory Exercise 4.8

Fill in the following chart for the major hexachord scale.

Solfège Syllable	Scale Degree Number
d	$\hat{1}$
r	
m	
f	
s	
l	

4.5   Exercise: Determining the Size and Quality of Intervals Between Notes of the Major Hexachord Scale

Exercise 4.9

Consider the major seconds and minor seconds used in the major hexachord scale. Complete the following chart using solfège syllables.

Whole Steps Major 2	Half Steps Minor 2
d–r	

4.6   Exercises: Writing a Major Hexachord Scale and Melodies Using Accidentals

Exercise 4.10

Write the following major hexachord scales in treble and bass clef using whole notes and accidentals ascending and descending. Include the solfège syllables and scale degrees, mark the half steps, and determine the accidentals.

1. G major

2. D major

3. A major

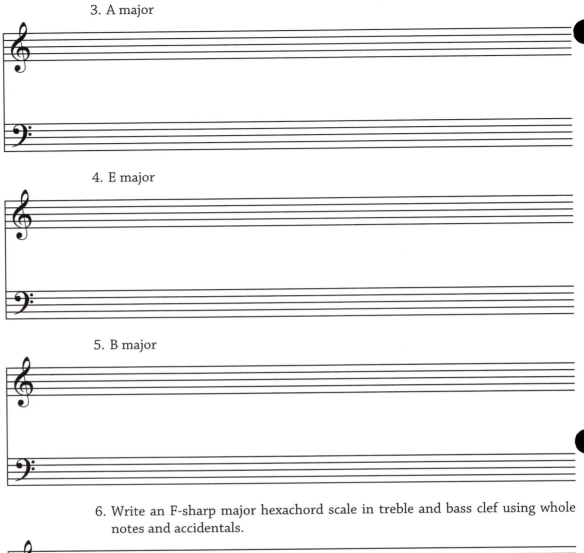

4. E major

5. B major

6. Write an F-sharp major hexachord scale in treble and bass clef using whole notes and accidentals.

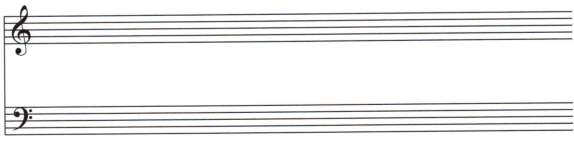

7. F major

8. B-flat major

9. E-flat major

10. A-flat major

11. D-flat major

12. G-flat major

Exercise 4.11

1. Write "Twinkle, Twinkle, Little Star" beginning on B-flat. Include the time signature, bar lines, and accidentals.

2. Write "Twinkle, Twinkle, Little Star" beginning on G. Include the time signature, bar lines, and accidentals.

3. Write "Twinkle, Twinkle, Little Star" beginning on F. Include the time signature, bar lines, and accidentals.

4. Write "Twinkle, Twinkle, Little Star" beginning on G. Include the time signature, bar lines, and accidentals.

4.7   Exercises: Major Pentatonic Scale and Melodies

Exercise 4.12

Consider the intervals in "Rocky Mountain." Bracket the whole steps and circle the minor-third intervals.

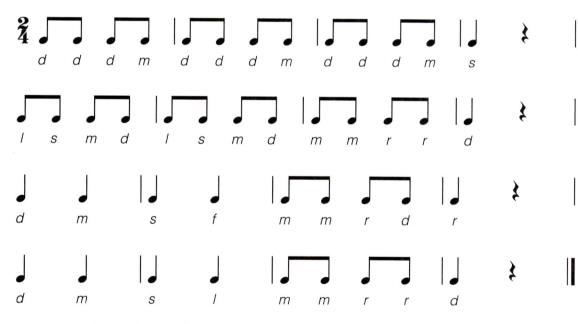

Exercise 4.13

Fill in the following chart for the major pentatonic scale.

Solfège Syllable	Scale Degree Number
d	$\hat{1}$
r	
m	
s	
l	

4.8   Exercises: Writing a Major Pentatonic Scale and Melodies Using Accidentals

Exercise 4.14

Write the following major pentatonic scales in treble and bass clef using whole notes and accidentals ascending and descending. Include the solfège syllables and scale degrees, and determine the accidentals.

1. G major pentatonic

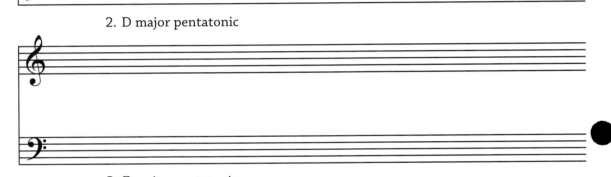

2. D major pentatonic

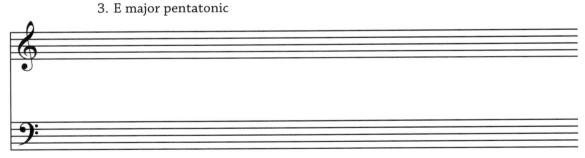

3. E major pentatonic

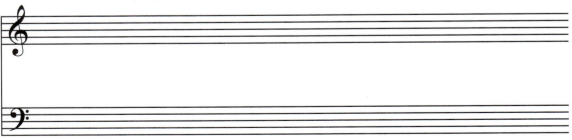

4. B major pentatonic

5. F-sharp major pentatonic

Exercise 4.15

1. Write "Rocky Mountain" beginning on B-flat. Include the time signature, bar lines, and accidentals.

2. Write "Rocky Mountain" beginning on A. Include the time signature, bar lines, and accidentals.

3. Write "Rocky Mountain" beginning on F. Include the time signature, bar lines, and accidentals.

4. Write "Rocky Mountain" beginning on G. Include the time signature, bar lines, and accidentals.

Chapter 5
The Major Scale

CHAPTER OVERVIEW

A scale is a sequence of notes ascending and descending stepwise and categorized by a particular arrangement of intervals. One form of the diatonic scale is represented by the white notes of the piano keyboard conventionally beginning and ending on C. Like the major pentachord and hexachord scale, the major scale is built on whole and half steps. All styles of music, from Bach, to Haydn, Mozart, Beethoven, popular, rock, and jazz, use these scales. In Chapter 4 you learned about the construction of the major pentachord, hexachord, and pentatonic scales. In this chapter you will build on this information to understand how to notate major scales and major-scale melodies with and without key signatures, as well as how to compose music based on the major scale. In order to understand music based on the major scale, it is important to develop notational skills as well as performance skills of singing and playing scales on the piano.

5.1 Major Diatonic Scales and Melodies

Sing, Memorize, and Analyze

13

Internalizing Music

1. Listen to "Alleluia" on Track 13. Memorize the song.
2. Sing "Alleluia" and keep the beat.
3. Sing "Alleluia" and clap the rhythm.
4. Pair off in the class. Facing your partner, sing "Alleluia" and clap the melodic contour.
5. Sing with rhythm names while clapping and showing the melodic contour.

Analyzing What You Hear

1. Sing the lowest note in the song.
2. Sing the highest note in the song.
3. Sing the beginning note of the song.
4. Sing the final note of the song.
5. Sing all the notes in the song from lowest to highest.
6. Sing all the notes in the song from the highest to the lowest.

Constructing a Melodic Representation from Memory

1. As you sing "Alleluia," draw a representation indicating the contour and pitches.
2. As you point to your representation, sing the melody with rhythm syllables.

Music Theory

Describing What You Hear with Solfège Syllables

We can describe the pitches in "Alleluia" with solfège syllables:

Alleluia
Phrase 1

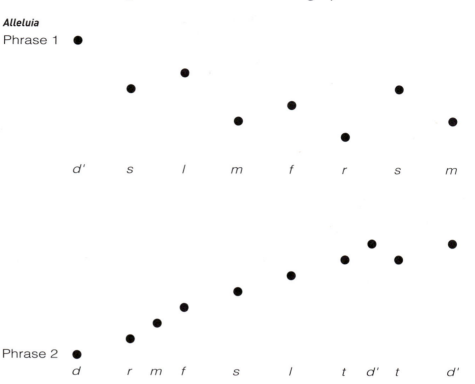

Phrase 2

Note that the pitch high *d'* is marked with a superscript (*d'*). Notes below *d* are marked with a subscript (*d,*). When we arrange the pitches of "Alleluia" in ascending order, we discover that there are seven adjacent pitches. From *d* to high *d* is an interval of an octave.

Notating What You Hear with Solfège Syllables

We can write "Alleluia" in rhythm notation with solfège syllables.

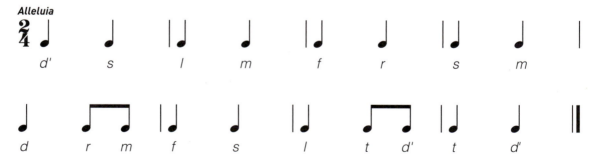

This piece of music is based on the major scale. A **major scale** is a series of eight adjacent pitches that uses successive letter names; half steps occur between the third and fourth degrees and seventh and first degrees of the scale. All other steps are whole steps. It is this pattern of half (m2) and whole steps (M2) that gives the major scale its particular configuration. We can find notes of the major pentachord scale, major hexachord scale, and major pentatonic scale in the major scale. The first note of the major scale is called the **tonic**, and this is the note that all of the other notes of the scale are related to.

Associating Solfège Syllables with Scale Degree Numbers

The following chart indicates how solfège syllables may be identified with **scale degree numbers**.

Solfège Syllable	Scale Degree Number
d'	$\hat{1}$
t	$\hat{7}$
l	$\hat{6}$
s	$\hat{5}$
f	$\hat{4}$
m	$\hat{3}$
r	$\hat{2}$
d	$\hat{1}$

Associating Scale Degree Numbers with Scale Degree Names

The scale degree numbers may also be identified with **scale degree names**. Each scale degree can be identified with a name that reflects its position in the scale. The tonic is sometimes referred to as the "home note." The tonic is the most important scale degree, followed by the fifth, the dominant. The subdominant is termed such because it is five notes, or degrees, below the tonic. The mediant lies halfway between the tonic and dominant. The second degree, supertonic (*super* in Latin means "above"), is above the tonic note. The leading tone leads to the tonic. The submediant is a third below the tonic note.

Scale Number	Scale Degree Name
$\hat{1}$	Tonic
$\hat{2}$	Supertonic
$\hat{3}$	Mediant
$\hat{4}$	Subdominant
$\hat{5}$	Dominant
$\hat{6}$	Submediant
$\hat{7}$	Leading Tone

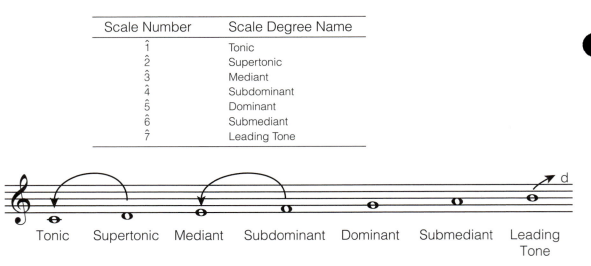

Tonic   Supertonic   Mediant   Subdominant   Dominant   Submediant   Leading Tone

It is important to note that all of the pitches of a scale are related to each other. For example, the tonic note is a stable note, but a note like the leading tone has a tendency to move toward the tonic note and the subdominant note has a tendency to move toward the mediant note. Notes that have an attraction for others are referred to as *tendency tones*.

5.2   Determining the Intervals Between Notes of the Major Scale

The following chart shows the whole- and half-step relationships of the C major scale on the keyboard. Look at the whole-step (W) and half-step (H) pattern of the scale.

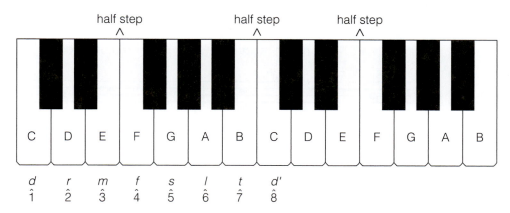

The following chart shows the whole- and half-step relationships of the C major scale on the staff. Look at the whole-step (W) and half-step (H) pattern.

Note that the major scale is made up of two *tetrachords* (a tetrachord is four adjacent notes).

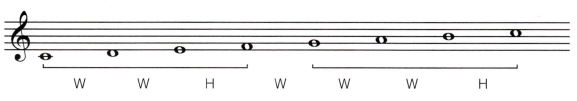

Note also that this pattern of whole and half steps that results in a major scale can begin on any note. This necessitates the use of sharps or flats to maintain the whole- and half-step relationships.

Note the intervals between *d* and *r*, *r* and *m*, *f* and *s*, *s* and *l*, and *l* and *t* are whole steps. The distance between *t* and *d'* and between *m* and *f* is a half step. We can refer to whole steps as major seconds (M2) and half steps as minor seconds (m2). The following chart is a summary of the major and minor seconds in the major scale.

Whole Steps Major 2	Half Steps Minor 2
d–r	
r–m	*m–f*
f–s	
s–l	
l–t	*t–d'*

Practice singing the intervals between each note of the major scale.

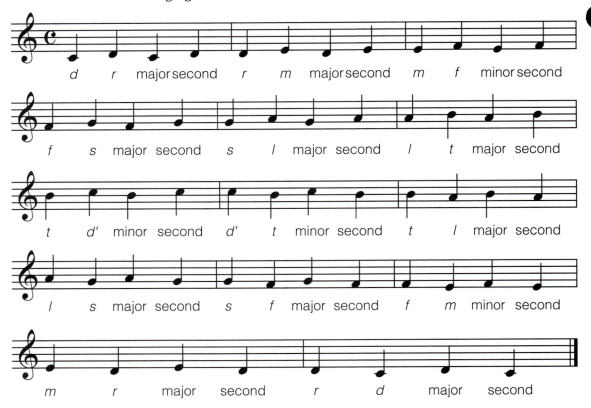

5.3   Writing a Major Scale and Melodies Using Accidentals

Writing a Major Scale on the Staff Using Accidentals

The following is a procedure for writing any major scale on the staff using accidentals. We will write this example as a D major scale in the treble clef.

1. Write the solfège syllables *d – r – m – f – s – l – t – d′* beneath the staff for the major scale.

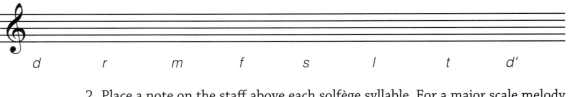

2. Place a note on the staff above each solfège syllable. For a major scale melody we use eight adjacent notes; therefore, the notes should also be adjacent on the staff. For example, if the tonic note is C, write C–D–E–F–G–A–B–C, or if the tonic note is D, write D–E–F–G–A–B–C–D.

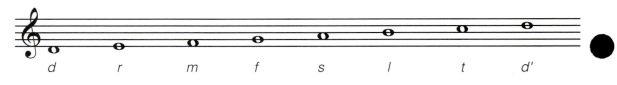

3. Mark the half step between scale degrees three and four and seven and eight and their corresponding pitches on the staff. Remember that the intervals between the other degrees will be whole steps.

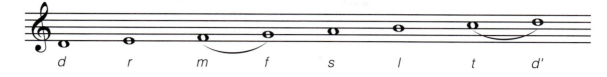

4. Check the intervallic relationship between the solfège syllables and the pitch names to insure the correct intervallic distance between the notes. If necessary, correct the intervals by using sharps or flats.

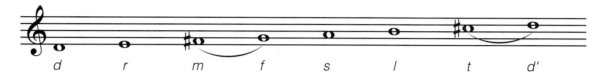

Writing a Major Melody on the Staff Using Accidentals

The following is a procedure for writing any major melody on the staff using accidentals. For an example, we will write "Alleluia" in the key of D major in treble clef using accidentals. Music based on a particular scale is said to be in the key of that scale. If music is built on the C major scale, the piece is in the key of C major and the tonic note of the music is C.

1. Write the D major scale on the staff using accidentals and mark the half steps.

2. Write the solfège syllables below the scale.

3. Write "Alleluia" on the staff by associating the solfège syllables with note names in the key of D major. "Alleluia" D = d. Note the placement of accidentals.

We can say that "Alleluia" is written in the key of D major as it uses the notes of the D major scale. The tonic of this piece is D.

5.4   Key Signatures

The **key signature** is a group of sharps or flats placed at the beginning of a composition (or after the clef) or during a composition (normally after a double bar) to indicate the key of the music that follows. By their positions on the staff, the signs show which notes are to be consistently sharped or flatted throughout in all octaves, thus establishing the prevailing **tonality** of the music. Reading a piece of music becomes much easier when we know what the key signature is, as it helps us organize the use of accidentals in tonal music.

How Key Signatures Facilitate Music Reading and Writing

Consider playing a B major scale from notation using accidentals or using a key signature. While the accidentals written in the music serve as a reminder, the score is clearer when a key signature is used. The same applies to a piece of music.

The following is the B major scale written with accidentals.

This is the B major scale written with a key signature.

The following is "Alleluia" written without a key signature.

The following is "Alleluia" with a key signature.

Major Key Signatures Using Sharps

The placement of sharps in a key signature follows a definite order. We must adhere to the order of sharps to maintain the same pattern as we progress through the keys.

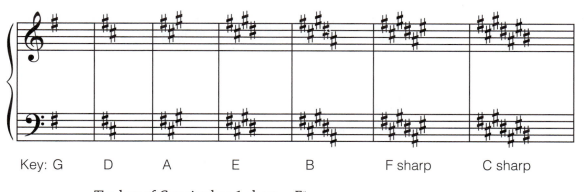

Key: G   D   A   E   B   F sharp   C sharp

The key of G major has 1 sharp—F♯.
The key of D major has 2 sharps—F♯, C♯.
The key of A major has 3 sharps—F♯, C♯, G♯.
The key of E major has 4 sharps—F♯, C♯, G♯, D♯.
The key of B major has 5 sharps—F♯, C♯, G♯, D♯, A♯.
The key of F-sharp major has 6 sharps—F♯, C♯, G♯, D♯, A♯, E♯.
The key of C-sharp major has 7 sharps—F♯, C♯, G♯, D♯, A♯, E♯, B♯.

Note that the last sharp in the key signature is the seventh degree of the major scale and is a half step below the tonic note. In the following example, G-sharp is the last sharp and the seventh degree of the scale, thus the tonic note is A. Therefore, A major has a key signature of three sharps. The following mnemonic device will help you remember the order of sharps:

Fat Cats Go Down Alleys Eating Bananas.

Major Key Signatures Using Flats

The placement of flats in a key signature follows a definite order. We must adhere to the order of flats to maintain the same pattern as we progress through the keys.

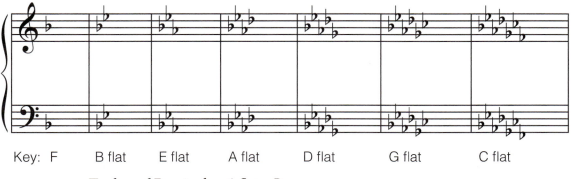

Key: F   B flat   E flat   A flat   D flat   G flat   C flat

The key of F major has 1 flat—B♭.
The key of B-flat major has 2 flats—B♭, E♭.
The key of E-flat major has 3 flats—B♭, E♭, A♭.
The key of A-flat major has 4 flats—B♭, E♭, A♭, D♭.

The key of D-flat major has 5 flats—B♭, E♭, A♭, D♭, G♭.
The key of G-flat major has 6 flats—B♭, E♭, A♭, D♭, G♭, C♭.
The key of C-flat major has 7 flats—B♭, E♭, A♭, D♭, G♭, C♭, F♭.

Note that the last flat in the key signature is the fourth degree of the major scale. To identify the major key using flat key signatures remember that the key is always the next to the last flat, the exception being F major, which has just one flat, B-flat. For example, in the following key signature the next to the last flat is E-flat; the key of E-flat has three flats in the key signature.

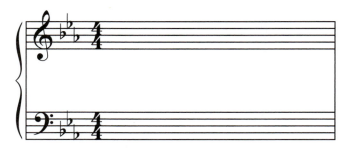

The Circle of Fifths

The order of the sharp and flat key signatures can be shown using a circle. This is a graphic representation of keynotes with their signatures. C is at the top of the circle, from where the notes progress clockwise in ascending fifths. Sharp keys progress around the circle in a clockwise direction and flat keys in a counterclockwise direction.

The Circle of Fifths and Enharmonic Keys

At the bottom of the circle of fifths, the note F-sharp is called also by its enharmonic name G-flat, and the same happens with the next note, C-sharp/D-flat; the notes on the return to C are then called by their flat names. Although the F-sharp scale is written differently from the G-flat scale, they sound the same when performed on the keyboard.

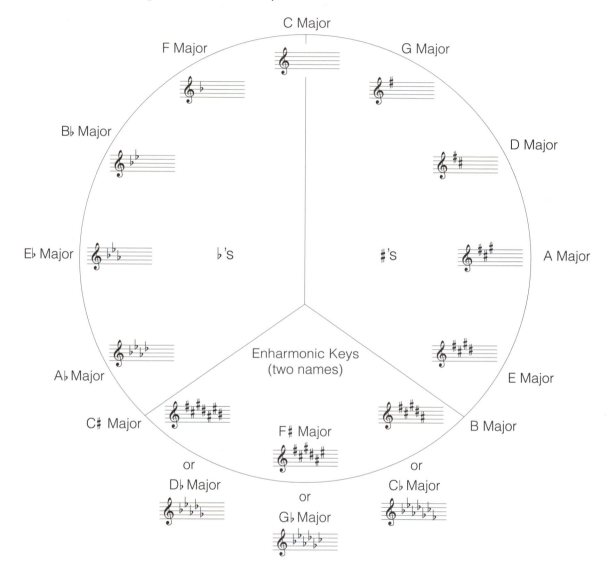

5.5 Writing Major Scales and Melodies Using a Key Signature

Writing a Major Scale Using a Key Signature

The following is a procedure for writing any scale with a key signature. We will write this example as an E major scale in the treble clef.

1. Put the key signature after the treble clef. Write the solfège syllables *d – r – m – f – s – l – t – d′* beneath the staff for the E major scale.

2. Place a note on the staff above each solfège syllable. Remember for a major scale we use eight adjacent notes. The tonic note is E; write E–F–G–A–B–C–D–E. Mark the half steps between the third and fourth degrees and the seventh and eighth degrees.

It is clearly evident that writing a scale using a key signature is an easier task than marking each note that is sharp or flat.

Writing a Major Melody Using a Key Signature

The following is a sample procedure for writing a major melody on the staff with a key signature.

1. Determine the key and write the scale of the melody on the staff. Mark the half steps.

2. Write the solfège syllables below the scale.

3. Associate the solfège syllables with the notes of the melody. Write the melody on the staff.

We can say that "Alleluia" is written in the key of E major, as it uses the notes of the E major scale. The tonic of this piece is E.

5.6   Transposition

In Chapter 4 we learned to transpose major pentachord and hexachord melodies. In this chapter we will learn to transpose major melodies into different keys. We can use the following process.

For example:
The following melody is written in D major. Let's transpose it to B-flat major.

1. Write solfège syllables or scale degree numbers under the melody to be transposed.

2. Add the new key signature and write the melody in the new key. Note that the solfège and scale degree numbers are the same in the original melody and the transposition.

5.7   Identifying the Key of a Major Scale or Composition from a Given Key Signature

Procedure for Identifying Major Sharp Key Signatures

1. Identify the last sharp in the key signature. This sharp is the solfège syllable *ti*.
2. Identify the solfège syllable *do* (one half step above *ti*). This note, *do*, represents the scale that has the given key signature.

Identify the scale having the following key signature.

The last sharp in the key signature is C-sharp. This C-sharp is the solfège syllable *ti*. If C-sharp is *ti,* then *do* is D. This note, D (*do*), is the major scale that has the above key signature.

Procedure for Identifying Major Flat Key Signatures

1. Identify the last flat in the key signature. This flat is the solfège syllable *fa*.
2. Identify the solfège syllable *do* (the note *do* is five half steps or four scale steps, or degrees, below *fa*). This note, *do*, represents the scale that has the given key signature.

Identify the scale having the following key signature.

The last flat in the key signature is E-flat. This flat is the solfège syllable *fa*. B-flat is the solfège syllable *do*. This note, B-flat (*do*), is the scale that has the given key signature.

Listening

For Children Vol. 1, No. 11, by Béla Bartók (1882–1945).

"All Through the Night" recorded by the Mormon Tabernacle Choir; also on the recording *A Nancy Wilson Christmas*, sung by Nancy Wilson.

"Ce fut en Mai," trouvère song.

"In Dulce Jubilo" recorded by the King's College Choir of Cambridge, conducted by Simon Preston and David Wilcox.

"Variations on a Theme by Haydn," Op. 56a, by Johannes Brahms (1833–1897).

"The Holly and the Ivy" as sung by Anonymous 4 from their recording *Wolcum Yule*.

"Rigadoon" by Henry Purcell (1659–1695). Two-part score found in the Supplemental Materials portion of Chapter 5, *The Major Scale*. From the recording *Purcell: Works for Harpsichord*, played by John Gibbons.

Minuet in G from *The Notebook of Anna Magdalena* by Johann Sebastian Bach (1685–1750). Two-part score found in the Supplementary Materials portion of Chapter 5 *The Major Scale*.

"Jupiter" from *The Planets*, <u>op</u>. 32, by Gustav Holst (1874–1934). Choral score found in the Supplemental Materials portion of Chapter 5, *The Major Scale*.

"Tallis Canon" from the album *Into the Light* by Harry Christophers, Kaori Muraji, and The Sixteen.

Singing and Listening

Sing the following theme in solfège before you listen to the principal melody of "Jupiter" from *The Planets*. The melody has been transposed for singing.

"Jupiter" from The Planets (choral version)   **Gustav Holst (1874–1934)**

Dvořák wrote the *New World* Symphony while visiting America in 1892. The slow movement begins with six measures of soft chords played by the brass and strings. Sing the following theme with solfège syllables before listening to a recording.

"Largo" from the New World Symphony (thematic reduction)   **Antonín Dvořák (1841–1904)**

Key Terms and Concepts

Major Scale	Scale Degree Names	Circle of Fifths
Tonic	Key Signatures	
Scale Degree Numbers	Tonality	

How to Practice

Here are some useful suggestions for practicing melody in a variety of ways. Remember to keep practicing in small groups with your peers.

Performing	Sing all of the melodies with rhythm syllables.
	Sing "Alleluia" with rhythm names and conduct as you sing. Sing "Alleluia" with solfège syllables and conduct as you sing. Sing "Alleluia" with numbers and conduct as you sing.
Sight Singing	Look at the meter and key. Choose a suitable tempo. Identify the phrases. Sing or speak the rhythm patterns of focus songs while tapping the beat. Sing with solfège syllables.
Echo Singing	Practice with a classmate or in class. One of you will hum or play on the piano an eight-beat melody. The other will "echo" what was played with solfège syllables.
Conducting	Sing and conduct at the same time.
Memorizing by Ear	The instructor or another student plays a melody on the piano or hums a melody: • Identify the meter. • Sing the example with rhythm names. • Identify the ending and starting pitches with solfège syllables. • Sing the example with solfège syllables.
Notating the Melody	Practice with a classmate or in class. One of you will sing a known melody with neutral syllables or play on the piano a melody from the chapter. The other will "echo" what was sung or played with solfège syllables and then notate the melody in a given meter and key.
Error Dictation	One student plays the melody, deliberately making a mistake. Another student follows the score and locates the error.
Dictation	Instructor hums or plays typical patterns from the dictation melody, and students must sing back with rhythm and solfège syllables. Instructor plays melody and students determine beginning and final note. Students sing the melody with rhythm and solfège syllables. Students notate melody in a key and meter provided by instructor.
Memorizing from a Score	Memorize an entire melody and notate it without referring to the notation. First analyze the form by looking for repeated and similar parts. This will simplify the task.
Improvisation/Composition	First select a meter and length for the composition, then decide what form to use (for example, ABBA). Create an improvisation or composition using only known rhythms and scales.
Performing a Canon	As you sing the melody, clap the rhythm in canon after two or four beats.

Using the Musical Skills CD

Access Chapter 5 on the skills CD to reinforce concepts associated with the major scale in this chapter through tutorials, exercises, and dictations. Please use the arrows on the top right of the page to move from one page to another.

In the Tutorial section, you can review information concerning the following:

1. The definition of a scale
2. Whole steps and half steps
3. Naming scale degrees
4. Key signatures
5. Identifying key signatures
6. Building key signatures with sharps and flats

Additionally, the major scale constructor will help you develop your skills of building major scales starting on any note. You can also listen to each scale. Make sure that you sing inside your head with solfège syllables as you play each scale.

In the Exercise section, you can review information concerning building a major scale from a given note. Each example is timed, so you should practice writing these examples many times until you become fluent and can do them quickly.

In the Dictation section, you will be provided with the opportunity to practice the notation of major scale melodies that include half, quarter, eighth, sixteenth, dotted half, dotted quarter, and dotted eighth notes. Listen to each example several times and try to clap, say the rhythm, and sing with solfège syllables before writing on the staff. You might also want to sing each example with letter names and point to the notes on the staff before attempting to notate them.

How to Read a Musical Score

Examine the following chorale by Johann Sebastian Bach.

Rhythm

Identify the key signature. What is the tempo of the chorale? Clap the rhythm of the treble clef while saying rhythm syllables. Clap the rhythm of the melody while counting with numbers.

Melody

Identify the phrase marks. Identify the dynamic markings. Identify the key signature.

What scale pattern do you find in the first two measures of the treble clef? Sing the first seven measures with solfège syllables, scale degree numbers, and letter names.

Chorale: *Eternity, O Mighty Word*

Johann Sebastian Bach (1685–1750)

Chapter 6
Intervals

CHAPTER OVERVIEW

Intervals have been briefly addressed in Chapters 2, 4, and 5. The distance between one pitch and another is called an interval, and you were introduced to different types of scales that contain interval patterns. Intervals are fundamental to understanding music as well as harmony. Interval patterns are the building blocks of tonal music.

In this chapter you will continue to learn how to identify all intervals found in tonal music. In the subsequent chapters you will continue to practice recognizing intervals both aurally and visually. Understanding intervals can help you develop your ear and your musicianship abilities as well as your ability to transpose a melody into another key. It is important to always sing the intervals once you have identified them correctly.

6.1 Interval Identification

Intervals are identified by their size and quality. The size of an interval refers to the number of notes the interval spans. Size is calculated by determining the distance between the first and the last pitch. Size is based on the letter names of the notes; count the first pitch as "one" and disregard accidentals. Adding the *quality* of the interval makes the designation more accurate.

Interval Size

The number of the interval is determined by counting the letter names or the number of lines and spaces from one pitch to another.

F   G   A   B   C

The number of the interval from F to C is five. Each letter name is counted only once when determining the size of the interval.

Note the size of intervals in the following familiar musical works.

Hungarian Canon

4.
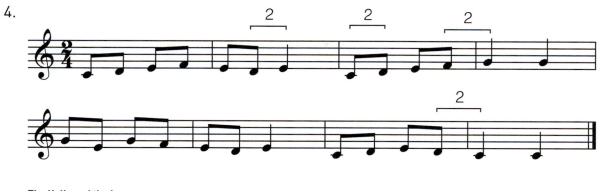

The Holly and the Ivy   **English Christmas Carol**

5.

Canon   **Luigi Cherubini (1760–1842)**

6.

Summary of Interval Size

Intervals of seconds always appear or are notated on adjacent lines or spaces.

Intervals of thirds appear or are notated on consecutive lines or spaces.

Intervals of fourths always appear or are notated on a line and space or a space and line.

Intervals of fifths always appear or are notated on lines or spaces.

Intervals of sixths and sevenths always appear or are notated on a line and space or a space and line.

6.2   Determining Interval Quality: Major, Minor, and Perfect

We use five terms to describe the quality of intervals: major (M), minor (m), **perfect** (P), **augmented**, (aug, A, or +) and **diminished** (dim or ⁰).

There are several ways to determine an interval. One is to memorize the number of half steps that are contained in each interval. Another is to remember the intervals that occur between the tonic and the other notes of the scale by using solfège syllables.

Let's review the intervals contained in the scales that we have studied. Note that there are only four types of perfect intervals: the unison, the fourth, the fifth, and the octave. In medieval and Renaissance music, these were considered the only intervals that were suitable for a cadence (point of rest).

Determining the Size and Quality of Intervals Between the Tonic of a Major Pentachord Scale and Each Note of the Scale

Note the sizes of intervals in the following:

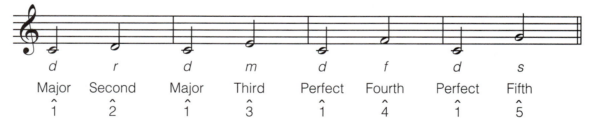

The interval between *d* and *d*—that is, between the tonic and itself—is referred to as a perfect unison.

The interval between *d* and *r* spans two letter names, and we refer to this as an interval of a second. The number of half steps contained in this interval is two. The quality is major. Therefore, we can refer to this interval as a major second.

The interval between *d* and *m* spans three letter names and is a skip. We refer to this as an interval of a third; the number of half steps contained in this interval, is four. The quality is major. Therefore, we can refer to this interval as a major third.

The interval between *d* and *f* spans four letter names. Since it is larger than a third, it is called a leap. We refer to this as an interval of a fourth; the number of half steps contained in this interval is five. The quality is perfect. Therefore, we can refer to this interval as a perfect fourth.

The interval between *d* and *s* spans five letter names, and we can refer to this as an interval of a fifth; the number of half steps contained in this interval is seven. The quality is perfect. Therefore, we can refer to this interval as a perfect fifth.

Determining the Size and Quality of Intervals Between the Fifth Degree of a Major Pentachord Scale and Each Note of the Scale

Note the size of intervals in the following:

s	*f*	*s*	*m*	*s*	*r*	*s*	*d*
Major	Second	minor	Third	Perfect	Fourth	Perfect	Fifth
$\hat{5}$	$\hat{4}$	$\hat{5}$	$\hat{3}$	$\hat{5}$	$\hat{2}$	$\hat{5}$	$\hat{1}$

The interval between *s* and *m* spans three notes and is a skip. We refer to this as an interval of a third; the number of half steps contained in this interval is three. The quality is minor. Therefore, we can refer to this interval as a minor third (m3). Note the relationships in the following table.

Scale Degree	Solfège Syllables	Size	Number of Half Steps	Name of Interval	Abbreviation
$\hat{1}$–$\hat{2}$	*d–r*	2	2	major second	M2
$\hat{1}$–$\hat{3}$	*d–m*	3	4	major third	M3
$\hat{1}$–$\hat{4}$	*d–f*	4	5	perfect fourth	P4
$\hat{1}$–$\hat{5}$	*d–s*	5	7	perfect fifth	P5

Determining the Size and Quality of Intervals Between the Tonic of a Major Hexachord Scale and Each Member of the Scale

Note the size of intervals in the following:

d	*r*	*d*	*m*	*d*	*f*	*d*	*s*	*d*	*l*
Major	Second	Major	Third	Perfect	Fourth	Perfect	Fifth	Major	Sixth
$\hat{1}$	$\hat{2}$	$\hat{1}$	$\hat{3}$	$\hat{1}$	$\hat{4}$	$\hat{1}$	$\hat{5}$	$\hat{1}$	$\hat{6}$

The interval between *d* and *l* ($\hat{1}$–$\hat{6}$) spans six notes, and we can refer to this as an interval of a sixth. The number of half steps contained in this interval is nine; the quality of this interval is major; we refer to this interval as a major sixth (M6).

Note the relationships in the following table.

Scale Degree	Solfège Syllables	Size	Number of Half Steps	Name of Interval
$\hat{1}$–$\hat{2}$	d–r	2	2	major second
$\hat{1}$–$\hat{3}$	d–m	3	4	major third
$\hat{1}$–$\hat{4}$	d–f	4	5	perfect fourth
$\hat{1}$–$\hat{5}$	d–s	5	7	perfect fifth
$\hat{1}$–$\hat{6}$	d–l	6	9	major sixth

The next section dealing with minor scales can be discussed in chapter 8.

Determining the Size and Quality of Intervals Between the Tonic of a Minor Pentachord Scale and Each Member of the Scale

Note the size of intervals in the following:

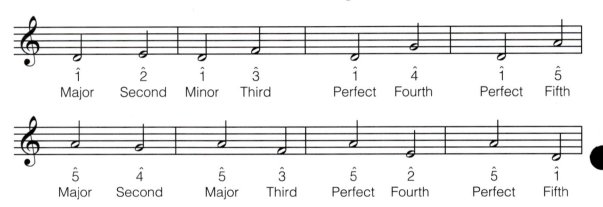

The interval between the first and second degrees of the scale spans two notes, and we can refer to this as an interval of a second; the number of half steps contained in this interval is two. The quality is major. We refer to this interval as a major second (M2).

The interval between the first and third degrees of the scale spans three notes, and we can refer to this as an interval of a third; the number of half steps contained in this interval is three. The quality is minor. We refer to this interval as a minor third. This interval is a half step smaller than a major third (M3).

The interval between the first and fourth degrees of the scale spans four notes, and we can refer to this as an interval of a fourth; the number of half steps contained in this interval is five. The quality is perfect. Therefore, we can refer to this interval as a perfect fourth (P4).

The interval between the first and fifth degrees of the scale spans five notes. We can refer to this as an interval of a fifth; the number of half steps contained in this interval is seven. The quality is perfect. We can refer to this interval as a perfect fifth (P5). Note the relationships in the following table.

Intervals in *La Minor*

Scale Degree	Solfège Syllables	Size	Number of Half Steps Contained in an Interval	Name of Interval	Abbreviation
1̂–2̂	l̩–t	2	2	major second	M2
1̂–3̂	t̩–d	3	3	minor third	m2
1̂–4̂	l̩–r	4	5	perfect fourth	P4
1̂–5̂	l̩–m	5	7	perfect fifth	P5

Intervals in *Do Minor*

Scale Degree	Solfège Syllables	Size	Number of Half Steps Contained in an Interval	Name of Interval	Abbreviation
1̂–2̂	d̩ r	2	2	major second	M2
1̂–3̂	d̩ m	3	3	minor third	m2
1̂–4̂	d̩ f	4	5	perfect fourth	P4
1̂–5̂	d̩ s	5	7	perfect fifth	P5

Determining the Size and Quality of Intervals Between the Tonic of a Minor Hexachord Scale and Each Note of the Scale

Note the size of intervals in the following:

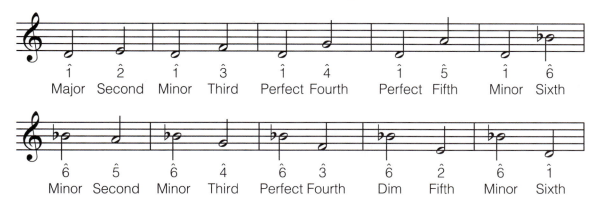

The interval between scale degrees one and six spans six notes, and we can refer to this as an interval of a sixth. The number of half steps contained in this interval is eight. The quality is minor. Therefore, we can refer to this interval as a minor sixth (m6). Note the relationships in the following table.

Scale Degree	Size	Number of Half Steps	Name of Interval	Abbreviation
1̂–2̂	2	2	major second	M2
1̂–3̂	3	4	minor third	m3
1̂–4̂	4	5	perfect fourth	P4
1̂–5̂	5	7	perfect fifth	P5
1̂–6̂	6	8	minor sixth	m6

When singing descending intervals, note the interval *f–t*. We refer to this as a diminished fifth. This particular interval is a diminished fifth because it contains two minor seconds (*f–m* and *d–t̩*) and is therefore smaller than a perfect fifth.

Determining the Intervallic Distance Between the Tonic Note of a Major Scale and Each Note of the Scale

The interval between *d* and *t* spans seven notes; we can refer to this as an interval of a seventh. The number of half steps contained in this interval is eleven. The quality is major. Therefore, we can refer to this interval as a major seventh.

Note the size of intervals in the following:

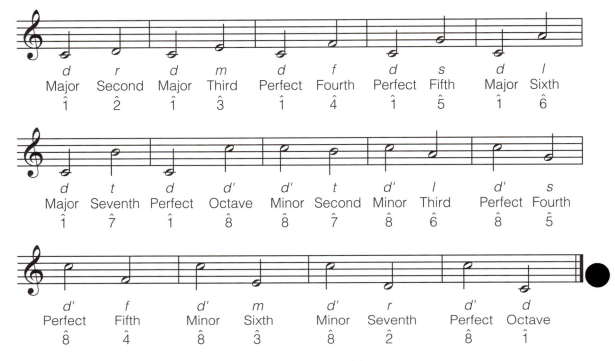

Note the relationships in the following table.

Scale Degree	Solfège Syllables	Size	Number of Half Steps Contained in an Interval	Name of Interval	Abbreviation
$\hat{1}$–$\hat{2}$	*d–r*	2	2	major second	M2
$\hat{1}$–$\hat{3}$	*d–m*	3	4	major third	M3
$\hat{1}$–$\hat{4}$	*d–f*	4	5	perfect fourth	P4
$\hat{1}$–$\hat{5}$	*d–s*	5	7	perfect fifth	P5
$\hat{1}$–$\hat{6}$	*d–l*	6	9	major sixth	M6
$\hat{1}$–$\hat{7}$	*d–t*	7	11	major seventh	M7
$\hat{1}$–$\hat{8}$	*d–d'*	8	12	perfect octave	P8

C major scale on the keyboard.

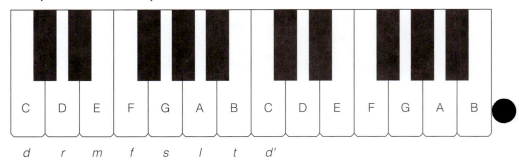

Intervals of the major scale.

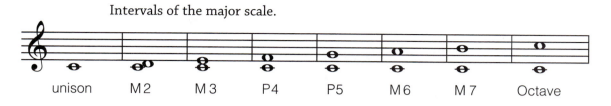

Intervals in Musical Compositions

Note the intervals in the following familiar musical works. Imagine that the first interval is the tonic of a scale.

Hungarian Canon

5.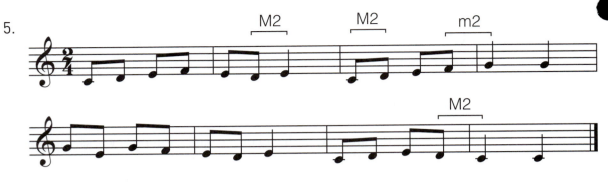

Rocky Mountain   **American Folk Song**

6.

Rock - y moun-tain, rock - y moun-tain, rock - y moun-tain high,

When you're on that rock - y moun-tain, hang your head and cry.

Do, do, do, do, do re - mem - ber me,

Do, do, do, do, do re - mem - ber me.

The Holly and the Ivy   **English Christmas Carol**

Canon for Four Voices   **Ludwig van** Beethoven (1770–1827)

Canon   **Luigi Cherubini (1760–1842)**

German Folk Song Fragment

10.

6.3   Determining Minor, Augmented, and Diminished Interval Relationships

Minor Intervals

A minor interval is one half step smaller than a major interval. A major interval is one half step larger than a minor interval. A diminished interval is one half step smaller than a minor interval.

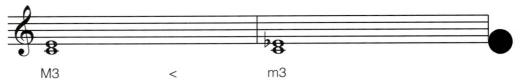

Augmented and Diminished Intervals

An augmented interval is one half step larger than a perfect or major interval. We use "A" as an abbreviation.

A diminished interval is one half step smaller than a perfect interval or minor interval. We use "d" as the abbreviation.

Perfect intervals do not become major or minor intervals; when altered, they are referred to as augmented or diminished.

Changing Major Scale Intervals Using Accidentals

Intervals in a major scale can be altered to make them larger or smaller. Using the lower note as the tonic, look at the intervals below and determine which have been made larger or smaller through the use of accidentals.

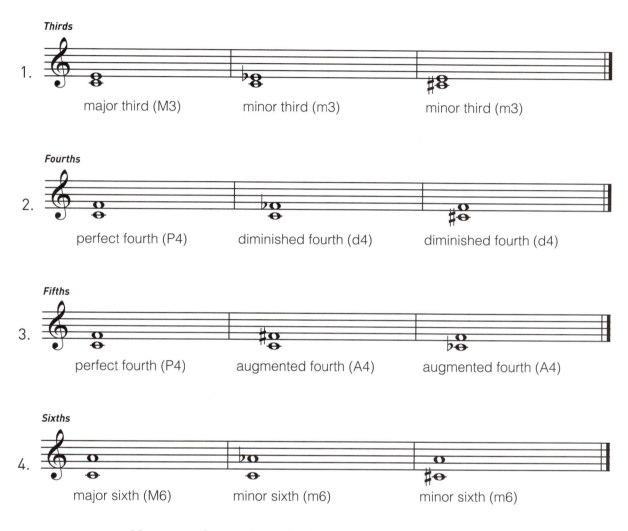

Thirds

1.
major third (M3)　　minor third (m3)　　minor third (m3)

Fourths

2.
perfect fourth (P4)　　diminished fourth (d4)　　diminished fourth (d4)

Fifths

3.
perfect fourth (P4)　　augmented fourth (A4)　　augmented fourth (A4)

Sixths

4.
major sixth (M6)　　minor sixth (m6)　　minor sixth (m6)

Harmonic and Melodic Intervals

When we sing or play two notes simultaneously, the resulting interval is described as a **harmonic interval**. When we play two notes one after the other, we describe the interval as a **melodic interval**. The following figures show an example of a melodic interval and a harmonic interval.

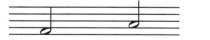

Melodic Interval　　　　　*Harmonic Interval*

Consonant and Dissonant Intervals

Harmonic intervals may be classified as consonant and dissonant. In general, consonant intervals sound stable while dissonant intervals sound unstable. In our culture, unisons, thirds, fourths (in some contexts considered a dissonance), fifths, sixths, and octaves are consonant intervals. Seconds and sevenths are sometimes considered dissonant. Consonance is the quality inherent in an interval or chord which in a traditional tonal or modal context seems satisfactorily complete and stable in itself. The opposite of consonance is dissonance, the quality of tension inherent in an interval or chord which in a traditional tonal or modal context involves a clash between adjacent notes of the scale and creates the expectation of resolution.

Summary of Intervals

The designation of perfect, augmented, and diminished can be used for the quality of intervals of a unison, fourth, fifth, and octave.

A major interval is one half step larger than a minor interval.

An augmented interval is one half step larger than a perfect interval.

A diminished interval is one half step smaller than a perfect interval.

An augmented interval is one half step larger than a major interval.

A diminished interval is one half step smaller than a minor interval.

Four Methods of Naming Intervals

Method 1: Comparing the Interval to the Notes of the Major Scale[2]

1. Treat the lower note as the tonic of the scale.
2. Determine the size of the interval.
3. Based on the intervals of the major scale, label the interval.

Method 2: Removing an Accidental

If the interval does not appear in the major scale, then compare the interval to a known interval. For identification purposes, simplify the given interval, either removing or adding an accidental, and then compare it to the original interval.

Consider D to G♯. This interval does not appear in the D major scale. However, the interval D–G appears as a perfect fourth in D major. The G♯ increases the size of the P4 interval by a half step. A perfect interval increased by a half step becomes an augmented interval, thus D–G♯ is augmented.

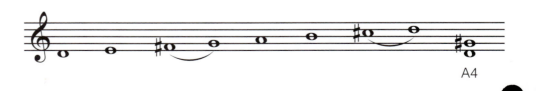

A4

---

[2] The same may be used to compare the interval to the notes in the minor scale. The minor scale is introduced in Chapter 8.

Method 3: Adding an Accidental

Consider F–B. This interval does not appear in the F major scale. However, the interval F–B♭ appears as a perfect fourth in F major. The B♭ decreases the distance of the interval by a half step and turns the interval into a perfect fourth. The interval F–B is one step larger than the perfect interval and is an augmented fourth.

A4

Method 4: Counting the Number of Half Steps

The quality of an interval can be determined by the number of half steps it contains.

The following chart provides a summary of how to identify the quality of intervals by counting the number of half steps. This is not the most effective way of naming intervals but is a useful reference.

Seconds	Diminished second 0 half steps (C♯–D♭)	Minor second 1 half step (C♯–D)	Major second 2 half steps (C–D)	Augmented second 3 half steps (C–D♯)
Thirds	Diminished third 2 half steps (C♯–E♭)	Minor third 3 half steps (C–E♭)	Major third 4 half steps (C–E)	Augmented third 5 half steps (C–E♯)
Sixths	Diminished sixth 7 half steps (C♯–A♭)	Minor sixth 8 half steps (C–A♭)	Major sixth 9 half steps (C–A)	Augmented sixth 10 half steps (C–A♯)
Sevenths	Diminished seventh 9 half steps (C♯–B♭)	Minor seventh 10 half steps (C–B♭)	Major seventh 11 half steps (C–B)	Augmented Seventh 12 half steps (C–B♯)

Unisons	Diminished unison (non-extant; no interval can have fewer than 0 half steps)	Perfect unison or Perfect prime 0 half steps (C–C)	Augmented unison 1 half step (C–C♯)
Fourths	Diminished fourth 4 half steps (C♭–F)	Perfect fourth 5 half steps (C–F)	Augmented fourth 6 half steps (C–F♯)
Fifths	Diminished fifth 6 half steps (C♯–G♭)	Perfect fifth 7 half steps (C–G)	Augmented fifth 8 half steps (C–G♯)
Octaves	Diminished octave 11 half steps (C–C♭)	Perfect octave 12 half steps (C–C)	Augmented octave 13 half steps (C–C♯)

6.4   Determining Harmonic Inversion of Intervals

Inversion involves moving either the lower pitch of an interval up an octave or the upper pitch down an octave.

Inversion is simply the reversal of the spatial relationship of the pitches. Sometimes inverting an interval simplifies the process of naming an interval. To determine the size of the inverted interval, subtract the number of the given interval from nine. The size of an interval plus its inversion will equal nine.

Inversion of Perfect Intervals

Perfect intervals remain perfect when inverted, but the number changes. For example:

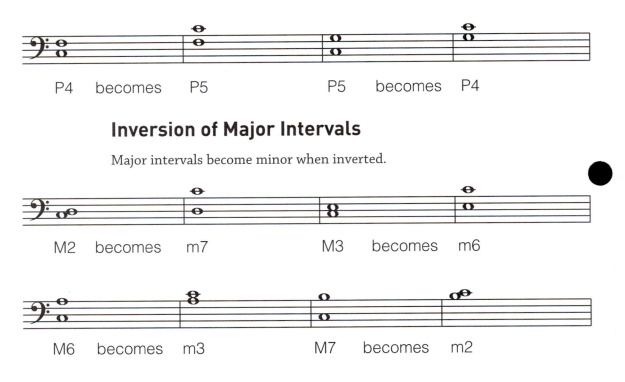

P4   becomes   P5   P5   becomes   P4

Inversion of Major Intervals

Major intervals become minor when inverted.

M2   becomes   m7   M3   becomes   m6

M6   becomes   m3   M7   becomes   m2

Inversion of Minor Intervals

Minor intervals become major when inverted

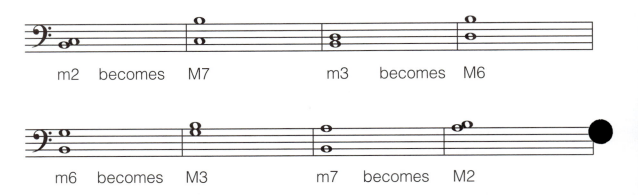

m2   becomes   M7   m3   becomes   M6

m6   becomes   M3   m7   becomes   M2

Inversion of Augmented Intervals

Augmented intervals become diminished when inverted. As illustrated below, an augmented fourth becomes a diminished fifth when inverted.

A4   becomes   d5

Inversion of Diminished Intervals

Diminished intervals become augmented when inverted.

d5   becomes   A4

Summary of Inversion of Intervals

d2	m2	M2	A2	d3	m3	M3	A3
↕	↕	↕	↕	↕	↕	↕	↕
A7	M7	m7	d7	A6	M6	m6	d6

6.5 **Compound Intervals**

Intervals that are an octave or smaller are called simple intervals. Intervals larger than an octave are known as compound intervals.

Simple Compound Intervals

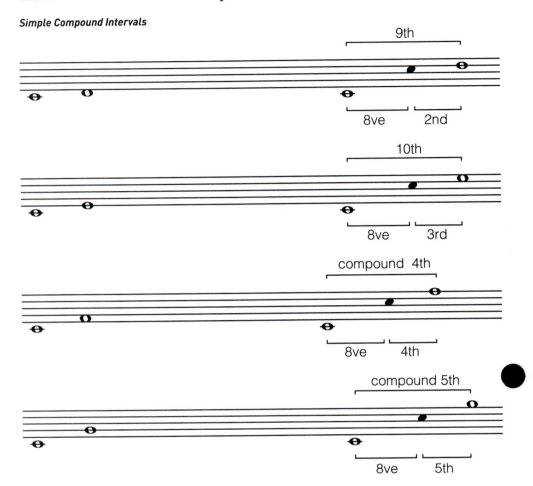

Method of Reading Compound Intervals

1. Reduce the intervals by an octave.
2. Name the resulting interval.
3. Add the word "compound" to the interval or add seven to the interval number to name the interval.

Key Terms and Concepts

Intervals
Major, Minor, and
   Perfect Intervals

Augmented and
   Diminished Intervals
Harmonic Intervals

Melodic Intervals
Inversion of Intervals

Using the Musical Skills CD

Access "Intervals" on the skills CD to reinforce your notation and recognition of intervals. Listen to each example several times. Try to sing with solfège syllables; there will probably be several solfège possibilities, depending on the interval.

You should make practicing and recognizing intervals a regular component of your daily practice.

How to Read a Musical Score

Look at Bach's Minuet in D Major. Find a partner in the class and test each other on identifying various melodic intervals throughout the piece. Remember to factor in the key signature and the effect that has on the notes and the relationship between the notes. Find examples of compound intervals.

Minuet in D Major   Johann Sebastian Bach (1685–1750)

Minuet in D Major (continued)

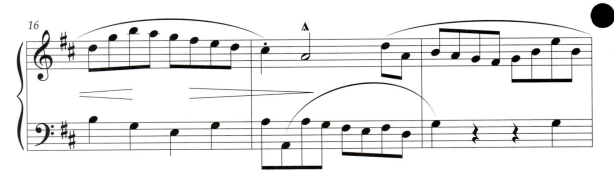

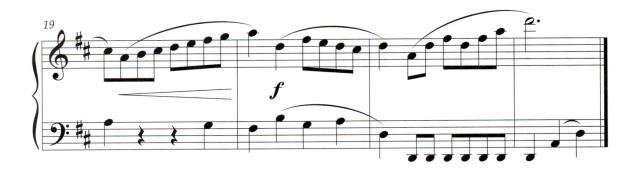

MUSIC THEORY EXERCISES

6.1 Exercises: Interval Identification

Exercise 6.1

Identify the size of the following melodic intervals in the treble and bass clefs.

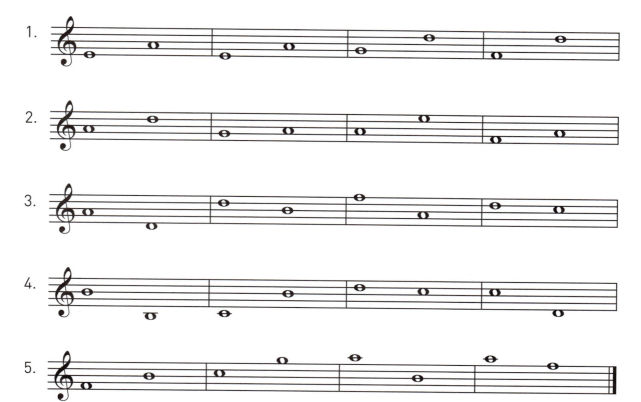

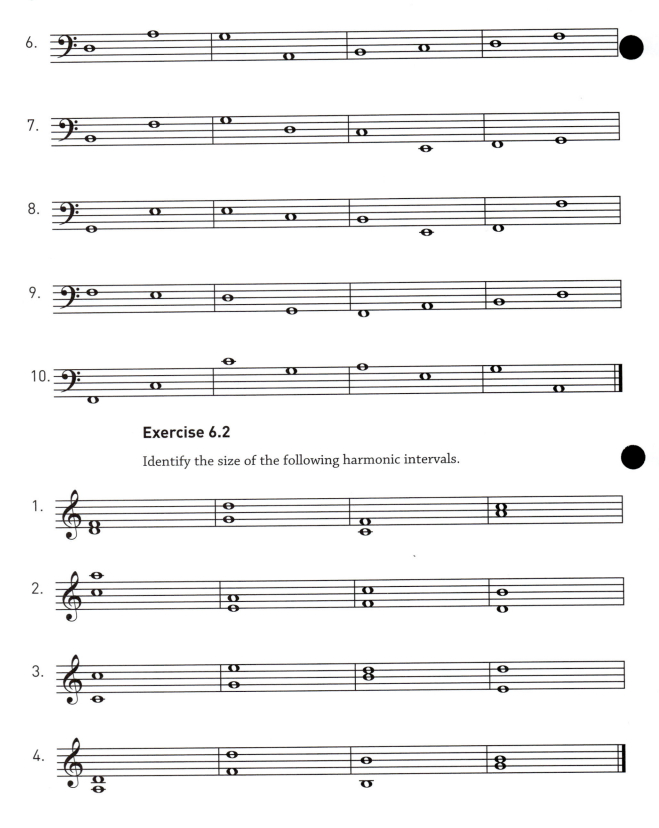

Exercise 6.2

Identify the size of the following harmonic intervals.

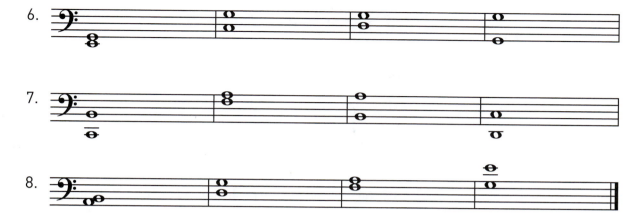

6.2 Exercises: Determining Interval Quality: Major and Minor

Exercise 6.3

1. Identify the size and quality of the following harmonic intervals:

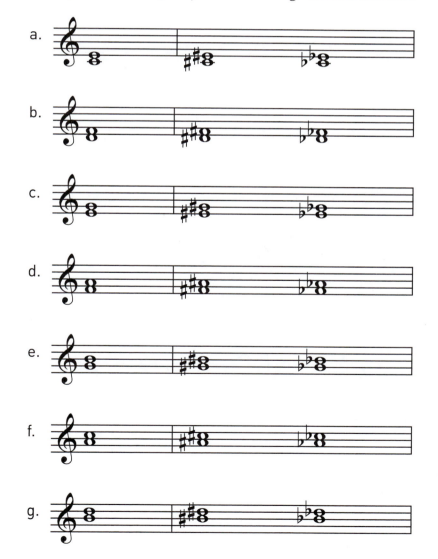

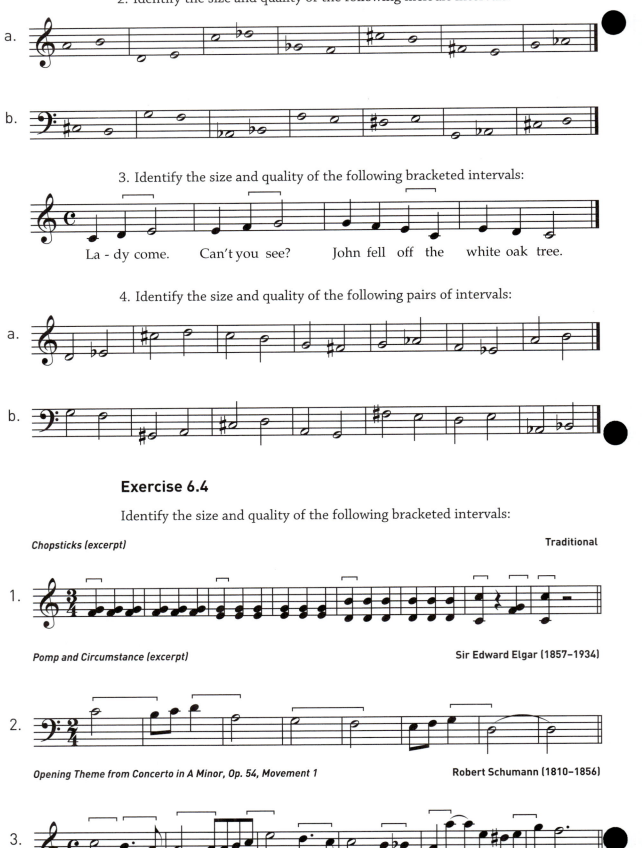

2. Identify the size and quality of the following melodic intervals:

a.

b.

3. Identify the size and quality of the following bracketed intervals:

La - dy come.   Can't you see?   John fell off the   white oak tree.

4. Identify the size and quality of the following pairs of intervals:

a.

b.

Exercise 6.4

Identify the size and quality of the following bracketed intervals:

Chopsticks (excerpt)   **Traditional**

1.

Pomp and Circumstance (excerpt)   **Sir Edward Elgar (1857–1934)**

2.

Opening Theme from Concerto in A Minor, Op. 54, Movement 1   **Robert Schumann (1810–1856)**

3.

Exercise 6.5

Write the abbreviated name of the bracketed interval on the dotted line.

Kis kece lányom   **Hungarian Folk Song**

Exercise 6.6

Write the abbreviated name of the interval above or below the bracket.

Twinkle, Twinkle, Little Star

1.

Slovak Folk Song

Exercise 6.7

Write the abbreviated name of the bracketed interval on the dotted line.

Alleluia

Variation on a Russian Folk Song

Louisiana Marching Song

6.3   Exercises: Determining Major, Minor, Augmented, and Diminished Interval Relationships

Exercise 6.8

Identify the following fourths and fifths. Keep in mind that a perfect interval made larger by a half step is called an augmented interval and a perfect interval made smaller by a half step is called diminished.

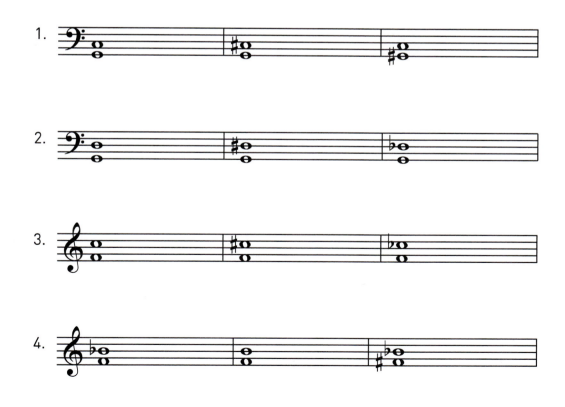

Exercise 6.9
Identify the following intervals.

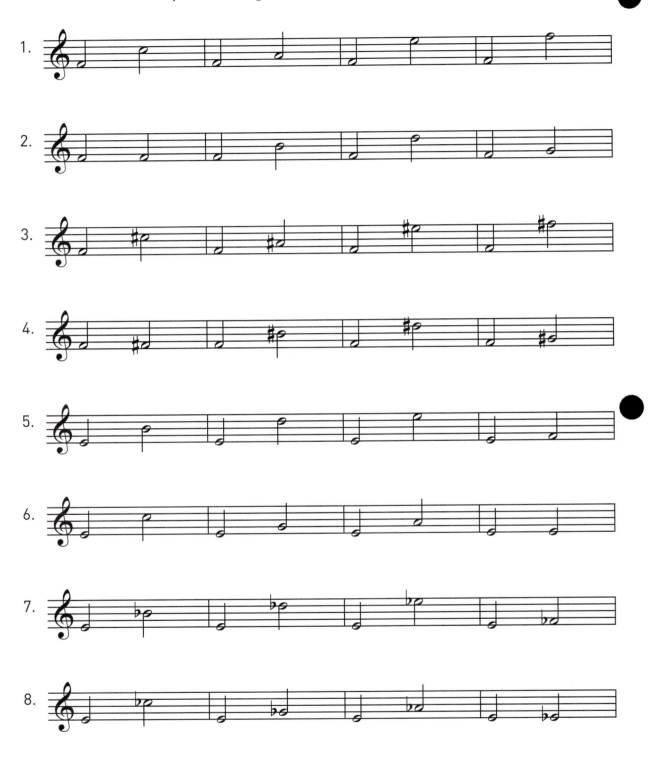

Exercise 6.10

Play the melodies, for major pentachord and hexachord, and the major scale on the keyboard. For each melody, name the intervals between each note played.

Exercise 6.11

1. Play G on the keyboard. Play the following in relation to this note:

M3 ↑ M2 ↓ M7 ↑ M6 ↑ P4 ↓ P5 ↑ Aug4 ↑ Dim 5 ↓ m2 ↑ m3 ↓

2. Play A-flat on the keyboard. Play the following in relation to this note:

M3 ↑ M2 ↓ M7 ↑ M6 ↑ P4 ↓ P5 ↑ Aug4 ↑ Dim 5 ↓ m2 ↑ m3 ↓

Exercise 6.12

Identify the interval size and the number of half steps in each example.

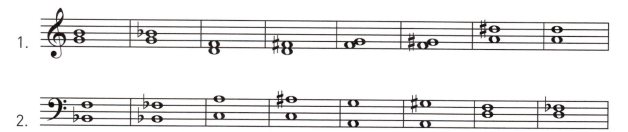

Exercise 6.13

Indicate the number of half steps in each interval and then name the interval.

Exercise 6.14

Name these intervals that are found in the major scales. The lower note is the tonic of the major scale.

6.4 Exercises: Determining Harmonic Inversion of Intervals

Exercise 6.15

Write the inversion of the interval to the right of the given interval. Write the abbreviated name of the interval below the notation. The key signature refers to the entire row of intervals.

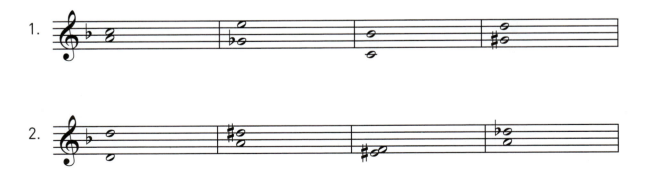

3.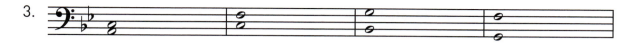

4.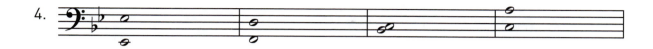

5.

6.

7.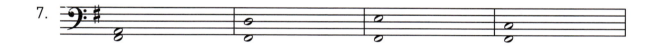

8.

Exercise 6.16

Write the inversion of the interval to the right of the given interval.

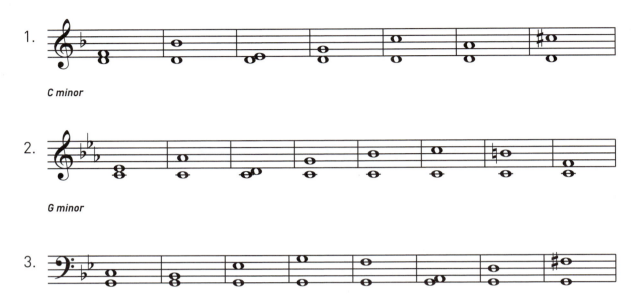

6.5   Exercises: Determining Compound Intervals

Exercise 6.17

Identify the following compound intervals.

Exercise 6.18

Identify the following compound intervals.

Chapter *7*
Compound Meter and Advanced Rhythmic Concepts

CHAPTER OVERVIEW

In previous chapters we learned that in simple meter the beat can be divided into two equal divisions. Now you will be introduced to another way to divide the pulse: into three equal divisions. We refer to this as compound meter. Well-known melodies such as "Row, Row, Row Your Boat" and "For He's a Jolly Good Fellow" are written in compound meter.

7.1 Rhythm Patterns in Compound Meter

All meters studied have a basic beat that can be divided into two; we refer to this as simple meter. We also have meters where the basic beat divides into three; we call this **compound meter**.

<table>
<tr><td>

Sing, Memorize, and Analyze

🔘

14

</td><td>

Internalizing Music

1. Listen to "Row, Row, Row Your Boat" on Track 14. Memorize the song.
2. Sing the melody and tap the beat.
3. Sing the melody and perform the division of the beat.
4. Sing the melody and conduct.
5. Sing the melody and clap the rhythm.
6. Pair off in the class. Student one performs the beat while student two performs the rhythm then switch.
7. Sing the song and perform the division of the beat as an ostinato. When the beat can be divided into three equal divisions, the composition is in compound meter. We use the term *duple compound meter* to describe the meter of "Row, Row, Row Your Boat."

Analyzing What You Hear

1. Consider the first of the four phrases. Each phrase is four beats long. Which beats have one sound? Which beat has two sounds? Are those two sounds even or uneven? Describe the sounds with the words "long" and "short."
2. Consider phrase two. On which beats do you sing the longest sound in the phrase? How many sounds do you sing on beat one? How many sounds do you sing on beat two? Are those sounds even or uneven? Describe the sounds with the words "long" and "short."
3. How many sounds do you sing on each beat in phrase three?
4. Describe the sounds on each beat of phrase four. Is the rhythm of phrase four the same as the rhythm of another phrase in the song?

Constructing a Representation from Memory

1. Using the information you acquired in the aural-awareness stage, create a visual representation of "Row, Row, Row Your Boat."
2. As you point to your representation of "Row, Row, Row Your Boat," sing the melody with solfège syllables.

</td></tr>
<tr><td>

Music Theory

</td><td>

Describing What You Hear with Rhythm Syllables

When we hear one sound on a beat, we call it *ta*. Three sounds that are evenly distributed over one beat are called *ta ki da*. Two sounds on a beat, one long

</td></tr>
</table>

followed by a short sound, is called *ta   da.* One sound lasting for two beats is called *ta-------ah,* or *ta* (and held).

The following are the rhythm syllables for "Row, Row, Row Your Boat."

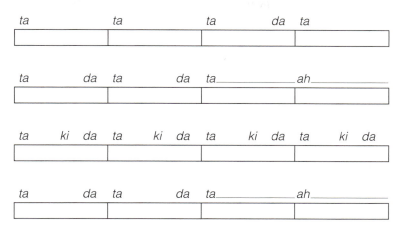

Notating What You Hear

We can notate "Row, Row, Row Your Boat" where the beat is equal to a dotted quarter note and there are two beats in a measure.

Row, Row, Row Your Boat

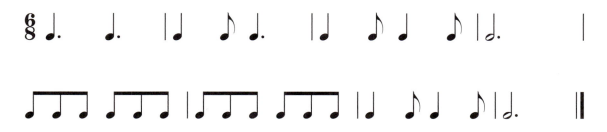

"Row, Row, Row Your Boat" is in duple compound meter, as there are two beats per measure. These are referred to as two *primary beats,* or *macrobeats,* per measure. Each of these beats can be divided into three *secondary beats,* or *microbeats.* We could say that there are two simultaneous pulses going on in each measure. Pulse one may refer to the dotted quarter notes and pulse two to the eighth notes. In fast tempos, we sense two pulses per measure, whereas in a slow tempo we have three pulses per measure.

We can state that the meter is duple compound meter because the macrobeats can be divided into three equal microbeats. We can use a $\frac{6}{8}$ time signature to indicate compound duple meter where the beat is equal to a dotted quarter note. Pulsation in $\frac{6}{8}$ may be indicated by two dotted quarter notes in each measure. There are six eighth notes in each measure or two groups of three beamed eighth notes. We can write "Row, Row, Row Your Boat" in traditional notation and use a $\frac{6}{8}$ time signature.

The following chart shows the relationship between rhythm syllables and notation:

Rhythm Syllable	**6/8** Meter
Ta ki da	♪♪♪
Ta	♩.
Ta da	♩ ♪
Ta	𝅗𝅥.

Reading with Rhythm Syllables

The following figure shows how we can use rhythm syllables to read "Row, Row, Row Your Boat."

Counting in 6/8 Meter with Numbers

The following figure shows how we can use numbers to count the rhythm of "Row, Row, Row Your Boat."

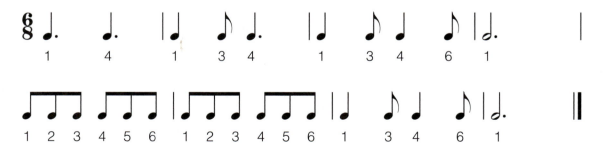

Conducting in $\frac{6}{8}$ Meter

We can conduct $\frac{6}{8}$ using a duple-meter pattern, conducting the macrobeats using the following pattern:

1 2

Or we can conduct the six microbeats in $\frac{6}{8}$ using the following conducting pattern:

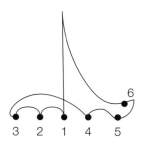

3 2 1 4 5

Notating a Rhythm Pattern into Additional Duple Compound Meters

"Row, Row, Row Your Boat" can be written in additional compound duple meters. The following chart will help you notate in additional meters.

Rhythm Syllable	$\frac{6}{8}$ Meter	$\frac{6}{4}$ Meter	$\frac{6}{16}$ Meter
Ta ki da	♪♪♪	♩♩♩	♬♬
Ta	♩.	♩.	♪.
Ta da	♩ ♪	♩ ♪	♪ ♪
Ta	♩.	𝅝.	♩.

$\frac{6}{4}$ can be used as a duple compound meter and indicates that there are two beats in a measure and that each beat is a dotted half note.

Scheherazade First Movement Theme   Nicolai Rimsky-Korsakov (1844–1908)

"Row, Row, Row Your Boat" can be written in $\frac{6}{4}$ as follows:

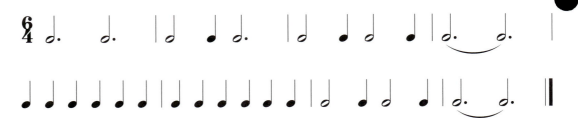

$\frac{6}{16}$ can be used as a duple compound meter and indicates that there are two beats in a measure and each beat is a dotted eighth note.

"Row, Row, Row Your Boat" can be written in $\frac{6}{16}$ as follows:

Distinguishing $\frac{3}{4}$ Meter from $\frac{6}{8}$ Meter

In both $\frac{3}{4}$ meter and $\frac{6}{8}$ meter there are six eighth notes in each measure. In the figure below, the accented pulses and the grouping of the notes will clearly show the difference:

In simple triple meter the eighth notes are grouped in twos, with three beats per measure. In compound duple meter the eighth notes are grouped in threes, with two beats per measure.

Compound Duple, Triple, and Quadruple Meters

Compound Duple Time Signatures

We have already discovered that $\frac{6}{8}$, $\frac{6}{4}$, and $\frac{6}{16}$ are compound meters.

Compound Triple Meters

$\frac{9}{8}$ is often used as a triple-compound-meter time signature and indicates that each beat is given the value of a dotted quarter note. There are nine eighth notes per measure, and these eighth notes are equal in length to three dotted-quarter-note beats per measure.

$\frac{9}{4}$ is often used as a triple-compound-meter time signature and indicates that each beat is given the value of a dotted half note. There are nine quarter notes per measure, and these nine quarter notes are equal in length to three dotted-half-note beats per measure.

The round "White Swans" is an example of a song in $\frac{9}{8}$ meter.

White Swans

White swans go   sail-ing a-long   sail-ing a-long   sail-ing a-long.

$\frac{9}{16}$ is often used as a triple-compound-meter time signature and indicates that each beat is given the value of a dotted eighth note. There are nine sixteenth notes per measure, and these nine sixteenth notes are equal in length to three dotted-eighth-note beats per measure.

Compound Quadruple Meter

$\frac{12}{8}$ is often used as a quadruple-compound-meter time signature and indicates that each beat is given the value of a dotted quarter note. There are twelve eighth notes per measure, and these eighth notes are equal in length to four dotted-quarter-note beats per measure.

Brandenburg Concerto No. 6, Movement 3   Johann Sebastian Bach (1685–1750)

$\frac{12}{4}$ is often used as a quadruple-compound-meter time signature and indicates that each beat is given the value of a dotted half note. There are twelve quarter notes per measure, and these twelve quarter notes are equal in length to four dotted-half-note beats per measure.

$\frac{12}{16}$ is often used as a quadruple-compound-meter time signature and indicates that each beat is given the value of a dotted eighth note. There are twelve sixteenth notes per measure, and these twelve sixteenth notes are equal in length to four dotted-eighth-note beats per measure.

The following chart provides a summary of compound meters.

Meter	Quarter Note as the Beat	Eighth Note as the Beat	Sixteenth Note as the Beat
Compound Duple Meter	$\frac{6}{4}$	$\frac{6}{8}$	$\frac{6}{16}$
Compound Triple Meter	$\frac{9}{4}$	$\frac{9}{8}$	$\frac{9}{16}$
Compound Quadruple Meter	$\frac{12}{4}$	$\frac{12}{8}$	$\frac{12}{16}$

Listening

"Memory" from *Cats*. Music by Andrew Lloyd Webber (1948–   ).
"Blue Rondo a la Turk" by Dave Brubeck (1920–   ).
"Rondo" from the Horn Concerto No. 4 in E-flat Major, K. 495, by Wolfgang Amadeus Mozart (1756–1791).

Summary of Note and Rest Values in Compound Meter

The following figure provides a summary of note and rest values in compound meter.

7.2 Subdivision of Rhythm Patterns in Compound Meter

Sing, Memorize, and Analyze

15

Internalizing Music

1. Listen to "Come, Let's Dance" on Track 15. Memorize the song.
2. Sing the melody and perform the beat.
3. Sing the melody and perform the division of the beat.
4. Sing the melody and conduct.

Analyzing What You Hear

1. How many phrases are there?
2. How many beats are in each phrase?
3. Consider phrase one. Which beats have two sounds? Are those sounds even or uneven?
4. Which beat has more than two sounds? Describe those sounds with the words "long" and "short."
5. Consider phrase two. Which beat has more than two sounds? How many sounds are on that beat? Describe those sounds with the words "long" and "short."
6. Sing "Come, Let's Dance," but sing beat three of phrases one and two with the words "short, short, long, long."

Constructing a Melodic Representation from Memory

1. Using the information you acquired in the aural-awareness stage, create a visual representation of "Come, Let's Dance."
2. Indicate the number of sounds on each beat and indicate the length of sounds on each beat.
3. Sing "Come, Let's Dance" with solfège syllables.

Music Theory

How to Describe What You Hear with Rhythm Syllables

In compound meter one sound on a beat is called *ta*. Four sounds on a beat, where there are two short sounds followed by two long sounds, are called *ta va ki da*. The rhythm syllables for "Come, Let's Dance" are sung as follows:

ta		*da*	*ta*		*da*	*ta va ki da*	*ta*		*da*

ta		*da*	*ta*		*da*	*ta va ki da*	*ta*

How to Notate What You Hear

We can write the rhythm of "Come, Let's Dance" as follows in simple duple meter when the beat is equal to a dotted quarter note.

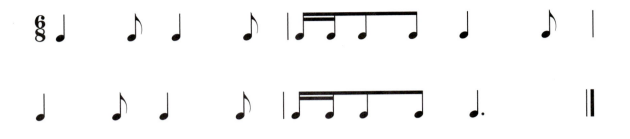

We can write "Come, Let's Dance" in $\frac{6}{8}$, $\frac{6}{4}$, and $\frac{6}{16}$ meter.

Rhythm Syllable	$\frac{6}{8}$ Meter	$\frac{6}{4}$ Meter	$\frac{6}{16}$ Meter
Ta ki da	♪♪♪	♩♩♩	♬♬
Ta	♩.	♩.	♪.
Ta da	♩ ♪	♩ ♩	♪ ♪
Tava ki da	♬♪	♫♩	♬♪

Reading Rhythms with Syllables

We can use rhythm syllables to read "Come, Let's Dance."

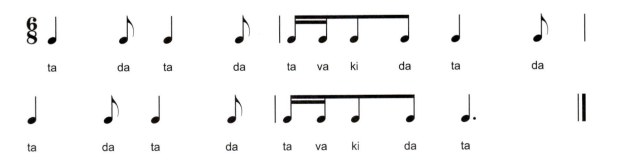

Counting with Numbers

The numbers below the rhythm of "Come, Let's Dance" indicate how to count the rhythm.

Come, Let's Dance   **French, Thirteenth Century**

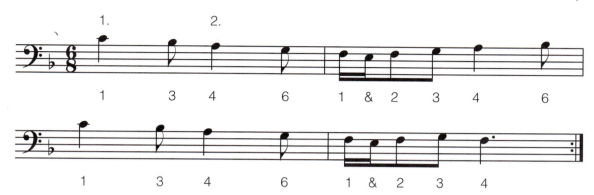

We can write the rhythm of "Come, Let's Dance" in $\frac{6}{4}$ meter as follows:

We can write the rhythm of "Come, Let's Dance" in $\frac{6}{16}$ as follows:

7.3   More Complex Rhythm Patterns in Compound Meter

Sing, Memorize, and Analyze

Internalizing Music

🔘 **16**

1. Listen to "Morning Is Come" on Track 16. Memorize the song.
2. Sing the melody and perform the beat.
3. Sing the melody and perform the division of the beat.

4. Sing the melody and conduct.

5. Sing the song and perform the division of the beat as an ostinato. When the beat can be divided into three equal divisions, the composition is in compound meter.

Analyzing What You Hear

1. How many beats are in each phrase?

2. Which beats in phrase one have one sound? Which beats in phrase one have three sounds?

3. Consider phrase two. Which beat has the most sounds? How many sounds are on that beat? Can you describe those sounds with the words "long" and "short"?

Constructing a Melodic Representation from Memory

1. Using the information you acquired in the aural-awareness stage, create a visual representation of "Morning Is Come."

2. Point to your representation as you sing "Morning Is Come" with solfège syllables.

Music Theory

Describing What You Hear with Rhythm Syllables

In compound meter one sound on a beat is called *ta*.

Three sounds that are evenly distributed over one beat are called *ta ki da*. Five sounds on the beat, where the first is longer, are called *ta ki di da ma*.

The following are the rhythm syllables for "Morning Is Come":

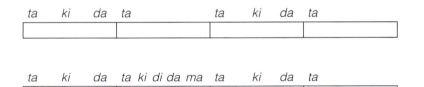

ta	ki	da	ta		ta	ki	da	ta

ta	ki	da	ta ki di da ma	ta	ki	da	ta

Notating What You Hear

In the second half of the third measure of "Morning Is Come," we have five sounds on a beat where the first sound is equal in length to a macrobeat and the next four sounds are equal to two microbeats. We can visually represent this in traditional notation using an eighth note followed by four sixteenth notes when the beat is equal to a dotted quarter note.

We can use the following chart to write "Morning Is Come" in different duple-meter key signatures:

Rhythm Syllable	$\frac{6}{8}$ Meter	$\frac{6}{4}$ Meter	$\frac{6}{16}$ Meter
Ta ki da	♪♪♪	♩♩♩	♬♬♬
Ta	♩.	♩.	♪.
Ta da	♩ ♪	♩ ♩	♪ ♪
Ta ki di da ma	♩ ♬	♩ ♬	♬♬

Here is an example of "Morning Is Come" written in $\frac{6}{8}$ meter.

Morning Is Come   **William H. Bradbury (1816–1868)**

Morn - ing   is   come,   Night   is   a - way,

Rise   with   the   sun_____ and__ wel - come   the   day.

Here is an example of "Morning Is Come" written in $\frac{6}{4}$ meter.

Here is an example of "Morning Is Come" written in $\frac{6}{16}$ meter.

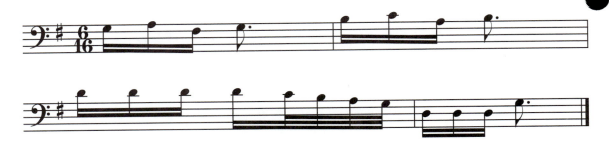

7.4   Dotted Rhythm Patterns in Compound Meter

Sing, Memorize, and Analyze

🔘
17

Internalizing Music

1. Listen to "Early to Bed" on Track 17. Memorize the song.
2. Sing the melody and perform the beat.
3. Sing the melody and perform the division of the beat.
4. Sing the melody and conduct.

Analyzing What You Hear

1. Consider phrase one. Which beats have one sound? Which beats have more than one sound?
2. Consider the beats that have three sounds on them. Are the three sounds evenly distributed within the beat?
3. Consider beat one in phrase one. Describe the three sounds.
4. Consider phrase two. How are the three sounds you sing on beat one different from the three sounds you sing on beats two and three?

Constructing a Melodic Representation from Memory

1. Using the information you acquired in the aural-awareness stage, create a visual representation of "Early to Bed."
2. Sing "Early to Bed" with solfège syllables as you point to your representation.

Music Theory

Describing What You Hear with Rhythm Syllables

In compound meter one sound on a beat is called *ta*. Three sounds that are evenly distributed over one beat are called *ta ki da*. Three uneven sounds on Early to Bed are called *ta   di da*.

The following are the rhythm syllables for "Early to Bed."

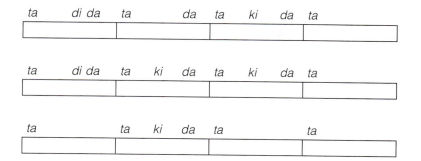

Notating What You Hear

We can write "Early to Bed" in $\frac{6}{8}$, $\frac{6}{4}$, and $\frac{6}{16}$ meter using the following chart:

Rhythm Syllable	$\frac{6}{8}$ Meter	$\frac{6}{4}$ Meter	$\frac{6}{16}$ Meter
Ta ki da			
Ta			
Ta da			
Ta di da			

We can write the rhythm of "Early to Bed" as follows in simple duple meter when the beat is equal to a dotted quarter note.

Early to Bed

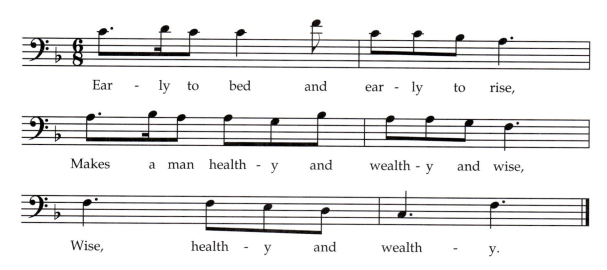

Ear - ly to bed and ear - ly to rise,

Makes a man health - y and wealth - y and wise,

Wise, health - y and wealth - y.

We can write the rhythm of "Early to Bed" in $\frac{6}{4}$ meter as follows.

We can write the rhythm of "Early to Bed" as follows in simple duple meter when the beat is equal to a dotted eighth note in $\frac{6}{16}$ meter.

Early to Bed

Beams in Compound Meter

The beat in $\frac{6}{8}$ meter is felt as two beats per measure and the dotted quarter note represents the beat. This beat is divisible by three. As a general rule, any combination of three eighth or sixteenth notes, including dotted notes, should be grouped or beamed together.

Using Rest Groupings in Compound Time

In $\frac{6}{8}$ meter, a one-beat rest is written as a dotted-quarter-note rest or as a quarter-note rest followed by an eighth-note rest.

In $\frac{6}{8}$, $\frac{9}{8}$, and $\frac{12}{8}$ meters, remember that each beat requires a new rest but in $\frac{12}{8}$ a dotted-half-note rest is used for the first two beats or the last two beats.

A silent measure in compound time is shown as a whole-note rest:

Listening 🎧   "Danza de la Moza Donosa," Op. 2, No. 2, from *Danzas Argentinas* for piano by Alberto E. Ginastera (1916–1983).

7.5 Triplets and Duplets

Sing, Memorize, and Analyze

18

Internalizing Music

1. Listen to the Greek folk song "Little Partridge" on Track 18. Memorize the song.
2. Sing "Little Partridge" and keep the beat.
3. Sing "Little Partridge" and conduct.
4. Sing "Little Partridge" and clap the rhythm.
5. Divide the class into two groups. Group A performs the beat while Group B performs the rhythm, and vice versa.
6. Sing "Little Partridge" tapping the beat with your left hand and tapping the rhythm with your right hand.

Analyzing What You Hear

1. As you sing "Little Partridge," determine the number of beats within each phrase.
2. Is there a place in phrase one where there are more than two sounds on a beat?
3. How many sounds do you hear on this beat?
4. Would you describe these sounds as even or uneven?

Constructing a Melodic Representation from Memory

1. Using the information you acquired in the aural-awareness stage, create a visual representation of "Little Partridge."

Music Theory   **Describing What You Hear with Rhythm Syllables**

We can sing "Little Partridge" with the following rhythm syllables.

ta	ta	ta	ta	di	ta	di	ta	di	ta	ki	da	ta	di

ta	di	ta	di	ta		ta	di	ta	di	ta	di	ta		ta

The pattern of three sounds occurring over one beat in simple meter is a **triplet** and can be read using *ta ki da* rhythm syllables. Note that three sounds occurring in one beat in compound meter is also called *ta ki da*. A triplet is defined as three notes performed in the time of two notes.

"Little Partridge" is in $\frac{2}{4}$ meter. Note that the seventh beat of the first phrase contains three evenly distributed sounds on the beat; this is a triplet.

How to Notate What You Hear

Three even sounds on one beat, when the beat is a quarter note, are written as three eighth notes with a 3 placed above or below the beam to denote that they are triplets; three eighth notes are equal in duration to two eighth notes. We can refer to this as a *borrowed division*, since we have a note that is usually subdivided into two but is now divided into three.

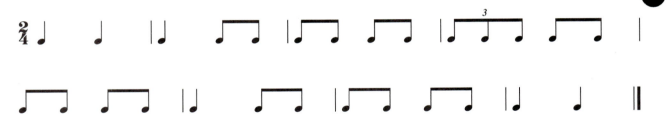

We can write "Little Partridge" in $\frac{2}{8}$ meter as follows.

We can write "Little Partridge" in $\frac{2}{2}$ meter as follows.

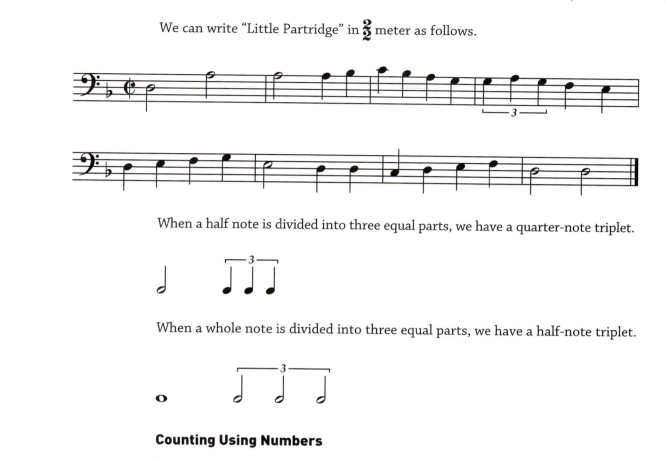

When a half note is divided into three equal parts, we have a quarter-note triplet.

When a whole note is divided into three equal parts, we have a half-note triplet.

Counting Using Numbers

When counting using numbers, we count the triplet as follows:

Little Partridge

Triplet Rest

If a rest appears within a triplet where the beat is equal to a quarter note, it is written like an eighth-note rest:

If a rest appears within a triplet where the beat is equal to an eighth note, it is written like an sixteenth-note rest. If a rest appears within a triplet where the beat is equal to a half note, it is written like a quarter-note rest.

Duplet

A **duplet** is a term used for two notes that are to be performed in the time of three. They are indicated by the number 2 placed above or below the two notes. In compound meter the beat can be divided into two equal parts called a duplet. Duplets appear as either two eighth notes with a 2 above them, or two dotted eighth notes. We use the rhythm syllables *ta di*, borrowed from simple meter, to count a duplet. The following figure illustrates a duplet in compound meter.

Listening 🎧   Triplets

Mikroskosmos Vol. 3, No. 75, by Béla Bartók (1882–1945).

"Sometimes I Feel Like a Motherless Child" (uses both triplets and syncopation).

"Jesu, Joy of Man's Desiring," chorale from Cantata no. 147 by Johann Sebastian Bach (1685–1750).

Duplets

Mikrokosmos Vol. 3, No. 85, by Béla Bartók (1882–1945).

7.6　Changing Meter and Asymmetric Meter

Some pieces of music have several different meter changes throughout. This is referred to as **mixed meter** or **changing meter**. In the following example, the basic beat of a quarter note remains the same even though the meter changes from $\frac{3}{4}$ to $\frac{2}{4}$, etc.

Little Swallow

Lit - tle　Swal - low　　　fly　　to　your　nest

who goes there　　fly　fly　a - way　now,　　Lit - tle Swal - low

fly　to　your nest,　　　Fly　oh　fly　a -　way.

Asymmetric Meter

Asymmetric meters contain an uneven number of beats per measure. More common asymmetric meters include $\frac{5}{4}$, $\frac{7}{4}$, $\frac{5}{8}$, and $\frac{7}{8}$.

$\frac{5}{4}$ meter indicates that each beat is given the value of a quarter note. There are five quarter-note beats per measure. These five quarter notes can appear as either a grouping of three followed by a grouping of two or a grouping of two followed by a grouping of three.

"Promenade" from Pictures at an Exhibition　　　　　　**Modest Mussorgsky (1839–1881)**

Finnish Folk Song

$\frac{5}{8}$ meter indicates that each beat is given the value of an eighth note; therefore, there are five eighth-note beats per measure. These five eighth notes can appear as either a grouping of three followed by a grouping of two or a grouping of two followed by a grouping of three.

$\frac{7}{4}$ meter indicates that each beat is given the value of a quarter note and therefore there are seven quarter-note beats per measure. These seven quarter notes can appear as either a grouping of three followed by two groupings of two or a grouping of two followed by a grouping of three followed by a grouping of two.

Folk Song

$\frac{7}{8}$ meter indicates that each beat is given the value of an eighth note. There are seven eighth-note beats per measure. These seven eighth notes can be grouped in a measure similarly to $\frac{7}{4}$.

Key Terms and Concepts

Compound Meter	Duplet	Changing Meter
Triplet	Mixed Meter	Asymmetric Meter

Using the Musical Skills CD

Access Chapter 7 on the *skills* CD to reinforce compound meter and the advanced rhythmic concepts introduced in this chapter through tutorials and dictation. Please use the arrows on the top right of the page to move from one page to another.

How to Practice

Here are suggestions for practicing rhythms in a variety of ways.

Performing	Sing all of the melodies with rhythm syllables.
	Sing "Row, Row, Row Your Boat" with words while tapping the beat. Sing "Row, Row, Row Your Boat" with rhythm syllables while tapping the beat. Sing "Row, Row, Row Your Boat" with rhythm syllables while conducting the beat.
	Sing "Early to Bed" with rhythm syllables and tap the microbeat. Sing "Early to Bed" with rhythm syllables and conduct. Sing "Early to Bed" using solfège syllables.
	Sing "Come, Let's Dance" with words while tapping the beat. Sing "Come, Let's Dance" with rhythm syllables while tapping the beat. Sing "Come, Let's Dance" with rhythm syllables while conducting the beat.
	Sing "Little Partridge" with rhythm syllables while conducting the beat. Sing "Little Partridge" with words while tapping the beat. Sing "Little Partridge" with rhythm syllables while tapping the beat. Sing "Little Partridge" with solfège syllables while conducting the beat.
	Sing "Little Swallow" with rhythm syllables while conducting the beat. Sing "Little Swallow" with words while tapping the beat. Sing "Little Swallow" with rhythm syllables while tapping the beat. Sing "Little Swallow" with solfège syllables while conducting the beat.
Performing the Rhythm and the Beat at the Same Time	Divide into three groups: one group performs the rhythm of the focus song, the other keeps the beat, and another group keeps the division. Practice this activity in different combinations: • Instructor/class • Class/instructor • Divided class Individually, keep the beat or division of the beat with one hand and tap the rhythm with the other hand.
Standard Practice	Sing or speak the rhythm patterns of focus songs while tapping the beat.
Echo Clapping	Practice with a classmate or in class. One of you will clap the rhythm of a melody or a rhythmic pattern. The other will "echo" what was clapped with rhythm syllables. Begin with the building blocks used in the compound-meter melody. Try to combine different building blocks from different focus songs.
Conducting	Sing and conduct at the same time. You can conduct compound meter using a duple-meter conducting pattern.
Aural Analysis	Identify which beat or beats contain specified rhythmic patterns.
Notating Your Rhythm	Practice with a classmate or in class. One of you will clap the rhythm of a melody or a rhythmic pattern. The other will "echo" what was clapped with rhythm syllables and then notate the pattern in a given meter.
Error Dictation	One student plays the melody, deliberately making a mistake. Another student follows the score and locates the error.
Memory	Memorize an entire exercise and notate it without referring to the notation. First analyze the form by looking for repeated and similar parts. This will simplify the task.
Improvisation/Composition	First select a meter and length for the composition, then decide what rhythmic form to use (for example, abba). Create an improvisation or composition using only known rhythms.
Performing a Rhythmic Canon	Say the rhythm syllables while clapping the rhythm of the melody. Think the rhythm syllables and clap the rhythm. Clap the rhythm while another person claps the melody starting after four beats. Perform the canon by yourself. Tap one part with one hand and use a pencil to tap the other part with the other hand.

How to Read a Musical Score

Examine the Minuet by Johann Sebastian Bach.

Identify the time signature. Identify the tempo of the piece. Identify the triplets. How would you count the rhythm of the treble clef with rhythm syllables?

Minuet in G Major

Johann Sebastian Bach (1685–1750)

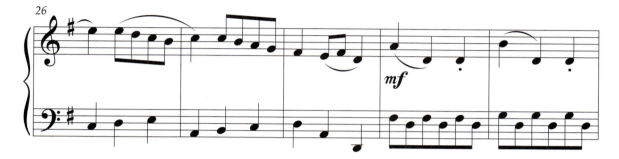

"Come, Let's Dance" in $\frac{6}{8}$, $\frac{6}{4}$, and $\frac{6}{16}$ meter.

Rhythm Syllable	$\frac{6}{8}$ Meter	$\frac{6}{4}$ Meter	$\frac{6}{16}$ Meter
	♪♪♪	♩ ♩ ♩	♬♬
	♩.	♩.	♪.
	♩ ♪	♩ ♩	♪ ♬
	♪♪♪♪	♪♪♩ ♩	♬♬♬

7.3   Exercise: More Complex Rhythm Patterns in Compound Meter

Exercise 7.5

Fill in the rhythm syllables for "Morning Is Come" in $\frac{6}{8}$, $\frac{6}{4}$, and $\frac{6}{16}$ meter.

Rhythm Syllable	$\frac{6}{8}$ Meter	$\frac{6}{4}$ Meter	$\frac{6}{16}$ Meter
	♪♪♪	♩ ♩ ♩	♬♬
	♩.	♩.	♪.
	♩ ♪	♩ ♩	♪ ♬
	♩ ♪♪♪	♩ ♪♪♪	♪ ♬♬

7.4 Exercises: Dotted Rhythm Patterns in Compound Meter

Exercise 7.6

Write the rhythm syllables for "Early to Bed" above the representation.

Exercise 7.7

Fill in the rhythm syllables for the following chart.

Rhythm Syllable	$\frac{6}{8}$ Meter	$\frac{6}{4}$ Meter	$\frac{6}{16}$ Meter
	♩♩♩	♩ ♩ ♩	♪♪♪
	♩.	♩.	♪.
	♩ ♪	♩ ♩	♪ ♪
	♩. ♪♪	♩. ♪♪	♪. ♪♪

Chapter 8

Orientation to the Minor Scale

CHAPTER OVERVIEW

In Chapter 4 you learned about the major pentachord, hexachord, and pentatonic scales, and in Chapter 5 you learned about the major scale. In this chapter you will learn how to construct, notate, and improvise with the minor pentachord, hexachord, and pentatonic scales. Like the other scales, the minor scale is built on whole and half steps. In order to understand music based on the minor scale, it is important to develop notational skills as well as the ability to sing and play scales on the piano.

8.1A Minor Pentachord Scale and Melodies

Sing, Memorize, and Analyze

19

Internalizing Music

1. Listen to "Kis kece lányom" on Track 19. Memorize the song.
2. Sing "Kis kece lányom" while you clap the melodic contour.

Analyzing What You Hear

1. As you sing "Kis kece lányom," determine the number of phrases.
2. As you sing "Kis kece lányom," determine the number of beats within the phrases.
3. Sing the lowest pitch in phrase one. On which beats in phrase one do you sing the lowest pitch?
4. Sing the highest pitch in phrase one.
5. Sing the beginning note of the song.
6. Sing the range of notes from the lowest to the highest.

Constructing the Melodic Contour of "Kis kece lányom"

1. As you sing "Kis kece lányom," draw a representation indicating the melodic contour of each phrase.
2. Point to your representation and sing "Kis kece lányom" with rhythm syllables.

Music Theory

Describing What You Hear with Solfège Syllables

There are two systems for labeling notes with solfège syllables in a minor key. System one is referred to as *la minor* and system two is referred to as *do minor*. Your instructor will select one of these systems. The following figure associates the pitches in "Kis kece lányom" with its corresponding solfège syllables.

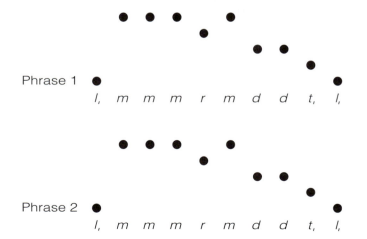

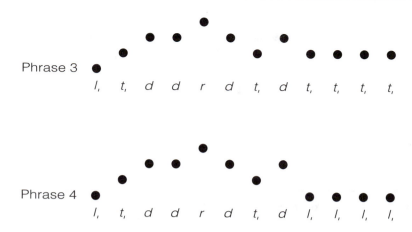

Phrase 3   l, t, d d r d t, d t, t, t, t,

Phrase 4   l, t, d d r d t, d l, l, l, l,

Note the subscript indicates notes lower than d.

Notating What You Hear with Solfège Syllables

We can write "Kis kece lányom" in rhythm notation with solfège syllables.

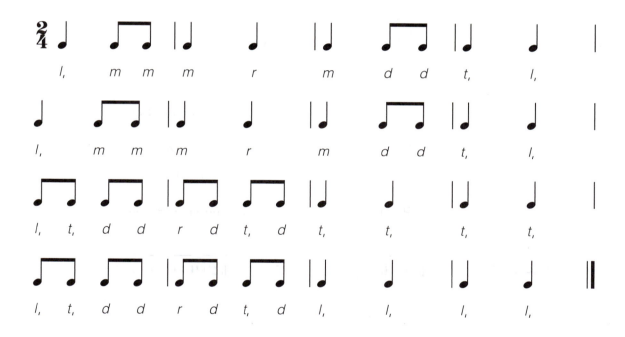

l,   m   m   m   r   m   d   d   t,   l,

l,   m   m   m   r   m   d   d   t,   l,

l,   t,   d   d   r   d   t,   d   t,   t,   t,   t,

l,   t,   d   d   r   d   t,   d   l,   l,   l,   l,

When we write the pitches of "Kis kece lányom" in ascending order, we discover that, just as in the major pentachord, there are five adjacent pitches: *l, – t, – d – r – m*. We refer to this pitch collection as a **minor pentachord scale**. The following chart illustrates the relationship between solfège syllables and scale degree numbers.

Solfège Syllable	Corresponding Number
m	$\hat{5}$
r	$\hat{4}$
d	$\hat{3}$
t,	$\hat{2}$
l,	$\hat{1}$

Notating What You Hear on the Staff

We can write "Kis kece lányom" on the staff beginning on D as follows:

| Listening 🎧 | The following listening examples include subsets of the minor pentachord scale. Can you sing the themes using solfège syllables? Can you write the themes of some of these examples using staff notation or stick notation with solfège syllables? |

For Children Vol. 1, No. 3, by Béla Bartók (1882–1945).

"Study for the Left Hand," *For Children* Vol. 1, by Béla Bartók (1882–1945).

"Round Dance," *For Children* Vol. 1, by Béla Bartók (1882–1945).

Mikrokosmos Vol. 1, Nos. 2b, 8, 21, and 23, by Béla Bartók (1882–1945).

"Táncnóta" (Dancing Song), choral composition by Zoltán Kodály (1882–1967).

8.2A Determining the Size and Quality of Intervals Between the Notes of the Minor Pentachord Scale

The following shows the whole- and half-step relationships of the minor pentachord scale on the keyboard. Look at the whole-step (W) and half-step (H) pattern.

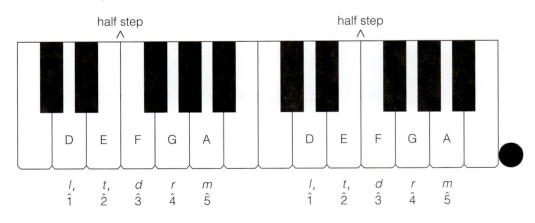

The following shows the whole- and half-step relationships of the minor pentachord scale on the staff.

W   H   W   W   W   W   H   W

The first degree of the scale is called the tonic note or keynote. There is a half step between the second and third degrees of the scale. There is a whole step between all other degrees of the minor pentachord scale (1 and 2, 3 and 4, 4 and 5). We can refer to whole steps as major seconds (M2) and half steps as minor seconds (m2).

Singing the following exercise will help you learn the size and quality of the intervals of the minor pentachord scale.

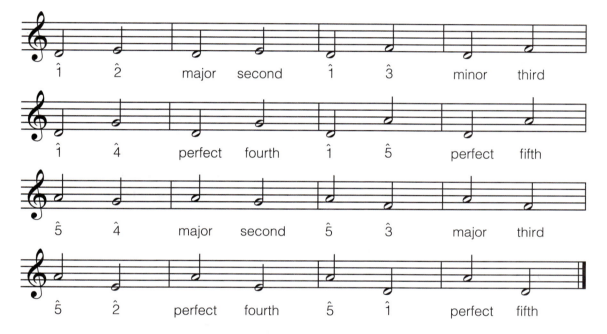

The following chart illustrates the intervals of the minor pentachord scale using the *la minor* system.

Scale Degree	Solfège Syllables	Size	Number of Half Steps Contained in an Interval	Name of Interval	Abbreviation
1–2	l–t,	2	2	major second	M2
1–3	t,–d	3	3	minor third	m3
1–4	l–r	4	5	perfect fourth	P4
1–5	l–m	5	7	perfect fifth	P5

8.3A   Writing Minor Pentachord Scales and Melodies Using Accidentals

Writing a Minor Pentachord Scale on the Staff Using Accidentals

The following is a procedure for writing any minor pentachord scale on the staff using accidentals. We will write this example as an e minor pentachord scale in the treble clef.

1. Write the solfège syllables *l, – t, – d – r – m* beneath the staff for the minor pentachord scale.

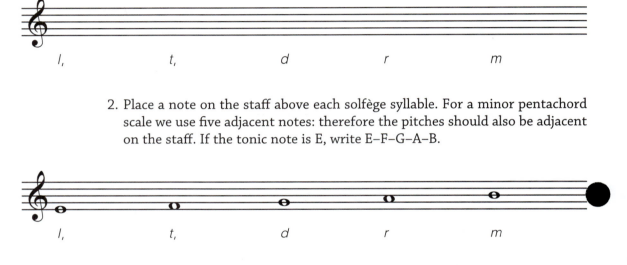

l,   *t,*   *d*   *r*   *m*

2. Place a note on the staff above each solfège syllable. For a minor pentachord scale we use five adjacent notes: therefore the pitches should also be adjacent on the staff. If the tonic note is E, write E–F–G–A–B.

l,   *t,*   *d*   *r*   *m*

3. Mark the half step between the second and third scale degrees and their corresponding pitches on the staff. Remember the intervals between the other degrees will be whole steps.

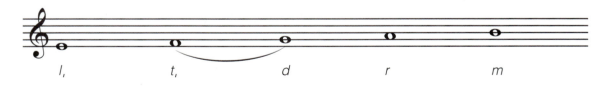

l,   *t,*   *d*   *r*   *m*

4. Check the intervallic relationship between the solfège syllables and the pitch names to insure the correct intervallic distance between the notes. Correct the intervallic relationship with accidentals. In the e minor pentachord we have an F-sharp.

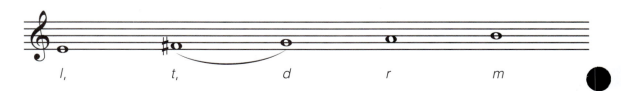

l,   *t,*   *d*   *r*   *m*

Writing a Minor Pentachord Melody Using Accidentals

The following is a procedure for writing any minor pentachord melody on the staff using accidentals. For example, we will write the melody "Kis kece lányom" in the key of e minor in treble clef.

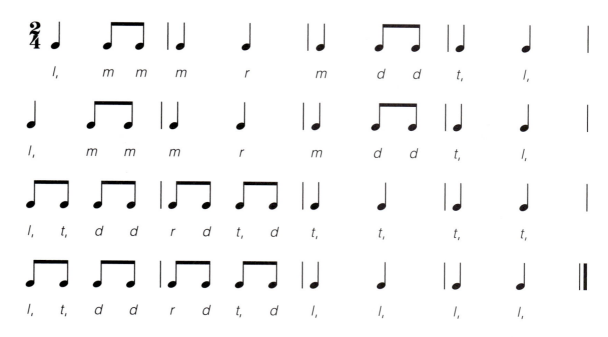

1. Write the e minor pentachord scale on the staff using accidentals.

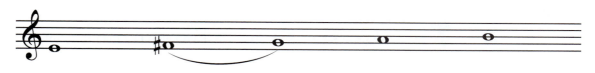

2. Write the solfège syllables below the scale.

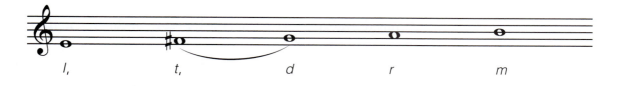

3. Write "Kis kece lányom" on the staff by associating the solfège syllables with note names in the e minor pentachord.

Kis kece lányom

8.4A   Minor Hexachord Scale and Melodies

Internalizing Music

1. Listen to the Slovak Folk Song on Track 20. Memorize the song.
2. Sing the Slovak Folk Song while you clap the melodic contour.

Analyzing What You Hear

1. As you sing the Slovak Folk Song, determine the number of phrases.
2. As you sing the Slovak Folk Song, determine the number of beats within the phrases.
3. Sing the range of notes from the lowest to the highest in the song.

Constructing the Melodic Contour of Slovak Folk Song

1. As you sing the Slovak Folk Song, draw a representation of the pitches in each phrase.
2. Point to your representation and sing the Slovak Folk Song with rhythm syllables.

| Music Theory | **Describing What You Hear with Solfège Syllables** |

We can describe the pitches in the Slovak Folk Song with solfège syllables. Notice that the melodic movement of both phrases is mostly stepwise.

Slovak Folk Song

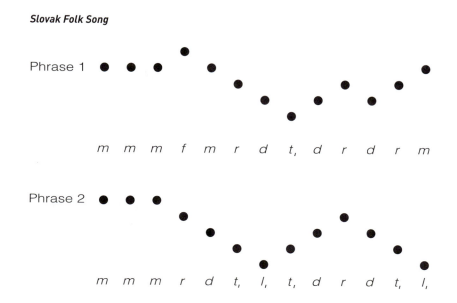

Notating What You Hear with Solfège Syllables

We can write the Slovak Folk Song in rhythm notation with solfège syllables.

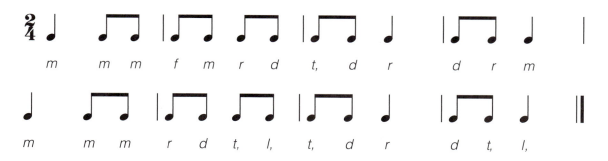

When we write the pitches of the Slovak Folk Song in ascending order, we discover that just as in the major hexachord, there are six adjacent pitches: *l, – t, – d – r – m – f*. We refer to this pitch collection as a **minor hexachord scale**. The following chart illustrates the relationship between solfège syllables and scale degree numbers.

Solfège Syllable	Corresponding Number
f	$\hat{6}$
m	$\hat{5}$
r	$\hat{4}$
d	$\hat{3}$
t,	$\hat{2}$
l,	$\hat{1}$

| **Listening** | The following listening example includes subsets of the minor hexachord scale. Can you sing the theme using solfège syllables? Can you write the theme using staff notation or stick notation with solfège syllables? |

"Dance," *For Children* Vol. 2, No. 8, by Béla Bartók (1882–1945).

8.5A   Determining the Intervals Between the Notes of the Minor Hexachord Scale

The following shows the whole- and half-step relationships of the d minor hexachord scale on the keyboard. The distances between *t,* and *d* and *m* and *f* are half steps (m2). The distances between *l,* and *t,* *d* and *r,* and *r* and *m* are whole steps (M2).

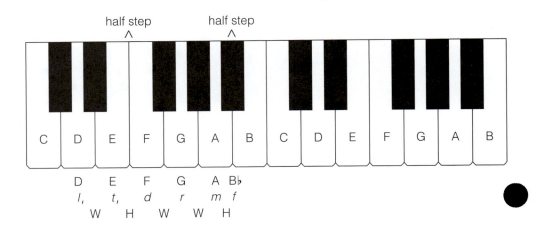

The following shows the whole- and half-step relationships of the d minor hexachord scale on the staff.

The first degree of the scale is called the tonic note or keynote. There is a half step between the second and third as well as the fifth and sixth degrees of the scale. There is a whole step between all other degrees of the scale (1 and 2, 3 and 4, 4 and 5).

Singing the following exercise will help you learn the size and quality of the intervals of the minor hexachord scale.

The following chart illustrates the intervals of the minor pentachord scale using the *la* minor system.

Scale Degree	Solfège Syllables	Size	Number of Half Steps Contained in an Interval	Name of Interval	Abbreviation
1–2	*l,–t,*	2	2	major second	M2
1–3	*t,–d*	3	3	minor third	m3
1–4	*l,–r*	4	5	perfect fourth	P4
1–5	*l,–m*	5	7	perfect fifth	P5
1–6	*l,–f*	6	8	minor sixth	m6
6–5	*f–m*	2	2	minor second	m2
6–4	*f–r*	3	3	minor third	m3
6–3	*f–d*	4	4	perfect fourth	P4
6–2	*f–t,*	5	6	diminished fifth	d5
6–1	*f–l,*	8	8	minor sixth	m6

8.6A   Writing Minor Hexachord Scales and Melodies Using Accidentals

Writing a Minor Hexachord Scale on the Staff Using Accidentals

The following is a procedure for writing any minor hexachord scale on the staff using accidentals. We will write this example as a d minor hexachord scale in the treble clef.

1. Write the solfège syllables *l, – t, – d – r – m – f* beneath the staff for the minor hexachord scale.

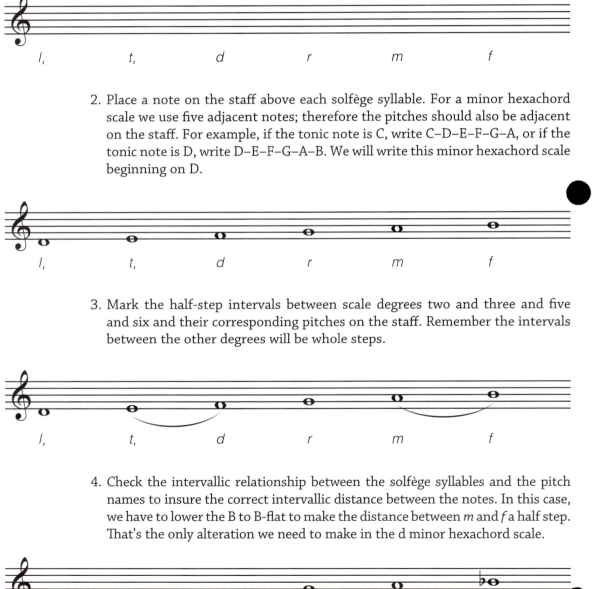

2. Place a note on the staff above each solfège syllable. For a minor hexachord scale we use five adjacent notes; therefore the pitches should also be adjacent on the staff. For example, if the tonic note is C, write C–D–E–F–G–A, or if the tonic note is D, write D–E–F–G–A–B. We will write this minor hexachord scale beginning on D.

3. Mark the half-step intervals between scale degrees two and three and five and six and their corresponding pitches on the staff. Remember the intervals between the other degrees will be whole steps.

4. Check the intervallic relationship between the solfège syllables and the pitch names to insure the correct intervallic distance between the notes. In this case, we have to lower the B to B-flat to make the distance between *m* and *f* a half step. That's the only alteration we need to make in the d minor hexachord scale.

Writing a Minor Hexachord Melody Using Accidentals

The following is a procedure for writing any minor hexachord melody on the staff using accidentals. For an example, we will write the Slovak Folk Song in the key of d minor hexachord in treble clef. Remember, music based on a particular scale is said to be in the key of that scale. If music is built on the d minor hexachord scale then the work is in the key of d minor hexachord and the tonic of the music is D.

1. Write the d minor hexachord scale on the staff using accidentals.

2. Write the solfège syllables below the scale.

3. Write the Slovak Folk Song on the staff by associating the solfège syllables with note names in the key of d minor hexachord. Note the placement of accidentals.

We can write the Slovak Folk Song on the staff as follows:

Listening 🎧 The following listening examples include subsets of the minor hexachord scale. Can you sing the themes using solfège syllables? Can you write the themes of some of these examples using staff notation or stick notation with solfège syllables?

"Ah! Vous dirai-je maman." Variations on "Twinkle, Twinkle, Little Star," K. 265, by Wolfgang Amadeus Mozart (1756–1791).

"Variations on a Nursery Song," Op. 25, by Ernö Dohnányi (1877–1960).

"Maypole Dance," No. 2 from *44 Duets for Two Violins* by Béla Bartók (1882–1945).

"Children at Play," *For Children* Vol. 1, No. 1, by Béla Bartók (1882–1945).

For Children Vol. 2, Nos. 2 and 3, by Béla Bartók (1882–1945).

8.7A   Minor Pentatonic Scale and Melodies

Sing, Memorize, and Analyze

21

Internalizing Music

1. Listen to "Gallows Pole" on Track 21. Memorize the song.
2. Sing "Gallows Pole" while you clap the melodic contour.

Analyzing What You Hear

1. Sing the lowest pitches in the song.
2. Sing the highest pitches in the song.
3. Sing the range of notes from the lowest to the highest.

Constructing the Melodic Contour of "Gallows Pole"

1. As you sing "Gallows Pole," draw a representation of the pitches in each phrase.
2. Point to your representation and sing "Gallows Pole" with rhythm syllables.

Music Theory

Describing What You Hear with Solfège Syllables

We can describe the pitches in "Gallows Pole" with solfège syllables.

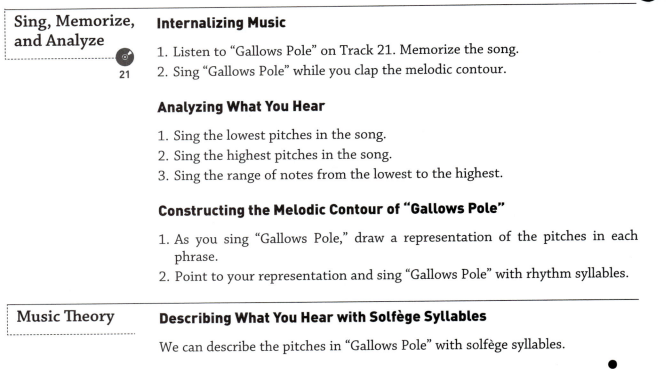

Notating What You Hear with Solfège Syllables

We can write "Gallows Pole" in rhythm notation with solfège syllables.

Gallows Pole

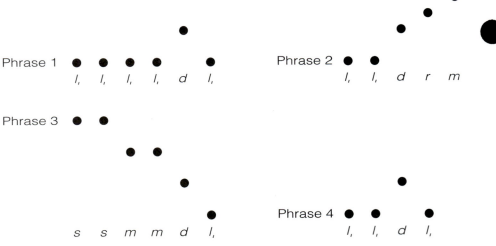

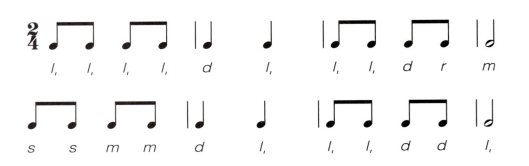

When we write the pitches of "Gallows Pole" in ascending order, we discover that there are five. We can label these pitches with the solfège syllables *l, — d – r – m — s*. We refer to this collection of notes as a **minor pentatonic scale**.

Notating What You Hear on the Staff

We can write "Gallows Pole" on the staff beginning on D as follows:

Listening 🎧

The following listening examples include subsets of the minor pentatonic scale. Can you sing the themes using solfège syllables? Can you write the themes of some of these examples using staff notation or stick notation with solfège syllables?

Mikrokosmos Vol. 5, No. 127, by Béla Bartók (1882–1945).

Mikrokosmos Vol. 3, No. 78, by Béla Bartók (1882–1945).

"An Evening in the Village" from *Hungarian Sketches* by Béla Bartók (1882–1945).

"Pentatonic Tune," *For Children* Vol. 1, No. 29, by Béla Bartók (1882–1945).

"Nuages," from *Nocturnes* by Claude Debussy (1862–1918).

8.8A   Determining the Intervals Between the Notes of the Minor Pentatonic Scale

The following shows the intervals between the notes of the minor pentatonic scale on the keyboard. There are two skips of a minor third. The distance between *l,* and *d,* as well as the distance between *m* and *s,* is a minor third (m3). The distance between *d* and between *r,* and *r* and *m,* is a whole step (M2).

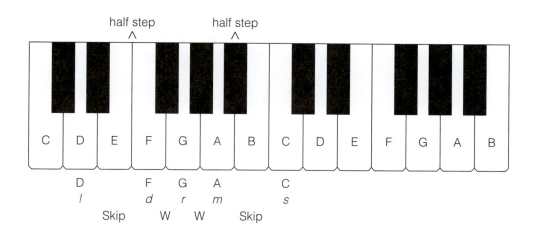

The following shows the intervals between the notes of the minor pentatonic scale on the staff.

Skip   W   W   Skip   Skip   W   W   Skip

Singing the following exercise will help you learn the size and quality of the intervals of the minor pentatonic scale. The exercise is written with solfège syllables instead of scale degree numbers. We believe that it is easier to sing with solfège syllables because singing with numbers could be confusing when considering the other scales we have encountered and will encounter.

l,   d   minor   third   l,   r   perfect   fourth

l,   m   perfect   fifth   l,   s   minor   seventh

l,   l   perfect   octave   l   s   major   second

l   m   perfect   fourth   l   r   perfect   fifth

l   d   major   sixth   l   l,   perfect   octave

The following chart illustrates the intervals of the minor pentatonic scale using the *la* minor system.

Solfège Syllables	Size	Number of Half Steps Contained in an Interval	Name of Interval	Abbreviation
l,–d	3	3	minor third	m3
l,–r	4	5	perfect fourth	P4
l,–m	5	7	perfect fifth	P5
l,–s	7	10	minor seventh	m7
l,–l	8	12	perfect octave	P8
l–s	2	2	major second	M2
l–m	4	5	perfect fourth	P4
l–r	5	7	perfect fifth	P5
l–d	6	8	major sixth	M6
l–l,	8	12	perfect octave	P8

8.9A Writing Minor Pentatonic Scales and Melodies Using Accidentals

Writing a Minor Pentatonic Scale on the Staff

The following is a procedure for writing any minor pentatonic scale on the staff. We will write this example as a d minor pentatonic scale in the treble clef.

1. Write the solfège syllables *l, – – d – r – m – – s* beneath the staff for the minor pentatonic scale.

2. Place a note on the staff above each solfège syllable. For a minor pentatonic scale we use five notes. There is a skip between the first and second degrees and a skip between degrees four and five. For example, if the tonic note is D, write D–F–G–A–C. We will write this minor pentatonic scale beginning on D. There are no half steps to mark. Remember the minor pentatonic scale consists of minor thirds and major seconds.

3. Check the intervallic relationship between the solfège syllables and the pitch names to insure the correct intervallic distance between the notes. There are no accidentals in the d minor pentatonic scale.

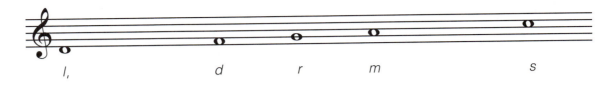

Writing a Minor Pentatonic Melody on the Staff

The following is a sample procedure for writing any minor pentatonic melody on the staff. As an example, we will write "Gallows Pole" in the key of d minor pentatonic in treble clef. Remember, music based on a particular scale is said to be in the key of that scale.

1. Write the d minor pentatonic scale on the staff using accidentals.

2. Write the solfège syllables below the scale.

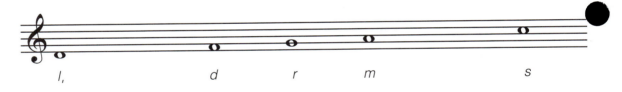

3. Write "Gallows Pole" on the staff by associating the solfège syllables with note names in the key of d minor pentatonic.

We can write "Gallows Pole" on the staff beginning on D as follows:

Key Terms and Concepts

Minor Pentachord Scale
Minor Hexachord Scale
Minor Pentatonic Scale

How to Practice

Here are some useful suggestions for practicing melody in a variety of ways. Remember to keep practicing in small groups with your peers.

Performing	Sing the minor pentachord, hexachord, and pentatonic melodies with rhythm syllables.
Singing with Solfège Syllables	Sing "Kis kece lányom" with rhythm syllables and conduct. Sing "Kis kece lányom" with solfège syllables and conduct. Sing "Kis kece lányom" with scale degree numbers and conduct. Sing the Slovak Folk Song with rhythm syllables and conduct. Sing the Slovak Folk Song with solfège syllables and conduct. Sing the Slovak Folk Song with scale degree numbers and conduct. Sing "Gallows Pole" with rhythm syllables and conduct. Sing "Gallows Pole" with solfège syllables and conduct.
Echo Singing	Practice with a classmate or in class. One of you will hum or play four-beat minor pentachord, hexachord, or pentatonic melodies on the piano. The other will "echo" what was played with solfège syllables.
Memorizing by Ear	The instructor or another student plays a minor pentachord, hexachord, or pentatonic melody on the piano: • Identify the meter. • Sing the example with rhythm names. • Identify the ending and starting pitches with solfège syllables. • Memorize and sing the example with solfège syllables.
Notating the Melody	Practice with a classmate or in class. One of you will sing a known minor pentachord, hexachord, or pentatonic melody with neutral syllables or play on the piano a melody from the chapter. The other will "echo" what was sung or played with solfège syllables and then notate the melody in a given meter and key.
Error Dictation	One student plays one of the melodies in this chapter deliberately making a mistake. Another student follows the score and locates the error.
Memorizing from a Score	Memorize an entire minor pentachord, hexachord, or pentatonic melody and notate it without referring to the notation. First analyze the form by looking for repeated and similar parts. This will simplify the task.
Improvisation/ Composition	First select a meter and length for the composition, then decide what form to use (for example, ABBA). Create an improvisation or composition using only known rhythms based on minor pentachord, hexachord, or pentatonic scales.
Performing a Canon	As you sing the melody, clap the rhythm in canon after two or four beats.

Using the Musical Skills CD

Access Chapter 8 on the skills CD to reinforce the notation of minor pentachord and hexachord melodies. You will be provided with the opportunity to practice the notation of minor pentachord and minor hexachord melodies that include half, quarter, and eighth notes and their corresponding rests on the staff.

How to Read a Musical Score

Look at "The Smoker's Reflection" by Johann Sebastian Bach.

Clap and say the rhythm syllables of the treble clef.

Say the rhythm syllables of the treble clef while clapping the rhythm of the bass clef.

Sing measures one through four of the treble clef using solfège syllables.

Identify minor second, major second, minor third, perfect fourth, and diminished fifth intervals.

The Smoker's Reflection

Johann Sebastian Bach (1685–1750)

Part B: **Do Minor**

8.1B   Minor Pentachord Scale and Melodies

Sing, Memorize, and Analyze

19

Internalizing Music

1. Listen to "Kis kece lányom" on Track 19. Memorize the song.
2. Sing "Kis kece lányom" while you clap the melodic contour.

Analyzing What You Hear

1. As you sing "Kis kece lányom," determine the number of phrases.
2. As you sing "Kis kece lányom," determine the number of beats within the phrases.
3. Sing the lowest pitch in phrase one. On which beats in phrase one do you sing the lowest pitch?
4. Sing the highest pitch in phrase one.
5. Sing the beginning note of the song.
6. Sing the range of notes from the lowest to the highest.

Constructing the Melodic Contour of "Kis kece lányom"

1. As you sing "Kis kece lányom," draw a representation indicating the melodic contour of each phrase.
2. Point to your representation and sing "Kis kece lányom" with rhythm syllables.

Music Theory

Describing What You Hear with Solfège Syllables

There are two systems for labeling notes with solfège syllables in a minor key. System one is referred to as *la minor* and system two is referred to as *do minor*. Your instructor will select one of these systems. The following figure associates the pitches in "Kis kece lányom" with its corresponding solfège syllables.

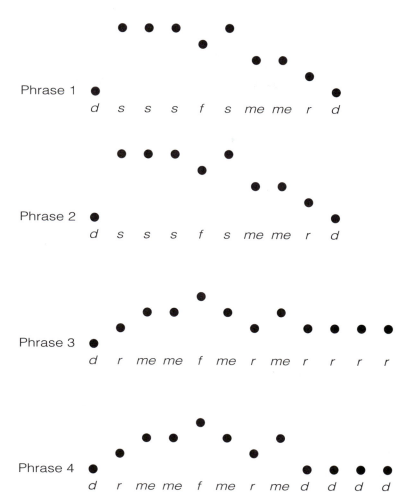

Notating What You Hear with Solfège Syllables

We can write "Kis kece lányom" in rhythm notation with solfège syllables.

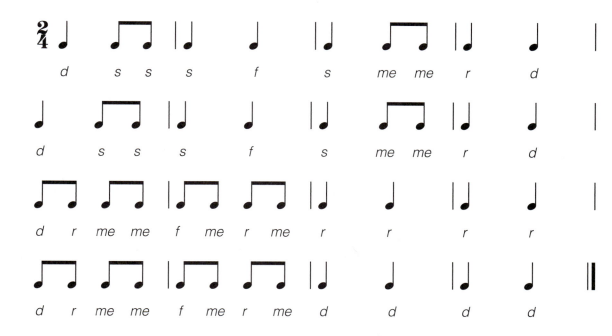

When we write the pitches of "Kis kece lányom" in ascending order, we discover that, just as in the major pentachord, there are five adjacent pitches: *d – r – me – f – s*. We refer to this pitch collection as a **minor pentachord scale**. The following chart illustrates the relationship between solfège syllables and scale degree numbers.

Solfège Syllable	Corresponding Number
s	5̂
f	4̂
me	3̂
f	2̂
d	1̂

Notating What You Hear on the Staff

We can write "Kis kece lányom" on the staff beginning on E as follows:

Listening 🎧 The following listening examples include subsets of the minor pentachord scale. Can you sing the themes using solfège syllables? Can you write the themes of some of these examples using staff notation or stick notation with solfège syllables?

For Children Vol. 1, No. 3, by Béla Bartók (1882–1945).

"Study for the Left Hand," *For Children* Vol. 1, by Béla Bartók (1882–1945).

"Round Dance," *For Children* Vol. 1, by Béla Bartók (1882–1945).

Mikrokosmos Vol. 1, Nos. 2b, 8, 21, and 23, by Béla Bartók (1882–1945).

"Táncnóta" (Dancing Song), choral composition by Zoltán Kodály (1882–1967).

8.2B   Determining the Size and Quality of Intervals Between the Notes of the Minor Pentachord Scale

The following shows the whole- and half-step relationships of the d minor pentachord scale on the keyboard. Look at the whole-step (W) and half-step (H) pattern.

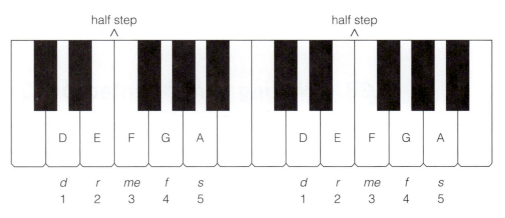

The following shows the whole- and half-step relationships of the d minor pentachord scale on the staff.

The first degree of the scale is called the tonic note or keynote. There is a half step between the second and third degrees of the scale. There is a whole step between all other degrees of the minor pentachord scale (1 and 2, 3 and 4, 4 and 5). We can refer to whole steps as major seconds (M2) and half steps as minor seconds (m2).

Singing the following exercise will help you learn the size and quality of the intervals of the minor pentachord scale.

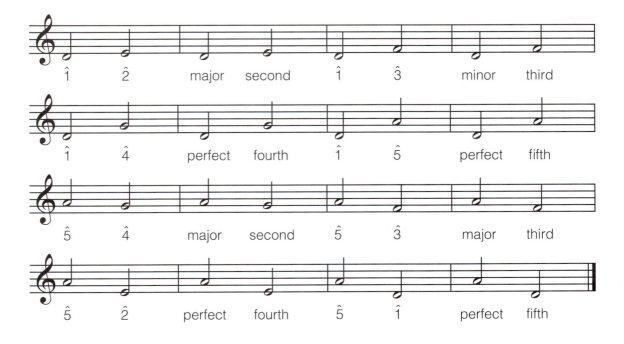

The following chart illustrates the intervals of the minor pentachord scale using the *do* minor system.

Scale Degree	Solfège Syllables	Size	Number of Half Steps Contained in an Interval	Name of Interval	Abbreviation
î–ĝ	d–r	2	2	major second	M2
î–ĝ	d–me	3	4	minor third	m3
î–â	d–f	4	5	perfect fourth	P4
î–ŝ	d–s	5	7	perfect fifth	P5

8.3B Writing Minor Pentachord Scales and Melodies Using Accidentals

Writing a Minor Pentachord Scale on the Staff Using Accidentals

The following is a procedure for writing any minor pentachord scale on the staff using accidentals. We will write this example as an e minor pentachord scale in the treble clef.

1. Write the solfège syllables *d – r – me – f – s* beneath the staff for the minor pentachord scale.

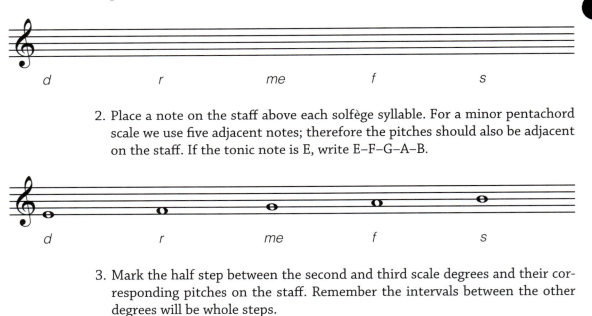

2. Place a note on the staff above each solfège syllable. For a minor pentachord scale we use five adjacent notes; therefore the pitches should also be adjacent on the staff. If the tonic note is E, write E–F–G–A–B.

3. Mark the half step between the second and third scale degrees and their corresponding pitches on the staff. Remember the intervals between the other degrees will be whole steps.

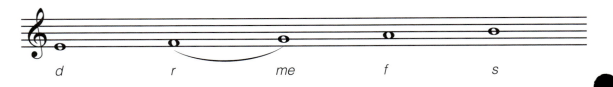

4. Check the intervallic relationship between the solfège syllables and the pitch names to insure the correct intervallic distance between the notes. Correct the intervallic relationship with accidentals. In the e minor pentachord we have an F-sharp.

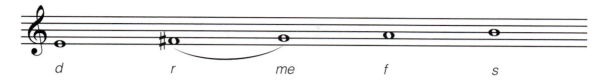

Writing a Minor Pentachord Melody Using Accidentals

The following is a procedure for writing any minor pentachord melody on the staff using accidentals. For example, we will write the melody "Kis kece lányom" in the key of e minor in treble clef.

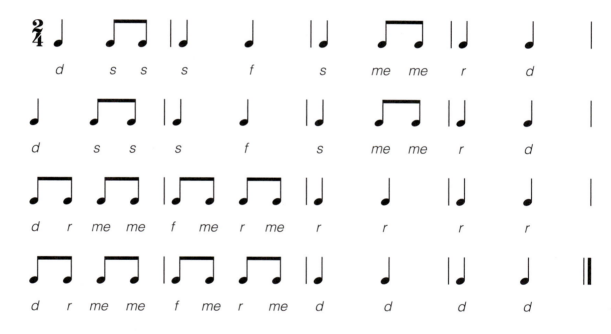

1. Write the e minor pentachord scale on the staff using accidentals.

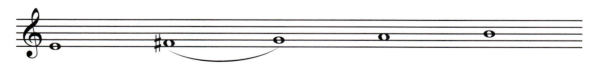

2. Write the solfège syllables below the scale.

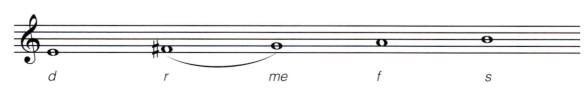

3. Write "Kis kece lányom" on the staff by associating the solfège syllables with note names in the e minor pentachord.

Kis kece lányom

8.4B   Minor Hexachord Scale and Melodies

Sing, Memorize, and Analyze

🎵
20

Internalizing Music

1. Listen to the Slovak Folk Song on Track 20. Memorize the song.
2. Sing the Slovak Folk Song while you clap the melodic contour.

Analyzing What You Hear

1. As you sing the Slovak Folk Song, determine the number of phrases.
2. As you sing the Slovak Folk Song, determine the number of beats within the phrases.
3. Sing the range of notes from the lowest to the highest in the song.

Constructing the Melodic Contour of Slovak Folk Song

1. As you sing the Slovak Folk Song, draw a representation of the pitches in each phrase.
2. Point to your representation and sing the Slovak Folk Song with rhythm syllables.

Music Theory

Describing What You Hear with Solfège Syllables

We can describe the pitches in the Slovak Folk Song with solfège syllables. Notice that the melodic movement of both phrases is mostly stepwise.

Slovak Folk Song

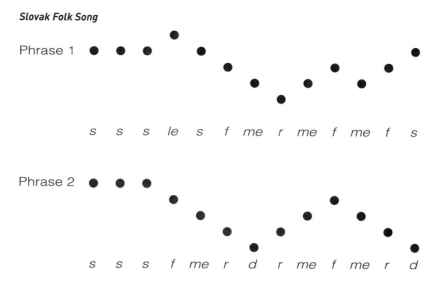

Notating What You Hear with Solfège Syllables

We can write the Slovak Folk Song in rhythm notation with solfège syllables.

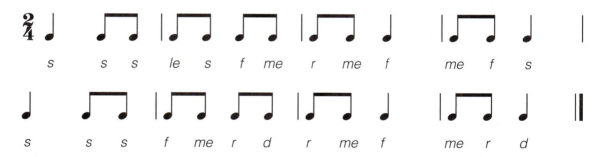

When we write the pitches of the Slovak Folk Song in ascending order, we discover that, just as in the major hexachord, there are six adjacent pitches: *d – r – me – f – s – le*. We refer to this pitch collection as a **minor hexachord scale**. The following chart illustrates the relationship between solfège syllables and scale degree numbers.

Solfège Syllable	Corresponding Number
le	$\hat{6}$
s	$\hat{5}$
f	$\hat{4}$
me	$\hat{3}$
r	$\hat{2}$
d	$\hat{1}$

Listening

The following listening example includes subsets of the minor pentachord scale. Can you sing the theme using solfège syllables? Can you write the theme using staff notation or stick notation with solfège syllables?

"Dance," *For Children* Vol. 2, No. 8, by Béla Bartók (1882–1945).

8.5B Determining the Intervals Between the Notes of the Minor Hexachord Scale

The following shows the whole- and half-step relationships of the d minor hexachord scale on the keyboard. The distances between *r*, and *me* and *s* and *le* are half steps (m2). The distances between *d*, and *r*, *me* and *f*, and *f* and *s* are whole steps (M2).

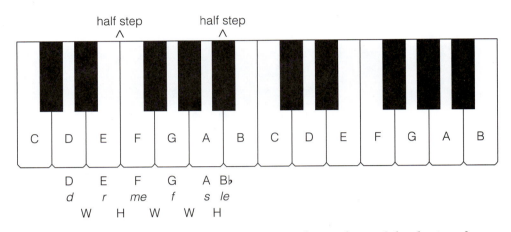

The following shows the whole- and half-step relationships of the d minor hexachord scale on the staff.

The first degree of the scale is called the tonic note or keynote. There is a half step between the second and third as well as the fifth and sixth degrees of the scale. There is a whole step between all other degrees of the scale (1 and 2, 3 and 4, 4 and 5).

Singing the following exercise will help you learn the size and quality of the intervals of the minor hexachord scale.

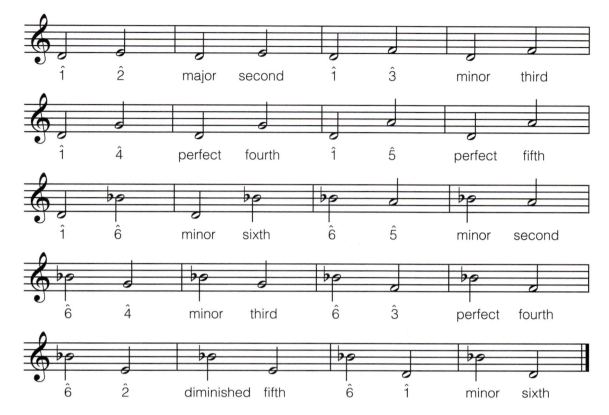

The following chart illustrates the intervals of the minor pentachord scale using the *do minor* system.

Scale Degree	Solfège Syllables	Size	Number of Half Steps Contained in an Interval	Name of Interval	Abbreviation
1–2	*d–r*	2	2	major second	M2
1–3	*d–me*	3	3	minor third	m3
1–4	*d–f*	4	5	perfect fourth	P4
1–5	*d–s*	5	7	perfect fifth	P5
1–6	*d–le*	6	8	minor sixth	m6
6–5	*le–s*	2	2	minor second	m2
6–4	*le–f*	3	3	minor third	m3
6–3	*le–me*	4	4	perfect fourth	P4
6–2	*le–r*	5	6	diminished fifth	d5
6–1	*le–d*	6	8	minor sixth	m6

8.6B Writing Minor Hexachord Scales and Melodies Using Accidentals

Writing a Minor Hexachord on the Staff Using Accidentals

There are fifteen different minor hexachord scales. The following is a sample procedure for writing any of them on the staff using accidentals. We will write this example as a d minor hexachord scale in the treble clef.

1. Write the solfège syllables *d – r – me – f – s – le* beneath the staff for the minor hexachord scale.

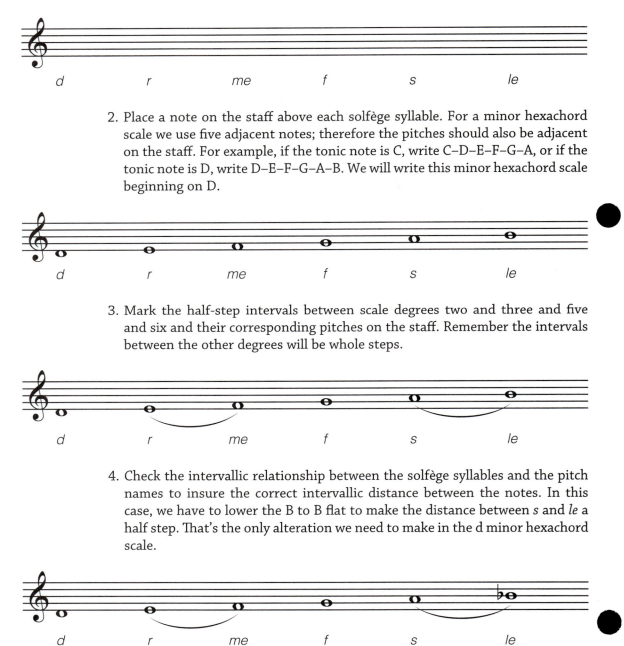

2. Place a note on the staff above each solfège syllable. For a minor hexachord scale we use five adjacent notes; therefore the pitches should also be adjacent on the staff. For example, if the tonic note is C, write C–D–E–F–G–A, or if the tonic note is D, write D–E–F–G–A–B. We will write this minor hexachord scale beginning on D.

3. Mark the half-step intervals between scale degrees two and three and five and six and their corresponding pitches on the staff. Remember the intervals between the other degrees will be whole steps.

4. Check the intervallic relationship between the solfège syllables and the pitch names to insure the correct intervallic distance between the notes. In this case, we have to lower the B to B flat to make the distance between *s* and *le* a half step. That's the only alteration we need to make in the d minor hexachord scale.

Writing a Minor Hexachord Melody Using Accidentals

The following is a procedure for writing any minor hexachord melody on the staff using accidentals. For an example, we will write the Slovak Folk Song in the key of d minor hexachord in treble clef. Remember, music based on a particular scale is said to be in the key of that scale. If music is built on the d minor hexachord scale, then the work is in the key of d minor hexachord and the tonic of the music is D.

1. Write the d minor hexachord scale on the staff using accidentals.

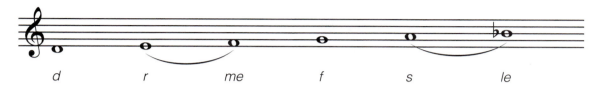

d   r   me   f   s   le

2. Write the solfège syllables below the scale.

3. Write the Slovak Folk Song on the staff by associating the solfège syllables with note names in the key of d minor hexachord. Note the placement of accidentals.

Listening 🎧   The following listening examples include subsets of the minor hexachord scale. Can you sing the themes using solfège syllables? Can you write the themes of some of these examples using staff notation or stick notation with solfège syllables?

"Ah! Vous dirai-je maman." Variations on "Twinkle, Twinkle, Little Star," K. 265, by Wolfgang Amadeus Mozart (1756–1791).

"Variations on a Nursery Song," Op. 25, by Ernö Dohnányi (1877–1960).

"Maypole Dance," No. 2 from *44 Duets for Two Violins* by Béla Bartók (1882–1945).

"Children at Play," *For Children* Vol. 1, No. 1, by Béla Bartók (1882–1945).

For Children Vol. 2, Nos. 2 and 3, by Béla Bartók (1882–1945).

8.7B Minor Pentatonic Scales and Melodies

Internalizing Music

1. Listen to "Gallows Pole" on Track 21. Memorize the song.
2. Sing "Gallows Pole" while you clap the melodic contour.

Analyzing What You Hear

1. Sing the lowest pitches in the song.
2. Sing the highest pitches in the song.
3. Sing the range of notes from the lowest to the highest.

Constructing the Melodic Contour of "Gallows Pole"

1. As you sing "Gallows Pole," draw a representation of the pitches in each phrase.
2. Point to your representation and sing "Gallows Pole" with rhythm syllables.

Music Theory

Describing What You Hear with Solfège Syllables

We can describe the pitches in "Gallows Pole" with solfège syllables.

Gallows Pole

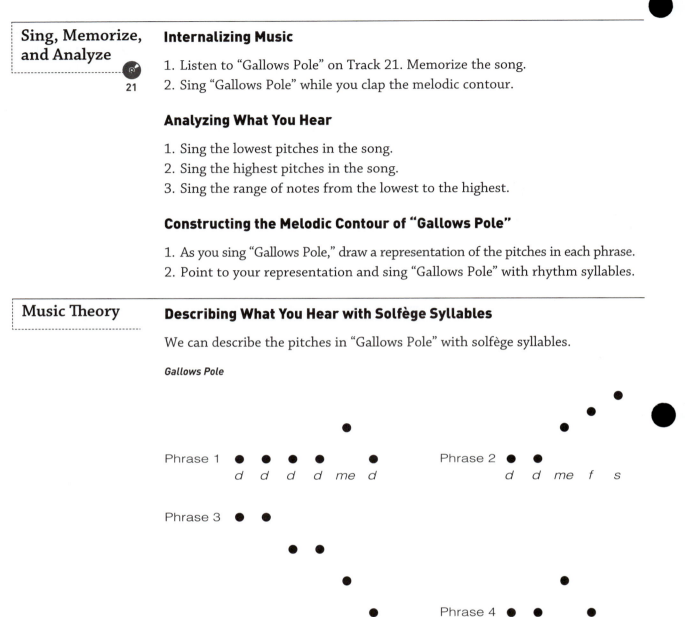

Notating What You Hear with Solfège Syllables

We can write "Gallows Pole" in rhythm notation with solfège syllables.

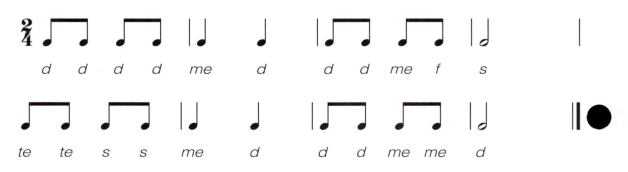

When we write the pitches of "Gallows Pole" in ascending order, we discover that there are five. We can label these pitches with the solfège syllables *d – me – f – s – – te*. We refer to this collection of notes as a **minor pentatonic scale.**

Notating What You Hear on the Staff

We can write "Gallows Pole" on the staff beginning on D as follows:

Listening 🎧

The following listening examples include subsets of the minor pentatonic scale. Can you sing the themes using solfège syllables? Can you write the themes of some of these examples using staff notation or stick notation with solfège syllables?

Mikrokosmos Vol. 5, No. 127, by Béla Bartók (1882–1945).

Mikrokosmos Vol. 3, No. 78, by Béla Bartók (1882–1945).

"An Evening in the Village," from *Hungarian Sketches* by Béla Bartók (1882–1945).

"Pentatonic Tune," *For Children* Vol. 1, No. 29, by Béla Bartók (1882–1945).

"Nuages" from *Nocturnes* by Claude Debussy (1862–1918).

8.8B   Determining the Intervals Between the Notes of the Minor Pentatonic Scale

The following shows the intervals between the notes of the minor pentatonic scale on the keyboard. There are two skips of a minor third. The distance between *d*, and *me*, as well as the distance between *s* and *te*, is a minor third (m3). The distance between *me* and *f*, and between *f* and *s*, is a whole step (M2).

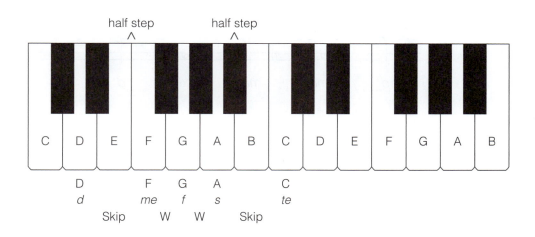

The following shows the intervals between the notes of the minor pentatonic scale on the staff.

Skip   W   W   Skip   Skip   W   W   Skip

Singing the following exercise will help you learn the size and quality of the intervals of the minor pentatonic scale. The exercise is written with solfège syllables instead of scale degree numbers. We believe that it is easier to sing with solfège syllables because singing with numbers could be confusing when considering the other scales we have encountered and will encounter.

d   me   minor   third   d   f   perfect   fourth

d   s   perfect   fifth   d   te   minor   seventh

d   d'   perfect   octave   d'   te   major   second

d'   s   perfect   fourth   d'   f   perfect   fifth

d'   me   major   sixth   d'   d   perfect   octave

8.9B Writing Minor Pentatonic Scales and Melodies Using Accidentals

Writing a Minor Pentatonic Scale on the Staff Using Accidentals

The following is a procedure for writing any minor pentatonic scale on the staff. We will write this example as a d minor pentatonic scale in the treble clef.

1. Write the solfège syllables *d – – me – f – s – – te* beneath the staff for the minor pentatonic scale.

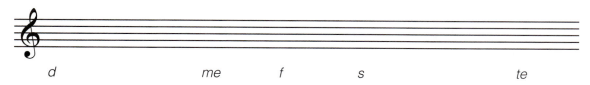

2. Place a note on the staff above each solfège syllable. For a minor pentatonic scale we use five notes. There is a skip between the first and second degrees and a skip between degrees four and five. For example, if the tonic note is D, write D––F–G–A––C. We will write this minor pentatonic scale beginning on D. There are no half steps to mark. Remember the minor pentatonic scale consists of minor thirds and major seconds.

3. Check the intervallic relationship between the solfège syllables and the pitch names to insure the correct intervallic distance between the notes. There are no accidentals in the d minor pentatonic scale.

Writing a Minor Pentatonic Melody on the Staff

The following is a sample procedure for writing any minor pentatonic melody on the staff. As an example we will write "Gallows Pole" in the key of d minor pentatonic in treble clef. Remember, music based on a particular scale is said to be in the key of that scale.

1. Write the d minor pentatonic scale on the staff using accidentals.

2. Write the solfège syllables below the scale.

d   me   f   s   te

3. Write "Gallows Pole" on the staff by associating the solfège syllables with note names in the key of d minor pentatonic. Note the placement of accidentals.

We can write "Gallows Pole" on the staff beginning on D as follows:

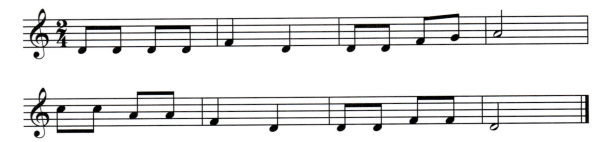

Key Terms and Concepts

Minor Pentachord Scale
Minor Hexachord Scale
Minor Pentatonic Scale

How to Practice

Here are some useful suggestions for practicing melody in a variety of ways. Remember to keep practicing in small groups with your peers.

Performing	Sing the minor pentachord, hexachord, and pentatonic melodies with rhythm syllables.
Singing with Solfège Syllables	Sing "Kis kece lányom" with rhythm syllables and conduct. Sing "Kis kece lányom" with solfège syllables and conduct. Sing "Kis kece lányom" with scale degree numbers and conduct. Sing the Slovak Folk Song with rhythm syllables and conduct. Sing the Slovak Folk Song with solfège syllables and conduct. Sing the Slovak Folk Song with scale degree numbers and conduct. Sing "Gallows Pole" with rhythm syllables and conduct. Sing "Gallows Pole" with solfège syllables and conduct.
Echo Singing	Practice with a classmate or in class. One of you will hum or play four-beat minor pentachord, hexachord, or pentatonic melodies on the piano. The other will "echo" what was played with solfège syllables.

Memorizing by Ear	The instructor or another student plays a minor pentachord, hexachord, or pentatonic melody on the piano: • Identify the meter. • Sing the example with rhythm names. • Identify the ending and starting pitches with solfège syllables. • Memorize and sing the example with solfège syllables.
Notating the Melody	Practice with a classmate or in class. One of you will sing a known minor pentachord, hexachord, or pentatonic melody with neutral syllables or play on the piano a melody from the chapter. The other will "echo" what was sung or played with solfège syllables and then notate the melody in a given meter and key.
Error Dictation	One student plays one of the melodies in this chapter deliberately making a mistake. Another student follows the score and locates the error.
Memorizing from a Score	Memorize an entire minor pentachord, hexachord, or pentatonic melody and notate it without referring to the notation. First analyze the form by looking for repeated and similar parts. This will simplify the task.
Improvisation/Composition	First select a meter and length for the composition, then decide what form to use (for example, ABBA). Create an improvisation or composition using only known rhythms based on minor pentachord, hexachord, or pentatonic scales.
Performing a Canon	As you sing the melody, clap the rhythm in canon after two or four beats.

Using the Musical Skills CD

Access Chapter 8 on the skills CD to reinforce the notation of minor pentachord and hexachord melodies. You will be provided with the opportunity to practice the notation of minor pentachord and minor hexachord melodies that include half, quarter, and eighth notes and their corresponding rests on the staff.

How to Read a Musical Score

Look at "The Smoker's Reflection" by Johann Sebastian Bach.

> Clap and say the rhythm syllables of the treble clef.
>
> Say the rhythm syllables of the treble clef while clapping the rhythm of the bass clef.
>
> Sing measures one through four of the treble clef using solfège syllables.
>
> Identify minor second, major second, minor third, perfect fourth, and diminished fifth intervals.

The Smoker's Reflection

Johann Sebastian Bach (1685–1750)

MUSIC THEORY EXERCISES

8.1 Exercises: Minor Pentachord Scale and Melodies

Exercise 8.1

Circle the half steps and put a bracket around the whole steps in "Kis kece lányom."

Kis kece lányom   **Hungarian Folk Song**

Exercise 8.2

Fill in the following chart by adding the correct solfège syllable for the minor pentachord scale degree numbers.

Solfège Syllable	Scale Degree Number
	1
	2
	3
	4
	5

8.2   Exercises: Determining the Size and Quality of Intervals Between the Notes of the Minor Pentachord Scale

Exercise 8.3

This chart illustrates the intervals of the minor pentachord scale using the *la* minor system. Fill in the missing information.

Scale Degree	Solfège Syllables	Size	Number of Half Steps Contained in an Interval	Name of Interval	Abbreviation
1–2					
1–3					
1–4					
1–5					

8.3   Exercises: Writing Minor Pentachord Scales and Melodies Using Accidentals

Exercise 8.4

Write the following minor pentachord scales in treble and bass clef using whole notes and accidentals, ascending and descending. Include the solfège syllables. Mark the half steps.

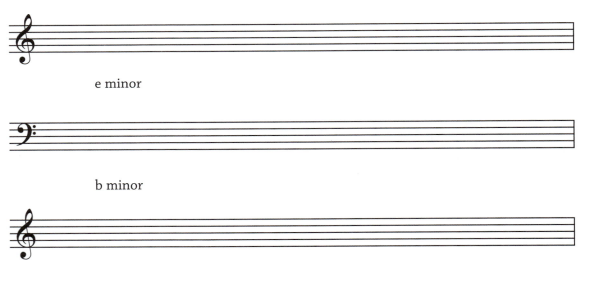

a minor

e minor

b minor

f-sharp minor

c-sharp minor

g-sharp minor

d-sharp minor

a-sharp minor

d minor

g minor

c minor

f minor

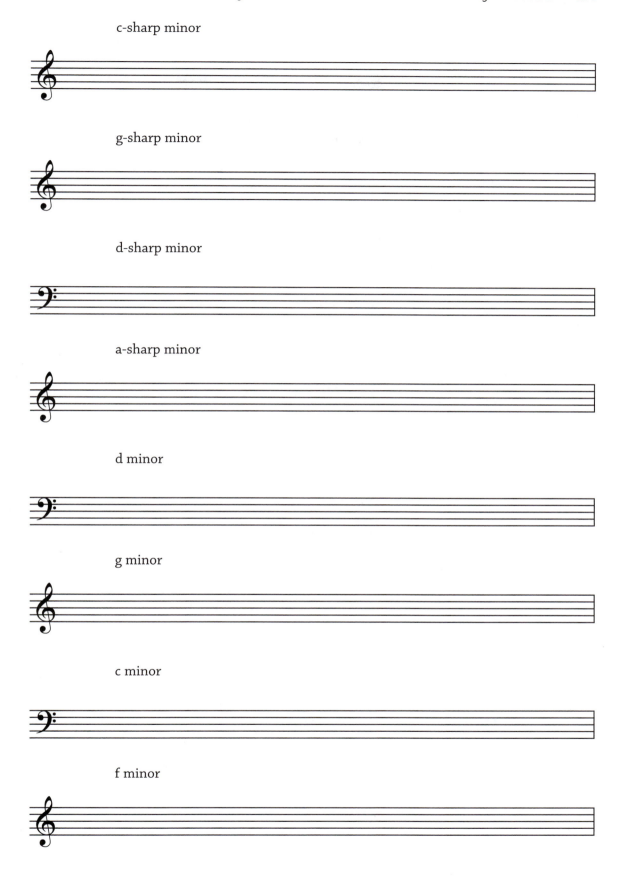

g-flat minor

c-flat minor

Exercise 8.5

Write in "Kis kece lányom" in e minor.

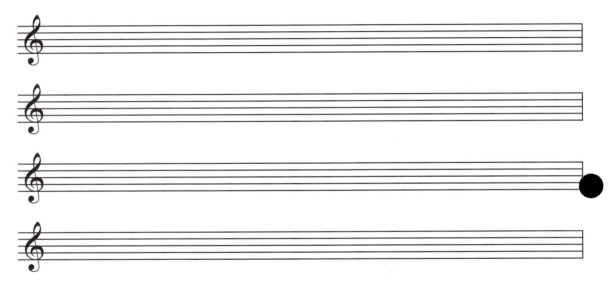

Exercise 8.6

Write in "Kis kece lányom" g minor.

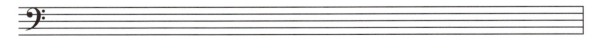

Exercise 8.7

Write "Kis kece lányom" in f-sharp minor.

Exercise 8.8

Write "Kis kece lányom" in c minor.

Exercise 8.9

Add accidentals to make this a minor pentachord melody.

8.4 Exercises: Minor Hexachord Scale and Melodies

Exercise 8.10

Circle the half steps and put a bracket around the whole steps in the Slovak Folk Song.

Exercise 8.11

Fill in the following chart by including the correct solfège syllable for the minor hexachord scale degrees.

Solfège Syllable	Scale Degree Number
	$\hat{1}$
	$\hat{2}$
	$\hat{3}$
	$\hat{4}$
	$\hat{5}$
	$\hat{6}$

8.5 Exercises: Determining the Intervals Between the Notes of the Minor Hexachord Scale

Exercise 8.12

Complete the missing information in the following chart.

Scale Degree	Solfège Syllables	Size	Number of Half Steps Contained in an Interval	Name of Interval	Abbreviation
$\hat{1}$–$\hat{2}$					
$\hat{1}$–$\hat{3}$					
$\hat{1}$–$\hat{4}$					
$\hat{1}$–$\hat{5}$					
$\hat{1}$–$\hat{6}$					
$\hat{6}$–$\hat{5}$					
$\hat{6}$–$\hat{4}$					

8.6 Exercises: Writing Minor Hexachord Scales and Melodies Using Accidentals

Exercise 8.13

Write the following minor hexachord scales. Write the solfège syllables and degree numbers under the notes on the staff. Be certain to mark the half-step intervals.

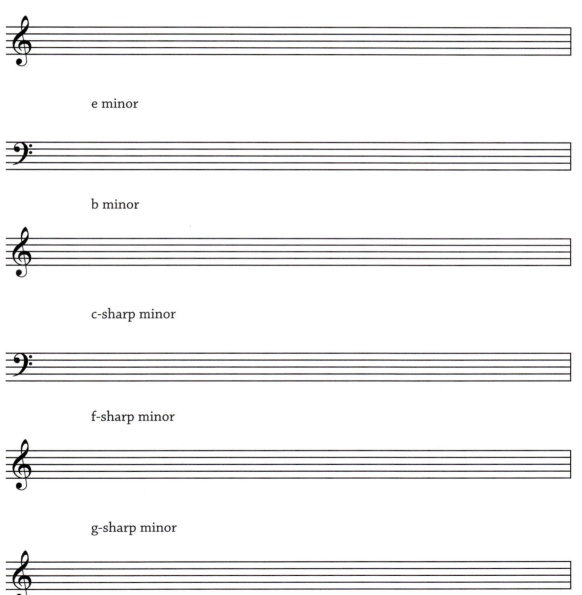

a minor

e minor

b minor

c-sharp minor

f-sharp minor

g-sharp minor

d-sharp minor

a-sharp minor

d minor

g minor

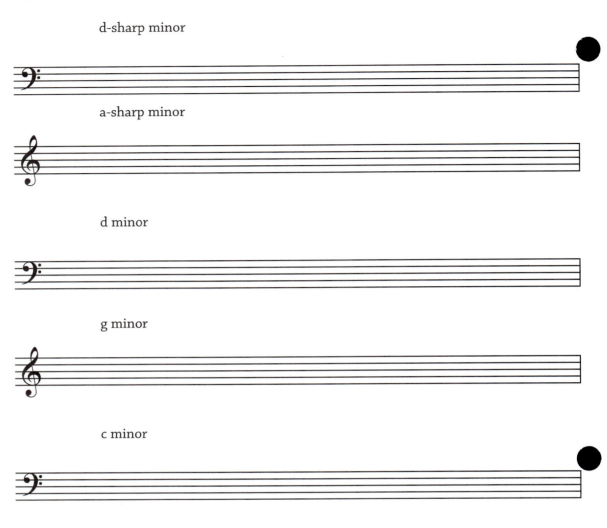

c minor

f minor

b-flat minor

g-flat minor

Exercise 8.14

Write the Slovak Folk Song in c minor.

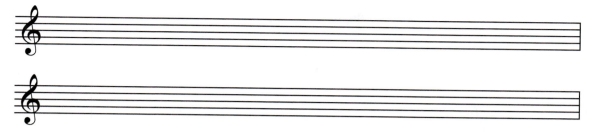

Exercise 8.15

Write the Slovak Folk Song in c-sharp minor.

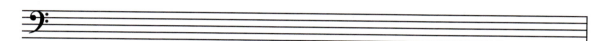

Exercise 8.16

Write the Slovak Folk Song in g-sharp minor.

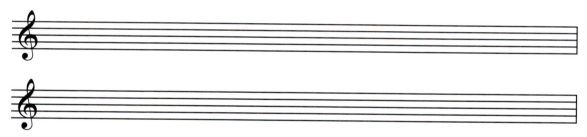

Exercise 8.17

Write the Slovak Folk Song in b minor.

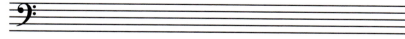

8.7 Exercises: Minor Pentatonic Scale and Melodies

Exercise 8.18

Circle the minor-third intervals and put a bracket around the major seconds in "Gallows Pole."

8.8 Exercises: Determining the Intervals Between the Notes of the Minor Pentatonic Scale

Exercise 8.19

The chart provides summary information concerning the intervals of the minor pentatonic scale. Complete the missing information.

Solfège Syllables	Size	Number of Half Steps Contained in an Interval	Name of Interval	Abbreviation
	3			m3
	4			P4
	5			P5
	7			m7
	8			P8

8.9 Exercises: Writing a Minor Pentatonic Scales and Melodies Using Accidentals

Exercise 8.20

Write the following minor pentatonic scales. Include the solfège syllables under the notes on the staff.

a minor pentatonic scale

e minor pentatonic scale

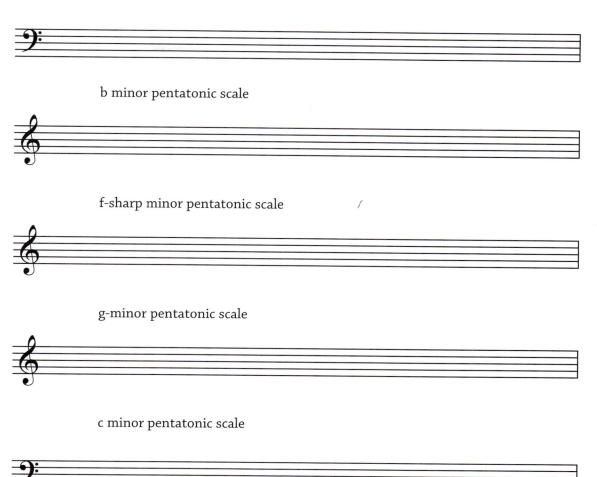

b minor pentatonic scale

f-sharp minor pentatonic scale

g-minor pentatonic scale

c minor pentatonic scale

f minor pentatonic scale

Exercise 8.21

Write "Gallows Pole" in c minor.

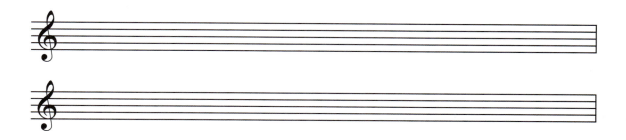

Exercise 8.22

Write "Gallows Pole" in e minor.

Exercise 8.23

Write "Gallows Pole" in g minor.

Chapter 9

The Minor Scale:

Natural Minor, Harmonic Minor, Melodic Minor

CHAPTER OVERVIEW

Both major and minor scales serve as the foundation for most tonal music. There are three forms of the minor scale: natural, harmonic and melodic. The minor scale is formed on the sixth degree of the major scale. Minor key signatures are related to major key signatures. As with the major scale each form has a particular arrangement of whole and half steps.

Although we will be studying the harmonic, and melodic forms of the minor scale separately, it should be pointed out that composers often use several forms of the minor scale within a piece.

Part A: La Minor

9.1A Natural Minor Scale and Melodies

Sing, Memorize, and Analyze

22

Internalizing Music

1. Listen to Variation on a Russian Folk Song on Track 22. Memorize the song.
2. Sing Variation on a Russian Folk Song and keep the beat.
3. Pair off in the class. Facing your partner, sing Variation on a Russian Folk Song and clap the melodic contour.
4. Sing with rhythm names while clapping and showing the melodic contour.

Analyzing What You Hear

1. Sing the lowest note in the song.
2. Sing the highest note in the song. Sing the beginning note of the song.
3. Sing all the notes in the song from the lowest to the highest.
4. Sing all the notes in the song from the highest to the lowest.

Constructing a Melodic Representation from Memory

1. As you sing Variation on a Russian Folk Song, draw a representation indicating the contour and pitches.
2. As you point to your representation, sing Variation on a Russian Folk Song with rhythm syllables.

Music Theory

Describing What You Hear with Solfège Syllables

These are the solfège syllables for Variation on a Russian Folk Song.

Variation on a Russian Folk Song

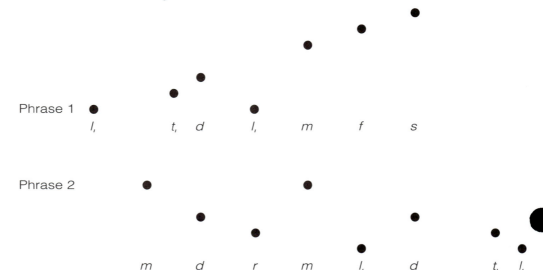

304

Notating What You Hear with Syllables

We can write Variation on a Russian Folk Song in rhythm notation with solfège syllables.

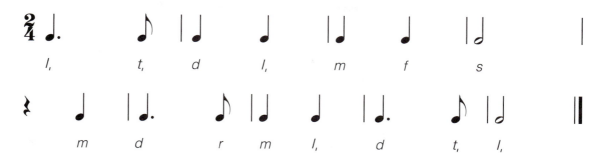

When we write the pitches of Variation on a Russian Folk Song in ascending order, we discover that there are seven adjacent pitches. We can label these pitches with solfège syllables *l,–t,–d–r–m–f–s–l*.

A **natural minor scale** is a series of eight adjacent pitches that uses successive letter names; half steps occur between the second and third degrees and fifth and sixth degrees of the scale. All other steps are whole steps. It is this pattern of half (m2) and whole steps (M2) that give the natural minor scale its particular configuration. We can find notes of the minor pentachord, minor hexachord, and minor pentatonic in this scale.

Associating Scale Degree Numbers with Solfège Syllables

The following figure illustrates that, as with the major scale, each solfège syllable of the natural minor scale can be identified with a scale degree name that reflects its position in the scale.

Solfège Syllable	Corresponding Number
l	1
s	7
f	6
m	5
r	4
d	3
t,	2
l,	1

Associating Scale Degree Numbers with Scale Degree Names

The following figures illustrate that, as with the major scale, each scale degree of the natural minor scale can be identified with a scale degree name that reflects its position in the scale.

Scale Numbers	Scale Degree Name
$\hat{1}$	Tonic
$\hat{2}$	Supertonic
$\hat{3}$	Mediant
$\hat{4}$	Subdominant
$\hat{5}$	Dominant
$\hat{6}$	Submediant
$\hat{7}$	Subtonic

Tonic   Supertonic   Mediant   Subdominant   Dominant   Submediant   Subtonic   Tonic

Listening

The following listening examples have themes based on the natural minor scale. Can you sing the themes using solfège syllables? Can you write the themes of some of these examples using staff notation or stick notation with solfège syllables?

"Sweet William." A similar version of this melody is sung by Alasdair Roberts on the recording *No Earthly Man*.

"Shalom Chaverim," sung by the Weavers in the recording *The Weavers at Carnegie Hall*, released by Vanguard Records in 1988.

"When Jesus Wept" by William Billings (1746–1800)

"Dona Dona," on the album released by Signum Classics, *From Jewish Life*. Musicians John Lenehan and Paul Marleyn. Also found on the album *Amulet*, sung by Nikitov, released by Chamsa Records, 2004.

"Hushabye," recorded by Mike and Peggy Seeger on *Album for Children*. Also found on the album *So Many Stars*, under the title of "The Little Horses," sung by Kathleen Battle.

Theme from *Psalmus Hungaricus* by Zoltán Kodály (1882–1967).

Theme from the "Peacock" Variations by Zoltán Kodály (1882–1967).

"Nights in White Satin," as recorded by the Moody Blues (1967).

9.2A   Determining the Intervals Between the Notes of the Natural Minor Scale

The following figure illustrates the whole-step (W) and half-step (H) patterns of the d natural minor scale on the keyboard.

d natural minor scale

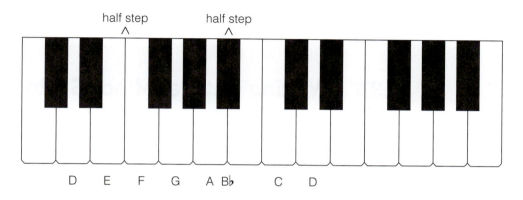

The following figure illustrates the whole-step (W) and half-step (H) patterns of the d natural minor scale on the staff.

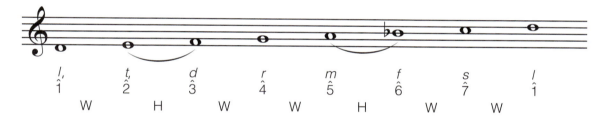

Note the intervals *d–r*, *r–m*, *f–s*, *s–l*, and *l–t* are whole steps. The distances between *t* and *d'* and *m* and *f* are half steps. We can refer to whole steps as major seconds (M2) and half steps as minor seconds (m2).

The following chart illustrates the major and minor seconds in the natural minor scale.

Whole Steps Major 2 (M2)	Half Steps Minor 2 (m2)
l,–t,	
	t,–d
d–r	
r–m	
	m–f
f–s	
s–l	

The following chart illustrates the intervallic distance between the tonic note of a natural minor scale and each member of the scale.

Scale Degree	Solfège Syllables	Size	Number of Half Steps Contained in an Interval	Name of Interval	Abbreviation
$\hat{1}$–$\hat{2}$	*l̦–ț*	2	2	major second	M2
$\hat{1}$–$\hat{3}$	*ț–d*	3	3	minor third	m3
$\hat{1}$–$\hat{4}$	*l̦–r*	4	5	perfect fourth	P4
$\hat{1}$–$\hat{5}$	*l̦–m*	5	7	perfect fifth	P5
$\hat{1}$–$\hat{6}$	*l̦–f*	6	8	minor sixth	m6
$\hat{1}$–$\hat{7}$	*l̦–s*	7	10	minor seventh	m7

9.3A Writing Natural Minor Scales and Melodies Using Accidentals

Writing a Natural Minor Scale on the Staff Using Accidentals

The following is a procedure for writing any natural minor scale on the staff using accidentals. We will write this example as a d minor scale in the treble clef.

1. Write the solfège syllables *l̦,–ț,–d–r–m–f–s–l* beneath the staff for the minor scale.

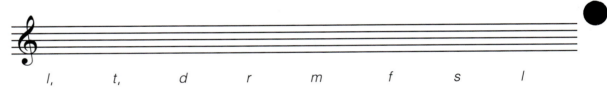

2. Place a note on the staff above each solfège syllable. For a minor scale we use eight adjacent notes; therefore the pitches should also be adjacent on the staff. First remember the sequential alphabetical spelling of scale and simply put the notes in order. If the tonic note is D, write D–E–F–G–A–B–C–D.

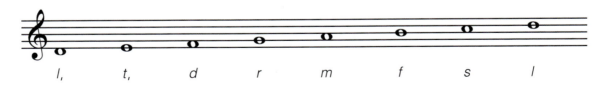

3. Mark the half steps between scale degrees two and three and five and six and their corresponding pitches on the staff. Remember the intervals between the other degrees will be whole steps.

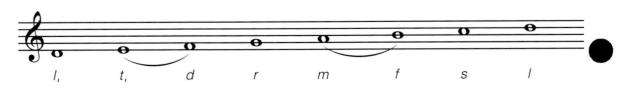

4. Check the intervallic relationship between the solfège syllables and the pitch names to insure the correct intervallic distance between the notes. If necessary, correct the intervals by using sharps or flats. In the case of d minor, we need to lower the sixth degree to B-flat.

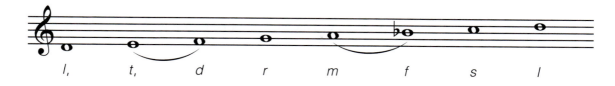

l,   t,   d   r   m   f   s   l

Writing a Minor Melody Using Accidentals

The following is a sample procedure for writing any minor melody on the staff using accidentals. For an example, we will write Variation on a Russian Folk Song in the key of d minor in treble clef.

1. Write the d minor scale on the staff using accidentals.

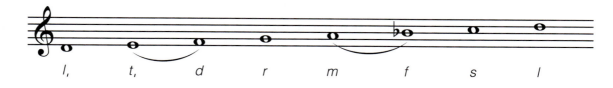

l,   t,   d   r   m   f   s   l

2. Write the solfège syllables below the scale and mark the half steps.

3. Write Variation on a Russian Folk Song on the staff by associating the solfège syllables with note names in the key of d minor.

Variation on a Russian Folk Song

9.4A   Minor Key Signatures

Minor key signatures are provided for both sharp and flat keys. We use lower-case letters to indicate minor keys. Note that the last sharp in the key signature is scale degree two of the minor scale. For example, in the key of f-sharp minor, G-sharp is the last sharp and the second degree of the scale. The following figure illustrates the placement of sharps for minor key signatures.

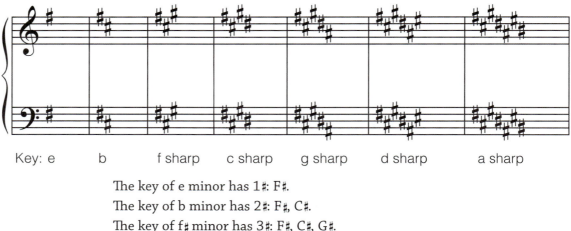

Key: e   b   f sharp   c sharp   g sharp   d sharp   a sharp

The key of e minor has 1♯: F♯.
The key of b minor has 2♯: F♯, C♯.
The key of f♯ minor has 3♯: F♯, C♯, G♯.
The key of c♯ minor has 4♯: F♯, C♯, G♯, D♯.
The key of g♯ minor has 5♯: F♯, C♯, G♯, D♯, A♯.
The key of d♯ minor has 6♯: F♯, C♯, G♯, D♯, A♯, E♯.
The key of a♯ minor has 7♯: F♯, C♯, G♯, D♯, A♯, E♯, B♯.

The last flat in the key signature is the sixth degree of the minor scale. For example, in the key of g minor, E-flat is the last flat and the sixth degree of the scale. The following figure illustrates the placement of flats for minor key signatures.

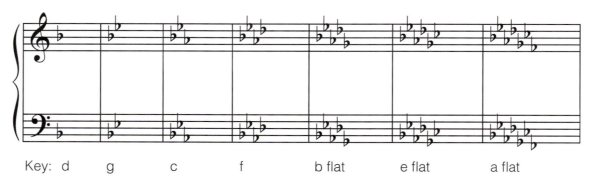

Key: d   g   c   f   b flat   e flat   a flat

The key of d minor has 1♭: B♭.
The key of g minor has 2♭: B♭, E♭.
The key of c minor has 3♭: B♭, E♭, A♭.
The key of f minor has 4♭: B♭, E♭, A♭, D♭.
The key of b♭ minor has 5♭: B♭, E♭, A♭, D♭, G♭.
The key of e♭ minor has 6♭: B♭, E♭, A♭, D♭, G♭, C♭.
The key of a♭ minor has 7♭: B♭, E♭, A♭, D♭, G♭, C♭, F♭.

Circle of Fifths Showing Minor Key Signatures

The circle of fifths provides another way of looking at minor key signatures.

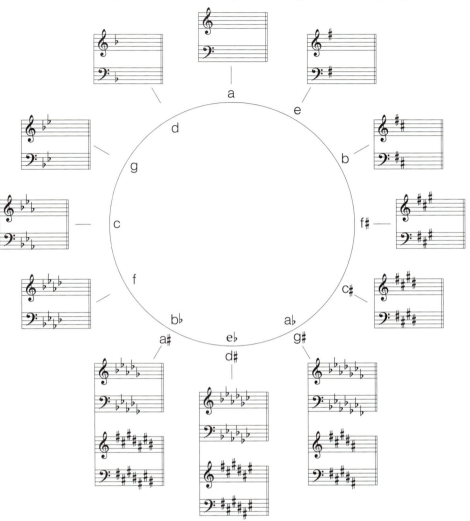

Determining the Key of a Minor Scale from a Given Key Signature

1. Identify the tonic note of the major scale that has this key signature.
2. Go down three half steps from this note.
3. This note is the tonic note of the minor scale.

For example:

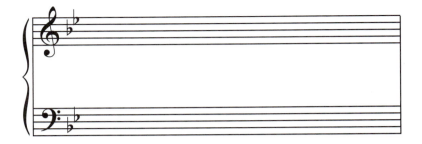

1. The tonic note of the major scale that has this key signature is B-flat.
2. The note G is three half steps down from B-flat. G is the tonic note of the g minor scale.
3. Therefore, g minor is the minor scale key for the key signature that has two flats.

9.5A   Writing Natural Minor Scales and Melodies with a Key Signature

Writing a Natural Minor Scale with a Key Signature

The following is a procedure for writing a natural minor scale with a key signature. We will write this example as a d natural minor scale in the treble clef.

1. Put the d minor key signature after the treble clef. Write the solfège syllables *l,–t,–d–r–m–f–s–l* beneath the staff for the d minor scale.

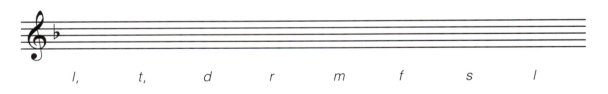

2. Place a note on the staff above each solfège syllable. For a minor scale we use eight adjacent notes; therefore the pitches should also be adjacent on the staff. The tonic note is D, so write D–E–F–G–A–B–C–D. It is important to remember the sequential alphabetical spelling of scales. Mark the half steps between the second and third degrees and the fifth and sixth degrees of the scale.

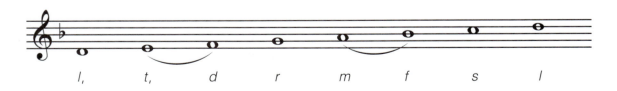

Writing a Minor Melody with a Key Signature

The following is a procedure for writing a minor melody on the staff with a key signature. We will write Variation on Russian Folk Song in d minor.

1. Determine the key and write the scale of the melody on the staff. Mark the half steps.

2. Write the solfège syllables below the scale.

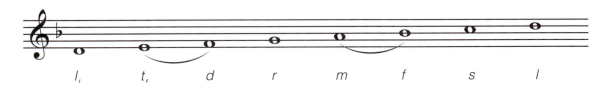

3. Associate the solfège syllables with the notes of the melody. Write the melody on the staff.

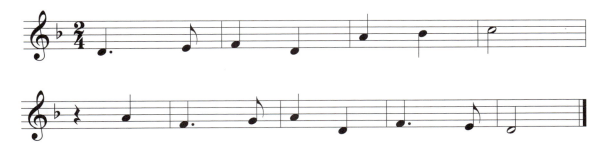

9.6A   Relative and Parallel Key Relationships

Relative Relationships

With the help of the following figures, compare the **a** natural minor scale with the **C** major scale.

a natural minor scale

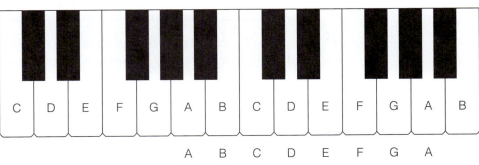

C major scale

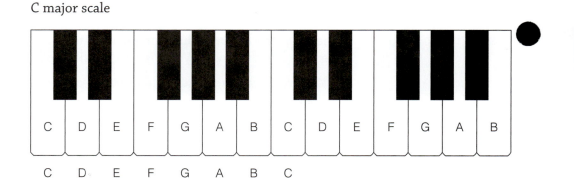

Now compare the d natural minor scale and the F major scale.

d natural minor scale

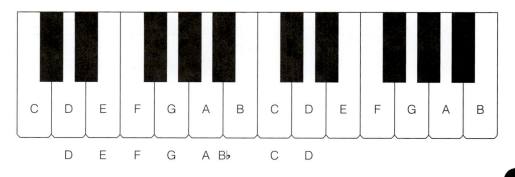

F major scale

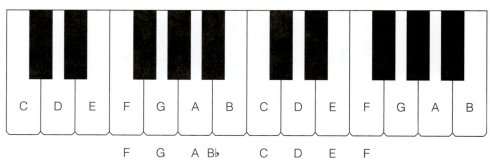

Both scales share the same pitch content, or tone set, and the same key signature. The keys of **a** minor and **C** major are related to each other. We can say that **a** minor is the relative minor of **C** major, or that **d** minor is the relative minor of F major, since these scales share the same notes and key signature. **C** major is the relative major of **a** minor; they both share the same key signature. **F** major is the relative major of **d** minor; they both share the same key signature.

The relative minor scale begins on the sixth degree of the major scale, or three half steps (a minor third) below the tonic of the major scale. The **a** natural minor scale begins on the sixth degree of the **C** major scale. The relationship between the minor and major scale is referred to as a *relative relationship*. The tonic of the major key is scale degree three of the minor scale.

To summarize, the relative minor scale begins three half steps below the relative major scale. The relative major scale begins three half steps above the related minor scale.

The composition "We Three Kings" contains an example of a relative relationship. The work begins in e minor and ends in G major.

We Three Kings   **John H. Hopkins (United States, mid-nineteenth century)**

e minor tonic

G major tonic

Parallel Relationships

The following figures illustrate the relationships between the **a** natural minor scale and the **A** major scale.

a natural minor scale

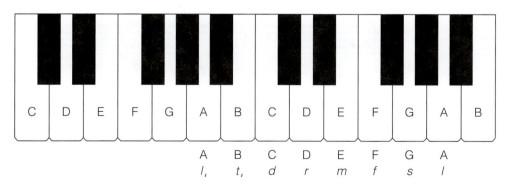

A major scale

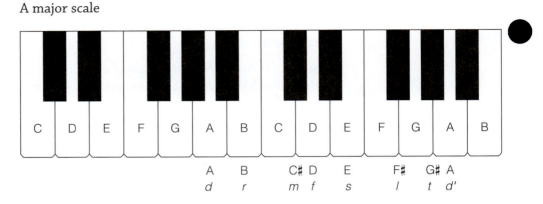

The relationship between the a minor and A major scales is referred to as a *parallel relationship*. When two keys share the same tonic note but different key signatures, we say that there is a parallel major/minor relationship.

The a natural minor scale is the relative minor of the C major scale and the parallel minor of A major; the C major scale is the relative major of the a natural minor scale and the A major scale is the parallel major of the a minor scale. If we raise the third, sixth, and seventh degrees of the minor scale, we will get the parallel major scale. It is important to emphasize that "parallel" means the same tonic but a different key signature.

In the following composition, the melody moves from the key of d minor to the key of D major.

9.7A   Harmonic Minor Scale and Melodies

Sing, Memorize, and Analyze

Internalizing Music

23

1. Listen to "Ah Poor Bird" on Track 23. Memorize the song.
2. Sing "Ah Poor Bird" and keep the beat.
3. Sing "Ah Poor Bird" and clap the rhythm.
4. Pair off in the class. Facing your partner, sing "Ah Poor Bird" and clap the melodic contour.
5. Sing with rhythm names while clapping and showing the melodic contour.

Analyzing What You Hear

1. Sing the lowest note in the song.
2. Sing the highest note in the song. Sing the beginning note of the song.
3. Sing the final note of the song.
4. Sing all the notes in the song from the lowest to the highest.
5. Sing all the notes in the song from the highest to the lowest.

Constructing a Melodic Representation from Memory

1. As you sing "Ah Poor Bird," draw a representation indicating the contour and pitches.
2. As you point to your representation, sing "Ah Poor Bird" with rhythm syllables.

Music Theory

Describing What You Hear with Solfège Syllables

We can describe the pitches in "Ah Poor Bird" with solfège syllables.

In "Ah Poor Bird" we find an accidental, the raised seventh degree that occurs frequently in the minor scale. This form of the minor is referred to as the harmonic minor. A **harmonic minor scale** is a series of eight adjacent notes; half steps occur between the second and third, fifth and sixth, and seventh and eighth degrees of the scale. All other steps are whole steps except for that between six and seven. When we write the pitches of "Ah Poor Bird" in ascending order and include *F*, we discover that the solfège syllables are *l,–t,–d–r–m–f–si–l* and the numbers are 1–2–3–4–5–6–7. We use the solfège syllable *si* to indicate that the seventh degree is raised a half step.

This tone set forms the harmonic minor scale. We also include the upper *l* in our diagram, as is customary when writing out the scale. When we compare the harmonic minor scale to the natural minor scale, we notice that the raised seventh degree in the harmonic minor scale creates a greater pull toward the tonic note. The raised seventh—the leading tone—is borrowed from the parallel major to replace the subtonic note.

The following are the solfège syllables for "Ah Poor Bird."

Ah Poor Bird

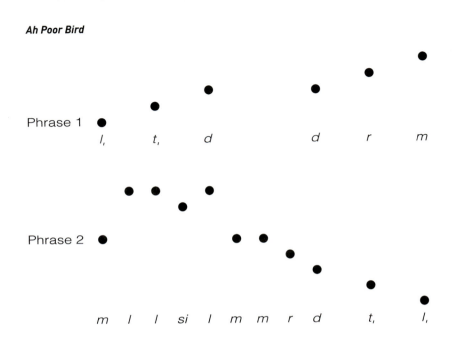

Phrase 1

l,   t,   d   d   r   m

Phrase 2

m l l si l m m r d   t,   l,

Notating What You Hear with Solfège Syllables

The following figure illustrates how to notate "Ah Poor Bird" with solfège syllables.

Ah Poor Bird

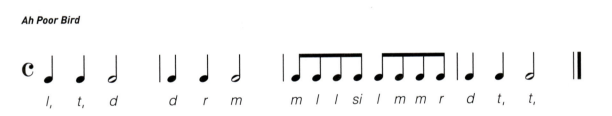

l,   t,   d   d   r   m   m l l si l m m r   d   t,   t,

Notating What You Hear on the Staff

The following figure illustrates how to notate "Ah Poor Bird" on the staff.

Listening The following listening examples have themes based on the harmonic minor scale. Can you sing the themes using solfège syllables? Can you write the themes of some of these examples using staff notation or stick notation with solfège syllables?

"Ah Poor Bird" from Mark Gilston's album *American Roots,* 2007.

"Rose Rose" from the album *Bowed Psaltery Psongsters.*

"Little Fugue in G Minor" by Johann Sebastian Bach (1685–1750).

Sonata No. 9 in E Major, Movement 2, by Ludwig van Beethoven (1770–1827).

"Joshua Fit the Battle of Jericho," recorded by Chris Barber's Jazz Band, 1957.

Passacaglia in C Minor, BWV 582, by Johann Sebastian Bach (1770–1827).

"The Wild Rider" from *Album for the Young* by Robert Schumann (1810–1856).

"Sunrise, Sunset" from the musical *Fiddler on the Roof,* music by Jerry Bock, lyrics by Sheldon Harnick.

9.8A   Determining the Intervals Between the Notes of the Harmonic Minor Scale

Intervals (*La Minor*)

Note the intervals *l,–t, d–r,* and *r–m* are whole steps. The distances between *t,* and *d* and *m* and *f* are half steps. We can refer to whole steps as major seconds (M2) and half steps as minor seconds (m2). The distance between *si* and *l* is a half step, or minor second. The distance between *f* and *si* is a step and a half, or three half steps. Since this interval is formed by two notes adjacent to each other, we describe it as an augmented second.

The following figure illustrates the intervals formed by adjacent notes of the harmonic minor scale.

Whole Steps Major 2	Half Steps Minor 2	Augmented Seconds
l,–t,		
	t,–d	
d–r		
r–m		
	m–f	
		f–si
	si–l	

The following figure illustrates the intervallic distance between the tonic note of a harmonic minor scale and each member of the scale.

Scale Degree	Solfège Syllables	Size	Number of Half Steps Contained in an Interval	Name of Interval	Abbreviation
1–2	*l,–t,*	2	2	major second	M2
1–3	*t,–d*	3	3	minor third	m3
1–4	*l,–r*	4	5	perfect fourth	P4
1–5	*l,–m*	5	7	perfect fifth	P5
1–6	*l,–f*	6	8	minor sixth	m6
1–7	*t,–si*	7	11	major seventh	M7

9.9 Writing Harmonic Minor Scales and Melodies on the Staff

Writing a Harmonic Minor Scale Using Accidentals

The following is a procedure for writing any harmonic minor scale on the staff using accidentals. We will write this example as a d harmonic minor scale in the treble clef.

1. Write the solfège syllables *l,–t,–d–r–m–f–si–l* beneath the staff for the harmonic minor scale.

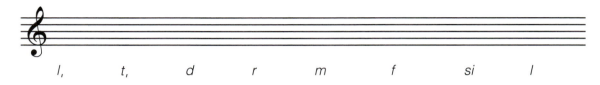

2. Place a note on the staff above each solfège syllable. For a minor scale we use eight adjacent notes; therefore the pitches should also be adjacent on the staff. Remember the sequential alphabetical spelling of scales, and simply put the notes in order. If the tonic note is D, write D–E–F–G–A–B–C–D.

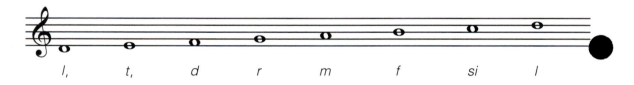

3. Mark the half steps between scale degrees two and three, five and six, and seven and eight and their corresponding pitches on the staff. Remember the intervals between the other degrees will be whole steps.

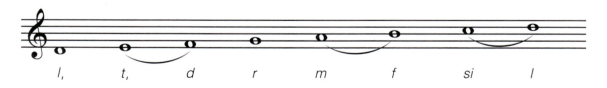

4. Check the intervallic relationship between the solfège syllables and the pitch names to insure the correct intervallic distance between the notes. If necessary, correct the intervals by using sharps or flats. In the case of d harmonic minor, we need to lower the sixth degree to B-flat and raise the seventh degree to C-sharp.

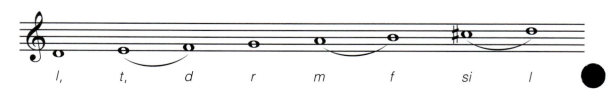

5. If we write the d harmonic minor scale with a key signature, the only alteration is the C-sharp. Because the B-flat is included in the key signature, it identifies each B as a flat. The following is the d harmonic minor scale written on the staff with a key signature.

Writing a Harmonic Minor Melody Using Accidentals

The following is a procedure for writing any minor melody on the staff using accidentals. For an example, we will write "Ah Poor Bird" in the key of d harmonic minor in treble clef.

1. Write the d harmonic minor scale on the staff using accidentals.

2. Write the solfège syllables below the scale.

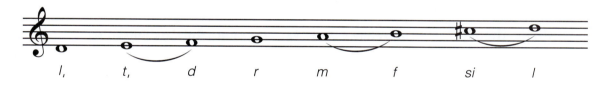

l,   t,   d   r   m   f   si   l

3. Write "Ah Poor Bird" on the staff by associating the solfège syllables with note names in the key of d minor.

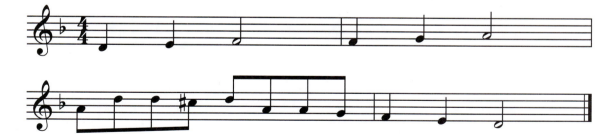

9.10A   Melodic Minor Scale and Melodies

24

Internalizing Music

1. Listen to "Louisiana Marching Song" on Track 24. Memorize the song.
2. Sing "Louisiana Marching Song" and keep the beat.
3. Pair off in the class. Facing your partner, sing "Louisiana Marching Song" and clap the melodic contour.
4. Sing with rhythm names while clapping and showing the melodic contour.

Analyzing What You Hear

1. Sing "Louisiana Marching Song" on "loo" and determine the number of phrases.
2. Sing the final note of the song.
3. Your instructor will sing or play ascending or descending patterns from the scale that "Louisiana Marching Song" is formed from. Try to sing back and identify the intervals between the adjacent notes.

Constructing a Melodic Representation from Memory

1. As you sing "Louisiana Marching Song," draw a representation indicating the contour and pitches.
2. As you point to your representation, sing "Louisiana Marching Song" with rhythm syllables.

Music Theory

Describing What You Hear with Solfège Syllables

These are the solfège syllables for "Louisiana Marching Song."

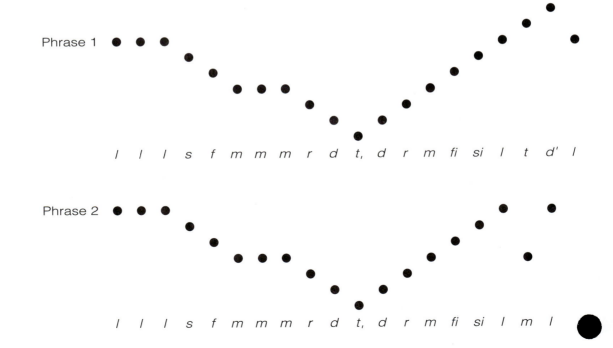

The notes contained in "Louisiana Marching Song" have patterns that are found in the **melodic minor scale**. The melodic minor scale has an ascending form and a descending form. In the ascending form of the scale, the sixth and seventh degrees are raised; in the descending form of the scale, these notes are lowered. We use the solfège syllable *fi* to indicate the raised sixth degree of the scale.

Melodic Minor Scale

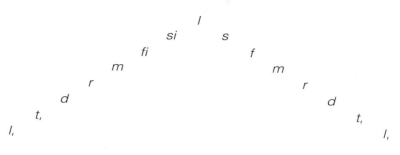

Note that the melodic minor scale avoids the use of the augmented second, an interval present in the harmonic minor scale.

Notating What You Hear with Solfège Syllables

The following are the solfège syllables for "Louisiana Marching Song."

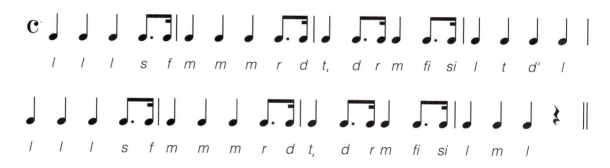

Associating Scale Degree Numbers with Solfège Syllables

The following figures illustrate that the scale degrees for the melodic minor scale may also be identified with scale degree names, reflecting the position of each in the scale.

Scale Numbers	Scale Degree Name
$\hat{1}$	Tonic
$\hat{2}$	Supertonic
$\hat{3}$	Mediant
$\hat{4}$	Subdominant
$\hat{5}$	Dominant
$\hat{6}$	Submediant
$\hat{7}$	Leading Tone

Solfège Syllable	Scale Degree Number
l	$\hat{1}$
si	$\hat{7}$
fi	$\hat{6}$
m	$\hat{5}$
r	$\hat{4}$
d	$\hat{3}$
t,	$\hat{2}$
l,	$\hat{1}$

9.11A   Determining the Intervals Between the Notes of the Melodic Minor Scale

The following figure illustrates the whole-step (W) and half-step (H) pattern of the d melodic minor scale on the staff.

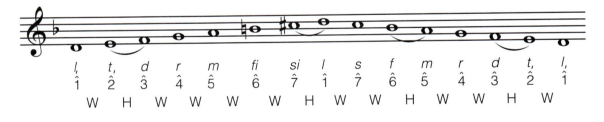

	l,	t,	d	r	m	fi	si	l	s	f	m	r	d	t,	l,
	$\hat{1}$	$\hat{2}$	$\hat{3}$	$\hat{4}$	$\hat{5}$	$\hat{6}$	$\hat{7}$	$\hat{1}$	$\hat{7}$	$\hat{6}$	$\hat{5}$	$\hat{4}$	$\hat{3}$	$\hat{2}$	$\hat{1}$
	W	H	W	W	W	W	H	W	W	H	W	W	H	W	

Intervallic Distance Between the Tonic Note of a Melodic Minor Scale and Each Member of the Scale (Ascending Only)

The following figure illustrates the relationships between the tonic of the melodic minor scale and each member of the scale.

Scale Degree	Solfège Syllables	Size	Number of Half Steps Contained in an Interval	Name of Interval	Abbreviation
1–2	*l,–t,*	2	2	major second	M2
1–3	*t,–d*	3	3	minor third	m3
1–4	*l,–r*	4	5	perfect fourth	P4
1–5	*l,–m*	5	7	perfect fifth	P5
1–6	*l,–fi*	6	9	major sixth	M6
1–7	*l,–si*	7	11	major seventh	M7
1–8	*l,–l*	8	12	perfect octave	P8

9.12A Writing Melodic Minor Scales and Melodies Using Accidentals

Writing a Melodic Minor Scale on the Staff Using Accidentals

The following is a procedure for writing a melodic minor scale on the staff using accidentals. We will write this example as a d melodic minor scale in the treble clef.

1. Write the solfège syllables *l,–t,–d–r–m–fi–si–l–s–f–m–r–d–t,–l,* beneath the staff for the melodic minor scale.

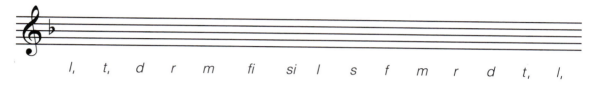

2. Place a note on the staff above each solfège syllable. Remember the sequential alphabetical spelling of scales, and simply put the notes in order both ascending and descending. To write d melodic minor, write D–E–F–G–A–B–C–D–C–B–A–G–F–E–D on the staff.

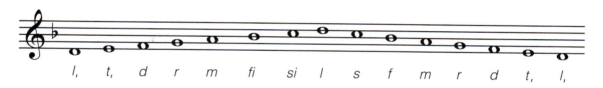

3. Mark the half steps between scale degrees two and three and seven and eight ascending, and (now consider the scale degrees in reverse order) degrees six and five and three and two descending, and their corresponding pitches on the staff. Remember the intervals between the other degrees will be whole steps.

4. Check the intervallic relationship between the solfège syllables and the pitch names to insure the correct intervallic distance between the notes. If necessary, correct the intervals by using sharps or flats. In the case of D melodic minor, we need to raise the sixth degree from B-flat to B-natural and raise the seventh degree to C-sharp in the ascending form. In the descending form, we lower the seventh degree to C-natural and lower the sixth degree to B-flat.

Writing a Melodic Minor Melody on the Staff Using Accidentals

The following procedure can be applied for writing a melodic minor melody on the staff using accidentals. For an example, we will write "Louisiana Marching Song" in the key of d melodic minor in treble clef.

1. Write the d melodic minor scale on the staff using accidentals.

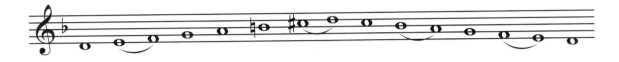

2. Write the solfège syllables below the scale.

l,   t,   d   r   m   fi   si   l   s   f   m   r   d   t,   l,

3. Write "Louisiana Marching Song" on the staff by associating the solfège syllables with note names in the key of d minor. The B and C are raised to B-natural and C-sharp where appropriate.

9.13A   Identifying the Key of a Composition

Minor and major scales use the same key signatures. A key signature can imply either a major or a minor key. You can determine the key of a piece by looking at the notes used (pitch collection).

Major or minor:

1. Look at the key signature.
2. Identify the tonic notes of the major scale and minor scale that share the same key signature.
3. Look for any accidentals used consistently that might indicate a minor key.
4. You may be able to determine the tonality of a musical example by simply looking at the final note. The final note is often the tonic of the major or minor key.
5. If a musical example is in a minor key, determine which form of the minor.

Key Terms and Concepts

Natural Minor Scale
Harmonic Minor Scale
Melodic Minor Scale

How to Practice

Here are some ways to practice the different forms of the minor scale.

Performing	Sing all of the melodies with rhythm syllables.
	Sing Variation on a Russian Folk Song with rhythm names and conduct as you sing.
	Sing Variation on a Russian Folk Song with solfège syllables and conduct as you sing.
	Sing Variation on a Russian Folk Song with numbers and conduct as you sing.
	Sing the harmonic minor scale with solfège syllables.
	Sing the intervals with solfège between the notes of the harmonic minor scale and name the intervals.
	Sing "Ah Poor Bird" with rhythm names and conduct as you sing.
	Sing "Ah Poor Bird" with solfège syllables and conduct as you sing.
	Sing "Ah Poor Bird" with numbers and conduct as you sing.
	Sing the melodic minor scale with solfège syllables.
	Sing the intervals with solfège between the notes of the melodic minor scale and name the intervals.
Singing Scales	Sing the natural minor scale with solfège syllables.
	Sing the harmonic minor scale with solfège syllables.
	Sing the melodic minor scale with solfège.
Playing on the piano	Play natural minor scales on the piano and sing with solfège and letter names.
	Play harmonic minor scales on the piano and sing with solfège and letter names.
	Play melodic minor scales on the piano and sing with solfège and letter names.
Echo Singing	Practice with a classmate or in class. One of you will hum or play on the piano an eight-beat melody. The other will "echo" what was played with solfège syllables.
Conducting	Sing and conduct at the same time.
Memorizing by Ear	The instructor or another student plays a minor melody on the piano or hums a melody.
	• Identify the meter.
	• Sing the example with rhythm names.
	• Identify the ending and starting pitches with solfège syllables.
	• Sing the example with solfège syllables.
Notating the Melody	Practice with a classmate or in class. One of you will sing a known minor melody with neutral syllables or play on the piano a melody from the chapter. The other will "echo" what was sung or played with solfège syllables and then notate the melody in a given meter and key.
Error Dictation	One student plays the melody, deliberately making a mistake. Another student follows the score and locates the error.
Dictation	Instructor hums or plays typical patterns from the dictation melody and students sing back with rhythm and solfège syllables.
	Instructor plays melody and students determine beginning and final note.
	Students sing the melody with rhythm and solfège syllables.
	Students notate the melody in a key and meter provided by the instructor.
Memorizing from a Score	Memorize an entire minor melody and notate it without referring to the notation. First analyze the form by looking for repeated and similar parts. This will simplify the task.
Improvisation/ Composition	First select a meter and length for the composition, then decide what form to use (for example, ABBA). Create an improvisation or composition using only known rhythms and scales.
Performing a Canon	As you sing the melody, clap the rhythm in canon after two or four beats.

Using the Musical Skills CD

Access Chapter 9 on the skills CD to reinforce the notation of minor melodies. You will be provided with the opportunity to practice the notation of different forms of the minor scale.

Listen to each example several times. Try to clap, say the rhythm, and sing with solfège syllables before notating each example. If you cannot memorize the complete example, try memorizing four measures. Once you can easily memorize four measures, then try to memorize eight measures. You might want to notate your example on staff paper before doing so on the computer. Try writing the example using rhythmic notation and solfège syllables before writing on the staff. You might also want to sing each example and point to the notes on the staff before attempting to notate it.

How to Read a Musical Score

Look through the Minuets and the Polonaise by Johann Sebastian Bach.

Say the upper part with rhythm syllables and numbers while you clap the lower part. Then clap the upper part while you say the rhythm of the lower part with syllables.

What is the key of each composition? Circle examples of melodic minor scale passages.

Minuet in D Minor   Johann Sebastian Bach (1685–1750)

Polonaise in G Minor

Minuet in G Minor

Johann Sebastian Bach (1685–1750)

9.1B   Natural Minor Scale and Melodies

Internalizing Music

22

1. Listen to Variation on a Russian Folk Song on Track 22. Memorize the song.
2. Sing Variation on a Russian Folk Song and keep the beat.
3. Pair off in the class. Facing your partner, sing Variation on a Russian Folk Song and clap the melodic contour.
4. Sing with rhythm names while clapping and showing the melodic contour.

Analyzing What You Hear

1. Sing the lowest note in the song.
2. Sing the highest note in the song. Sing the beginning note of the song.
3. Sing all the notes in the song from the lowest to the highest.
4. Sing all the notes in the song from the highest to the lowest.

Constructing a Melodic Representation from Memory

1. As you sing "Variation on a Russian Folk Song," draw a representation indicating the contour and pitches.
2. As you point to your representation, sing Variation on a Russian Folk Song with rhythm syllables.

Music Theory   **Describing What You Hear with Solfège Syllables**

These are the solfège syllables for Variation on a Russian Folk Song.

Variation on a Russian Folk Song

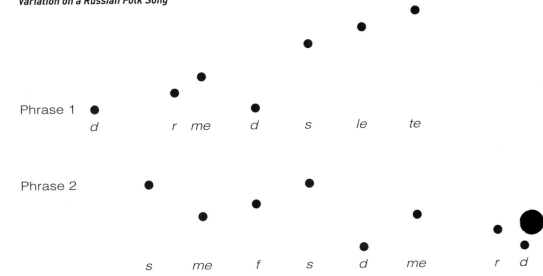

Notating What You Hear with Syllables

We can write Variation on a Russian Folk Song in rhythm notation with solfège syllables.

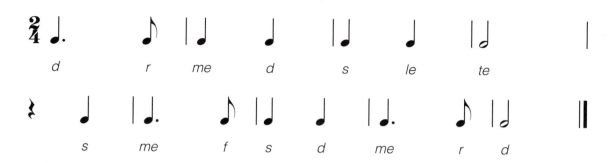

When we write the pitches of Variation on a Russian Folk Song in ascending order, we discover that there are seven adjacent pitches. We can label these pitches with solfège syllables *d–r–me–f–s–le–te–d'*.

A **natural minor scale** is a series of eight adjacent pitches that uses successive letter names; half steps occur between the second and third degrees and fifth and sixth degrees of the scale. All other steps are whole steps. It is this pattern of half (m2) and whole steps (M2) that gives the minor scale its particular configuration. We can find notes of the minor pentachord, minor hexachord, and minor pentatonic in this scale.

Associating Scale Degree Numbers with Solfège Syllables

The following figures illustrate that, as with the major scale, each scale degree of the harmonic minor scale can be identified with a scale degree name that reflects its position in the scale.

Scale Numbers	Scale Degree Name
$\hat{1}$	Tonic
$\hat{2}$	Supertonic
$\hat{3}$	Mediant
$\hat{4}$	Subdominant
$\hat{5}$	Dominant
$\hat{6}$	Submediant
$\hat{7}$	Subtonic

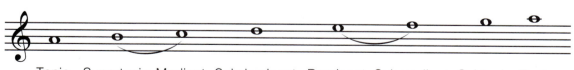

Tonic   Supertonic Mediant Subdominant   Dominant Submediant Subtonic Tonic

Listening 🎧 The following listening examples have themes based on the natural minor scale. Can you sing the themes using solfège syllables? Can you write the themes of some of these examples using staff notation or stick notation with solfège syllables?

"Sweet William." A similar version of this melody is sung by Alasdair Roberts on the recording *No Earthly Man.*

"Shalom Chaverim," sung by the Weavers in the recording *The Weavers at Carnegie Hall,* released by Vanguard Records in 1988.

"When Jesus Wept" by William Billings (1746–1800)

"Dona Dona," on the album released by Signum Classics, *From Jewish Life.* Musicians John Lenehan and Paul Marleyn. Also found on the album *Amulet,* sung by Nikitov, released by Chamsa Records, 2004.

"Hushabye," recorded by Mike and Peggy Seeger on *Album for Children.* Also found on the album *So Many Stars,* under the title of "The Little Horses," sung by Kathleen Battle.

Theme from *Psalmus Hungaricus* by Zoltán Kodály (1882–1967).

Theme from the "Peacock" Variations by Zoltán Kodály (1882–1967).

"Nights in White Satin," as recorded by the Moody Blues (1967).

9.2B Determining the Intervals Between the Notes of the Natural Minor Scale

The following figure illustrates the whole-step (W) and half-step (H) patterns of the d natural minor scale on the keyboard.

d natural minor scale

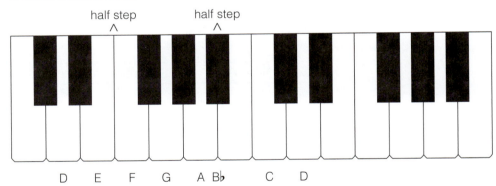

The following figure illustrates the whole-step (W) and half-step (H) patterns of the d natural minor scale on the staff.

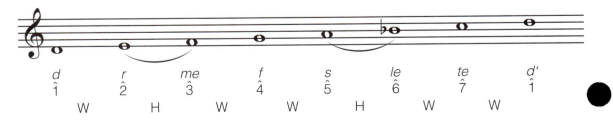

Note the intervals *d–r, me–f,* and *f–s, le–te* are whole steps. The distances between *r* and *me* and *s* and *le* are half steps. We can refer to whole steps as major seconds (M2) and half steps as minor seconds (m2).

Whole Steps Major 2 (M2)	Half Steps Minor 2 (m2)
d–r	
	r–me
me–f	
f–s	
	s–le
le–te	
te–d	

The following illustrates the intervallic distance between the tonic note of a natural minor scale and each member of the scale.

Scale Degree	Solfège Syllables	Size	Number of Half Steps Contained in an Interval	Name of Interval	Abbreviation
1̂–2̂	*d–r*	2	2	major second	M2
1̂–3̂	*d–me*	3	3	minor third	m3
1̂–4̂	*d–f*	4	5	perfect fourth	P4
1̂–5̂	*d–s*	5	7	perfect fifth	P5
1̂–6̂	*d–le*	6	8	minor sixth	m6
1̂–7̂	*d–te*	7	10	minor seventh	m7

9.3B   Writing Natural Minor Scales and Melodies Using Accidentals

Writing a Natural Minor Scale Using Accidentals

The following is a procedure for writing a minor scale on the staff using accidentals. We will write this example as a d minor scale in the treble clef.

1. Write the solfège syllables *d–r–me–f–s–le–te–d'* beneath the staff for the minor scale.

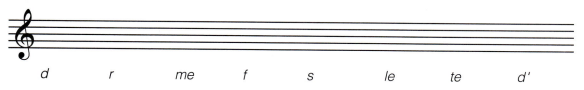

    d   *r*   *me*   *f*   *s*   *le*   *te*   *d'*

2. Place a note on the staff above each solfège syllable. For a minor scale we use eight adjacent notes. The pitches should also be adjacent on the staff. First remember the sequential alphabetical spelling of scales. If the tonic note is D, write D–E–F–G–A–B–C–D.

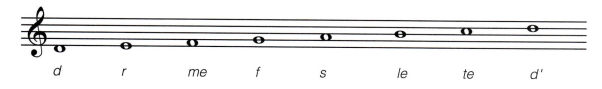

    d   *r*   *me*   *f*   *s*   *le*   *te*   *d'*

3. Mark the half steps between scale degrees two and three and five and six and their corresponding pitches on the staff. Remember the intervals between the other degrees will be whole steps.

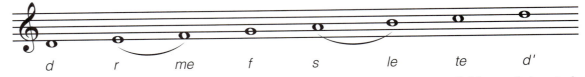

d   r   me   f   s   le   te   d'

4. Check the intervallic relationship between the solfège syllables and the pitch names to insure the correct intervallic distance between the notes. If necessary, correct the intervals by using sharps or flats. In the case of d minor, we need to lower the sixth degree to B-flat.

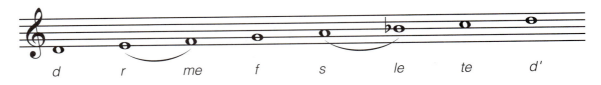

d   r   me   f   s   le   te   d'

Writing a Minor Melody Using Accidentals

The following is a sample procedure for writing any minor melody on the staff using accidentals. For an example we will write Variation on a Russian Folk Song in the key of d minor in treble clef.

1. Write the d minor scale on the staff using accidentals.

2. Write the solfège syllables below the scale.

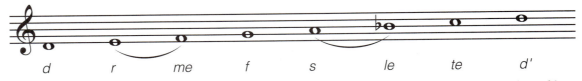

d   r   me   f   s   le   te   d'

3. Write Variation on a Russian Folk Song on the staff by associating the solfège syllables with note names in the key of d minor.

9.4B Minor Key Signatures

Minor key signatures are provided for both sharp and flat keys. We use lower-case letters to indicate minor keys. Note that the last sharp in the key signature is scale degree two of the minor scale. For example, in the key of f-sharp minor, G-sharp is the last sharp and the second degree of the scale. The following figure illustrates the placement of sharps for minor key signatures.

Key: e   b   f sharp   c sharp   g sharp   d sharp   a sharp

The key of e minor has 1♯: F♯.
The key of b minor has 2♯: F♯, C♯.
The key of f♯ minor has 3♯: F♯, C♯, G♯.
The key of c♯ minor has 4♯: F♯, C♯, G♯, D♯.
The key of g♯ minor has 5♯: F♯, C♯, G♯, D♯, A♯.
The key of d♯ minor has 6♯: F♯, C♯, G♯, D♯, A♯, E♯.
The key of a♯ minor has 7♯: F♯, C♯, G♯, D♯, A♯, E♯, B♯.

The last flat in the key signature is the sixth degree of the minor scale. For example, in the key of g minor, E-flat is the last flat and the sixth degree of the scale. The following figure illustrates the placement of flats for minor key signatures.

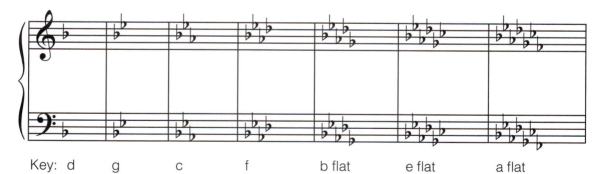

Key: d   g   c   f   b flat   e flat   a flat

The key of d minor has 1♭: B♭.
The key of g minor has 2♭: B♭, E♭.
The key of c minor has 3♭: B♭, E♭, A♭.
The key of f minor has 4♭: B♭, E♭, A♭, D♭.
The key of b♭ minor has 5♭: B♭, E♭, A♭, D♭, G♭.
The key of e♭ minor has 6♭: B♭, E♭, A♭, D♭, G♭, C♭.
The key of a♭ minor has 7♭: B♭, E♭, A♭, D♭, G♭, C♭, F♭.

Circle of Fifths Showing Minor Key Signatures

The circle of fifths provides another way of looking at minor key signatures.

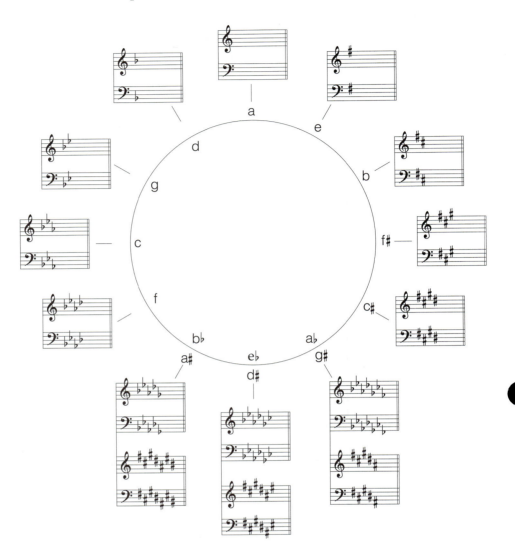

Determining the Key of a Minor Scale from a Given Key Signature

1. Identify the tonic note of the major scale that has this key signature.
2. Go down three half steps from this note.
3. This note is the tonic note of the minor scale.

For example:

1. The tonic note of the major scale that has this key signature is B-flat.
2. The note G is three half steps down from B-flat. G is the *tonic note* of the g minor scale.
3. Therefore, g minor is the minor scale key for the key signature that has two flats.

9.5B   Writing Natural Minor Scales and Melodies with a Key Signature

Writing a Natural Minor Scale with a Key Signature

The following is a procedure for writing a natural minor scale with a key signature. We will write this example as a d natural minor scale in the treble clef.

1. Put the d minor key signature after the treble clef. Write the solfège syllables *d–r–me–f–s–le–te–d'* beneath the staff for the d minor scale.

2. Place a note on the staff above each solfège syllable. For a minor scale we use eight adjacent notes. The pitches should also be adjacent on the staff. If the tonic note is D, write D–E–F–G–A–B–C–D. Mark the half steps between the second and third degrees and the fifth and sixth degrees of the scale.

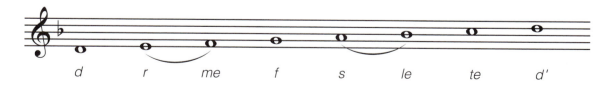

Writing a Minor Melody with a Key Signature

The following is a sample procedure for writing a minor melody on the staff with a key signature. We will write Variation on a Russian Folk Song in d minor.

1. Determine the key and write the scale of the melody on the staff. Mark the half steps.

2. Write the solfège syllables below the scale.

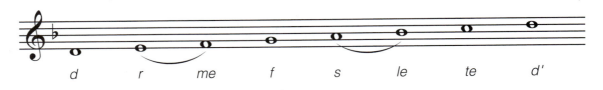

3. Associate the solfège syllables with the notes of the melody. Write the melody on the staff.

9.6B   Relative and Parallel Key Relationships

Relative Relationships

With the help of the following figures, compare the **a** natural minor scale with the **C** major scale.

a natural minor scale

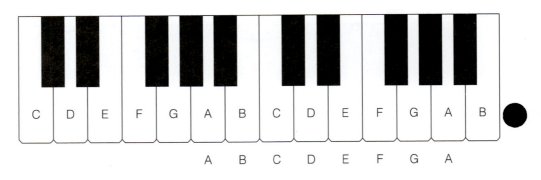

C major scale

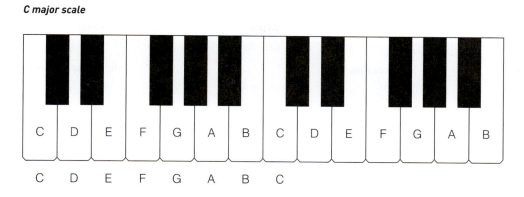

C   D   E   F   G   A   B   C

Now compare the d natural minor scale and the F major scale.

d natural minor scale

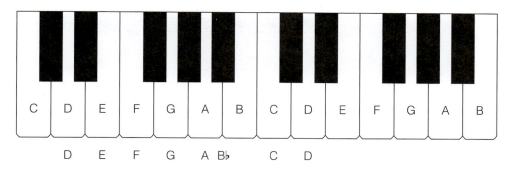

D   E   F   G   A B♭   C   D

F major scale

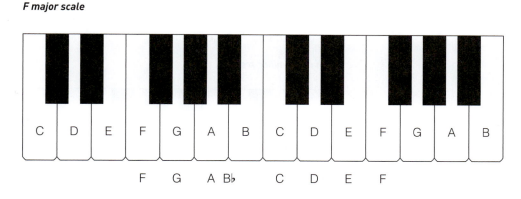

F   G   A B♭   C   D   E   F

Both scales share the same pitch content, or tone set, and the same key signature. The keys of **a** minor and **C** major are related to each other. We can say that **a** minor is the relative minor of **C** major, or that **d** minor is the relative minor of **F** major, since these scales share the same notes and key signature. **C** major is the relative major of **a** minor; they both share the same key signature. **F** major is the relative major of **d** minor; they both share the same key signature.

The relative minor scale begins on the sixth degree of the major scale, or three half steps (a minor third) below the tonic of the major scale. The **a** natural minor scale begins on the sixth degree of the **C** major scale. The relationship between the minor and major scale is referred to as a *relative relationship*. The tonic of the major key is scale degree three of the minor scale.

To summarize, the relative minor scale begins three half steps below the relative major scale. The relative major scale begins three half steps above the related minor scale.

The composition "We Three Kings" contains an example of a relative relationship. The work begins in e minor and ends in G major.

We Three Kings   **John H. Hopkins (United States, mid-nineteenth century)**

e minor tonic

G major tonic

Parallel Relationships

The following figures illustrate the relationships between the **a** natural minor scale and the **A** major scale.

a natural minor scale

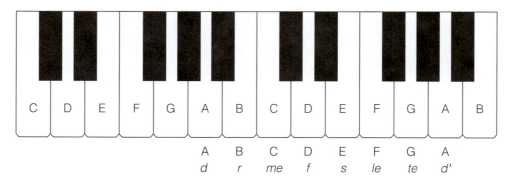

A major scale

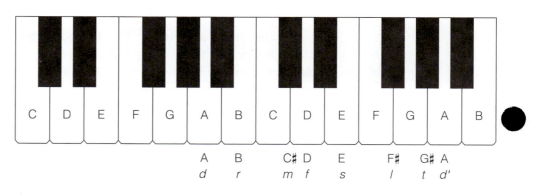

The relationship between the **a** minor and **A** major scales is referred to as a *parallel relationship*. When two keys share the same tonic note but different key signatures, we say that there is a parallel major/minor relationship.

The **a** natural minor scale is the relative minor of the **C** major scale and the parallel minor of **A** major; the **C** major scale is the relative major of the **a** natural minor scale and the A major scale is the parallel major of the a minor scale. If we raise the third, sixth, and seventh degrees of the minor scale, we will get the parallel major scale. It is important to emphasize that "parallel" means the same tonic but a different key signature.

In the following composition, the melody moves from the key of **d** minor to the key of **D** major.

9.7B   Harmonic Minor Scale and Melodies

Sing, Memorize, and Analyze

23

Internalizing Music

1. Listen to "Ah Poor Bird" on Track 23. Memorize the song.
2. Sing "Ah Poor Bird" and keep the beat.
3. Sing "Ah Poor Bird" and clap the rhythm.
4. Pair off in the class. Facing your partner, sing "Ah Poor Bird" and clap the melodic contour.
5. Sing with rhythm names while clapping and showing the melodic contour.

Analyzing What You Hear

1. Sing the lowest note in the song.
2. Sing the highest note in the song. Sing the beginning note of the song.
3. Sing the final note of the song.
4. Sing all the notes in the song from the lowest to the highest.
5. Sing all the notes in the song from the highest to the lowest.

Constructing a Melodic Representation from Memory

1. As you sing "Ah Poor Bird," draw a representation indicating the contour and pitches.
2. As you point to your representation, sing "Ah Poor Bird" with rhythm syllables.

How to Describe What You Hear with Solfège Syllables

We can describe the pitches in "Ah Poor Bird" with solfège syllables. In "Ah Poor Bird" we find an accidental, the raised seventh degree that occurs frequently in the minor scale. This form of the minor is referred to as the harmonic minor. A **harmonic minor scale** is a series of eight adjacent notes; half steps occur between the second and third, fifth and sixth, and seventh and eighth degrees of the scale. All other steps are whole steps except for steps six and seven. When we write the pitches of "Ah Poor Bird" in ascending order and include *F*, we discover that the solfège syllables are *d–r–me–f–s–le–t–d* and the numbers are 1–2–3–4–5–6–7. We use the solfège syllable *si* to indicate that the seventh degree is raised a half step.

The following are the solfège syllables for "Ah Poor Bird."

Ah Poor Bird

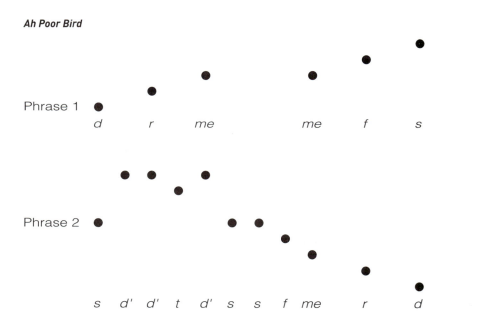

Notating What You Hear with Solfège Syllables

The following figure illustrates how to notate "Ah Poor Bird" with solfège syllables.

Ah Poor Bird

Notating What You Hear on the Staff

The following figure illustrates how to notate "Ah Poor Bird" on the staff.

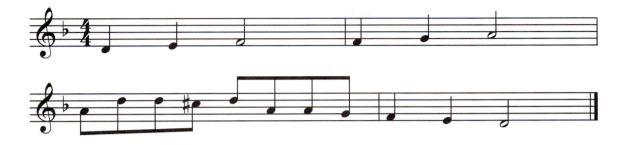

Listening 🎧	The following listening examples have themes based on the harmonic minor scale. Can you sing the themes using solfège syllables? Can you write the themes of some of these examples using staff notation or stick notation with solfège syllables?

"Ah Poor Bird" from Mark Gilston's album *American Roots,* 2007.

"Rose Rose" from the album *Bowed Psaltery Psongsters.*

"Little" Fugue in G Minor by Johann Sebastian Bach (1685–1750).

Sonata No. 9 in E Major, movement 2, by Ludwig van Beethoven (1770–1827).

"Joshua Fit the Battle of Jericho," recorded by Chris Barber's Jazz Band, 1957.

Passacaglia in C Minor, BWV 582, by Johann Sebastian Bach (1770–1827).

"The Wild Rider" from *Album for the Young* by Robert Schumann (1810–1856).

"Sunrise, Sunset" from the musical *Fiddler on the Roof,* music by Jerry Bock, lyrics by Sheldon Harnick.

9.8B   Determining the Intervals Between the Notes of the Harmonic Minor Scale

Intervals (*Do* minor)

Note the intervals *d–r*, *me–f*, *f–s*, and *le–t* are whole steps. The distances between *r* and *me*, *s* and *le*, *t* and *d* are half steps. We can refer to whole steps as major seconds (M2) and half steps as minor seconds (m2). The distance between *f* and *s* is a step and a half, or three half steps. Since this interval is formed by two notes adjacent to each other, we describe it as an augmented second. The following figure illustrates the intervals formed by adjacent notes of the harmonic minor scale.

Whole Steps Major 2	Half Steps Minor 2
d–r	
	r–m
me–f	
f–s	
	s–le
le–t	
	t–d'

The following figure illustrates the intervallic distance between the tonic note of a harmonic minor scale and each member of the scale.

Scale Degree	Solfège Syllables	Size	Number of Half Steps Contained in an Interval	Name of Interval	Abbreviation
1–2	d–r	2	2	major second	M2
1–3	d–me	3	3	minor third	m3
1–4	d–f	4	5	perfect fourth	P4
1–5	d–s	5	7	perfect fifth	P5
1–6	d–le	6	8	minor sixth	m6
1–7	d–t	7	11	major seventh	M7

9.9B Writing Harmonic Minor Scales and Melodies on the Staff

Writing a Harmonic Minor Scale Using Accidentals

The following is a procedure for writing any harmonic minor scale on the staff using accidentals. We will write this example as a d harmonic minor scale in the treble clef.

1. Write the solfège syllables *d–r–me–f–s–le–t–d'* beneath the staff for the harmonic minor scale.

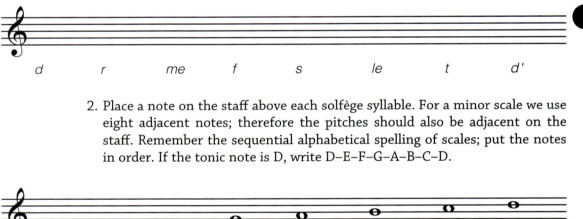

2. Place a note on the staff above each solfège syllable. For a minor scale we use eight adjacent notes; therefore the pitches should also be adjacent on the staff. Remember the sequential alphabetical spelling of scales; put the notes in order. If the tonic note is D, write D–E–F–G–A–B–C–D.

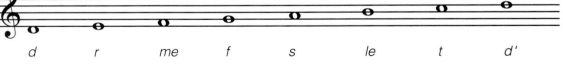

3. Mark the half step between scale degrees two and three, five and six, and seven and eight and their corresponding pitches on the staff. Remember the intervals between the other degrees will be whole steps.

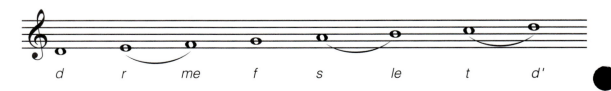

4. Check the intervallic relationship between the solfège syllables and the pitch names to insure the correct intervallic distance between the notes. If necessary, correct the intervals by using sharps or flats. In the case of d harmonic minor, we need to lower the sixth degree to B-flat and raise the seventh degree to C-sharp.

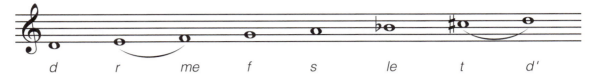

d   r   me   f   s   le   t   d'

5. If we wrote the d harmonic minor scale with a key signature, the only alteration would be the C-sharp. Because the B-flat is included in the key signature, it identifies each B as a flat. The following is the d harmonic minor scale written on the staff with a key signature.

Writing a Harmonic Minor Melody on the Staff Using Accidentals

The following is a sample procedure for writing any major melody on the staff using accidentals. For an example we will write "Ah Poor Bird" in the key of d harmonic minor in treble clef using accidentals.

1. Write the d harmonic minor scale on the staff using accidentals.

2. Write the solfège syllables below the scale.

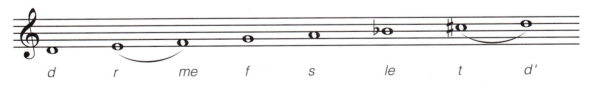

d   r   me   f   s   le   t   d'

3. Write "Ah Poor Bird" on the staff by associating the solfège syllables with note names in the key of d minor.

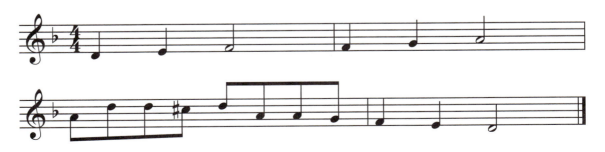

9.10B   Melodic Minor Scale and Melodies

Sing, Memorize, and Analyze

24

Internalizing Music

1. Listen to "Louisiana Marching Song" on Track 24. Memorize the song.
2. Sing "Louisiana Marching Song" and keep the beat.
3. Pair off in the class. Facing your partner, sing "Louisiana Marching Song" and clap the melodic contour.
4. Sing with rhythm names while clapping and showing the melodic contour.

Analyzing What You Hear

1. Sing "Louisiana Marching Song" on "loo" and determine the number of phrases.
2. Sing the final note of the song.
3. Your instructor will sing or play ascending or descending patterns from the scale that "Louisiana Marching Song" is formed from. Try to sing back and identify the intervals between the adjacent notes.

Constructing a Melodic Representation from Memory

1. As you sing "Louisiana Marching Song," draw a representation indicating the contour and pitches.
2. As you point to your representation sing "Louisiana Marching Song" with rhythm syllables.

Music Theory

Describing What You Hear with Solfège Syllables

These are the solfège syllables for "Louisiana Marching Song."

Louisiana Marching Song

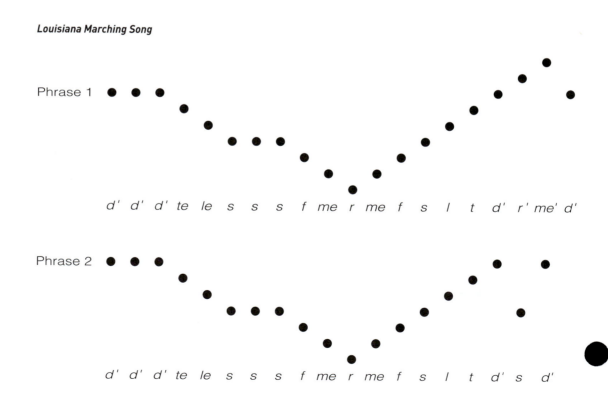

The notes contained in "Louisiana Marching Song" have patterns that are found in the **melodic minor scale**. The melodic minor scale has an ascending form and a descending form. In the ascending form of the scale, the sixth and seventh degrees are raised; in the descending form of the scale these notes are lowered.

Melodic Minor Scale

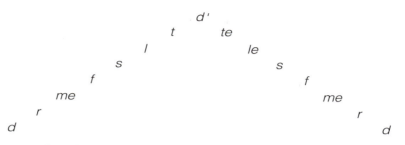

Note that the melodic minor scale avoids the use of the augmented second, an interval present in the harmonic minor scale.

Notating What You Hear with Solfège Syllables

The following are the solfège syllables for the "Louisiana Marching Song."

Associating Scale Degree Numbers with Solfège Syllables

The following figures illustrate that the scale degrees for the melodic minor scale may also be identified with scale degree names, reflecting the position of each in the scale.

Scale Numbers	Scale Degree Name
$\hat{1}$	Tonic
$\hat{2}$	Supertonic
$\hat{3}$	Mediant
$\hat{4}$	Subdominant
$\hat{5}$	Dominant
$\hat{6}$	Submediant
$\hat{7}$	Leading Tone

Solfège Syllable	Scale Degree Number
d'	$\hat{1}$
te	$\hat{7}$
le	$\hat{6}$
s	$\hat{5}$
f	$\hat{4}$
me	$\hat{3}$
r	$\hat{2}$
d	$\hat{1}$

9.11B   Determining the Intervals Between the Notes of the Melodic Minor Scale

The following figure illustrates the whole-step (W) and half-step (H) pattern of the d melodic minor scale on the keyboard.

Intervallic Distance Between the Tonic Note of a Melodic Minor Scale and Each Member of the Scale (Ascending Only)

The following figure illustrates the relationships between the tonic of the melodic minor scale and each member of the scale.

Scale Degree	Solfège Syllables	Size	Number of Half Steps Contained in an Interval	Name of Interval	Abbreviation
$\hat{1}$–$\hat{2}$	d–r	2	2	major second	M2
$\hat{1}$–$\hat{3}$	d–me	3	3	minor third	m3
$\hat{1}$–$\hat{4}$	d–f	4	5	perfect fourth	P4
$\hat{1}$–$\hat{5}$	d–s	5	7	perfect fifth	P5
$\hat{1}$–$\hat{6}$	d–l	6	9	major sixth	M6
$\hat{1}$–$\hat{7}$	d–t	7	11	major seventh	M7
$\hat{1}$–$\hat{8}$	d–d'	8	12	perfect octave	P8

9.12B   Writing Melodic Minor Scales and Melodies Using Accidentals

Writing a Melodic Minor Scale Using Accidentals

The following is a procedure for writing a melodic minor scale on the staff using accidentals. We will write this example as a d melodic minor scale in the treble clef.

1. Write the solfège syllables *d–r–me–f–s–l–t–d'–te–le–s–f–me–r–d* beneath the staff for the melodic minor scale.

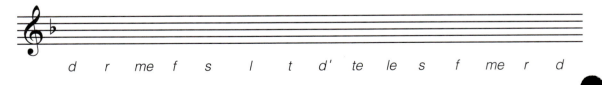

2. Place a note on the staff above each solfège syllable. For a melodic minor scale we use eight adjacent notes ascending and descending. The pitches should also be adjacent on the staff. Remember the sequential alphabetical spelling of scales, and write D–E–F–G–A–B–C–D–C–B–A–G–F–E–D.

3. Mark the half steps between scale degrees two and three and seven and eight ascending, and (now consider the scale degrees in reverse order) degrees six and five and three and two descending, and their corresponding pitches on the staff. Remember the intervals between the other degrees will be whole steps.

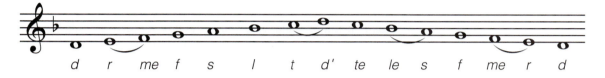

4. Check the intervallic relationship between the solfège syllables and the pitch names to ensure the correct intervallic distance between the notes. If necessary, correct the intervals by using sharps or flats. In the case of d melodic minor, we need to raise the sixth degree from B-flat to B-natural and raise the seventh degree to C-sharp in the ascending form. In the descending form we lower the seventh degree to C-natural and lower the sixth degree to B-flat.

Writing a Melodic Minor Melody Using Accidentals

The following procedure can be applied for writing a melodic minor melody on the staff using accidentals. For an example, we will write "Louisiana Marching Song" in the key of d melodic minor in treble clef.

1. Write the d melodic minor scale on the staff using accidentals.

2. Write the solfège syllables below the scale.

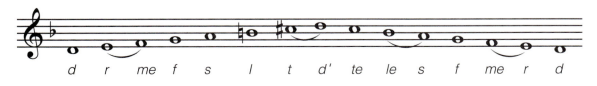

Write "Louisiana Marching Song" on the staff by associating the solfège syllables with note names in the key of d minor. The B♭ and C are raised to B-natural and C-sharp where appropriate.

9.13B   Identifying the Key of a Composition

Minor and major scales use the same key signatures. A key signature can imply either a major or a minor key. You can determine the key of a piece by looking at the notes used (pitch collection).

Major or minor:

1. Look at the key signature.
2. Identify the tonic notes of the major scale and minor scale that share the same key signature.
3. Look for any accidentals used consistently that might indicate a minor key.
4. You may be able to determine the tonality of a musical example by simply looking at the final note. The final note is often the tonic of the major or minor key.
5. If a musical example is in a minor key, determine which form of the minor.

Key Terms and Concepts

Natural Minor Scale
Harmonic Minor Scale
Melodic Minor Scale

How to Practice

Here are some ways to practice the different forms of the minor scale.

Performing	Sing all of the melodies with rhythm syllables.
	Sing Variation on a Russian Folk Song with rhythm names and conduct as you sing.
	Sing Variation on a Russian Folk Song with solfège syllables and conduct as you sing.
	Sing Variation on a Russian Folk Song with numbers and conduct as you sing.
	Sing the harmonic minor scale with solfège syllables.
	Sing the intervals with solfège between the notes of the harmonic minor scale and name the intervals.
	Sing "Ah Poor Bird" with rhythm names and conduct as you sing.
	Sing "Ah Poor Bird" with solfège syllables and conduct as you sing.
	Sing "Ah Poor Bird" with numbers and conduct as you sing.
	Sing the melodic minor scale with solfège syllables.
	Sing the intervals with solfège between the notes of the melodic minor scale and name the intervals.
Singing Scales	Sing the natural minor scale with solfège syllables.
	Sing the harmonic minor scale with solfège syllables.
	Sing the melodic minor scale with solfège.
Playing on the piano	Play natural minor scales on the piano and sing with solfège and letter names.
	Play harmonic minor scales on the piano and sing with solfège and letter names.
	Play melodic minor scales on the piano and sing with solfège and letter names.
Echo Singing	Practice with a classmate or in class. One of you will hum or play on the piano an eight-beat melody. The other will "echo" what was played with solfège syllables.
Conducting	Sing and conduct at the same time.
Memorizing by Ear	The instructor or another student plays a minor melody on the piano or hums a melody.
	• Identify the meter.
	• Sing the example with rhythm names.
	• Identify the ending and starting pitches with solfège syllables.
	• Sing the example with solfège syllables.
Notating the Melody	Practice with a classmate or in class. One of you will sing a known minor melody with neutral syllables or play on the piano a melody from the chapter. The other will "echo" what was sung or played with solfège syllables and then notate the melody in a given meter and key.
Error Dictation	One student plays the melody, deliberately making a mistake. Another student follows the score and locates the error.
Dictation	Instructor hums or plays typical patterns from the dictation melody and students sing back with rhythm and solfège syllables.
	Instructor plays melody and students determine beginning and final note.
	Students sing the melody with rhythm and solfège syllables.
	Students notate the melody in a key and meter provided by the instructor.
Memorizing from a Score	Memorize an entire minor melody and notate it without referring to the notation. First analyze the form by looking for repeated and similar parts. This will simplify the task.
Improvisation/ Composition	First select a meter and length for the composition, then decide what form to use (for example, ABBA). Create an improvisation or composition using only known rhythms and scales.
Performing a Canon	As you sing the melody, clap the rhythm in canon after two or four beats.

Using the Musical Skills CD

Access Chapter 9 on the skills CD to reinforce the notation of minor melodies. You will be provided with the opportunity to practice the notation of different forms of the minor scale.

Listen to each example several times. Try to clap, say the rhythm, and sing with solfège syllables before notating each example. If you cannot memorize the complete example, try memorizing four measures. Once you can easily memorize four measures, then try to memorize eight measures. You might want to notate your example on staff paper before doing so on the computer. Try writing the example using rhythmic notation and solfège syllables before writing on the staff. You might also want to sing each example and point to the notes on the staff before attempting to notate it.

How to Read a Musical Score

Look through the Minuets and the Polonaise by Johann Sebastian Bach.

Say the upper part with rhythm syllables and numbers while you clap the lower part. Then clap the upper part while you say the rhythm of the lower part with syllables.

What is the key of each composition? Circle examples of melodic minor scale passages.

Minuet in D Minor   Johann Sebastian Bach (1685–1750)

(continues on next page)

Polonaise

Johann Sebastian Bach (1685–1750)

Minuet in G Minor

Johann Sebastian Bach (1685–1750)

Minuet in G Minor (continued)   **Johann Sebastian Bach (1685–1750)**

MUSIC THEORY EXERCISES

9.1 Exercises: Natural Minor Scale and Melodies

Exercise 9.1

Fill in the solfège syllables for the natural minor scale.

Solfège Syllable	Corresponding Number
	$\hat{1}$
	$\hat{7}$
	$\hat{6}$
	$\hat{5}$
	$\hat{4}$
	$\hat{3}$
	$\hat{2}$
	$\hat{1}$

Exercise 9.2

Add the solfège syllables below the dots for the Variation on a Russian Folk Song.

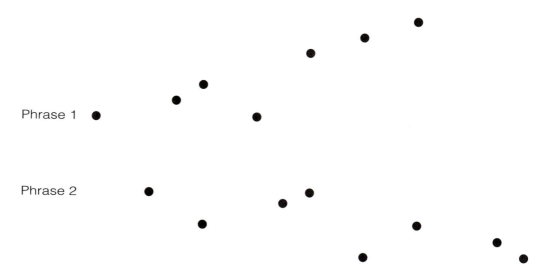

9.2   Exercises: Determining the Intervals Between the Notes of the Natural Minor Scale

Exercise 9.3

Complete the chart for the natural minor scale.

Scale Degree	Solfège Syllables	Size	Number of Half Steps Contained in an Interval	Name of Interval	Abbreviation
1̂–2̂			2		M2
1̂–3̂			3		m3
1̂–4̂			5		P4
1̂–5̂			7		P5
1̂–6̂			8		m6
1̂–7̂			10		m7

9.3   Exercises: Writing Natural Minor Scales and Melodies on the Staff Using Accidentals

Exercise 9.4

Write the following scales in treble and bass clef using whole notes and accidentals ascending and descending. Include the solfège syllables and scale degrees, mark the half steps, and determine the accidentals.

a minor

e minor

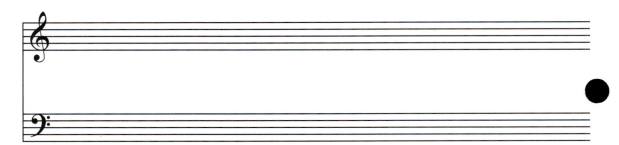

b minor

f-sharp minor

c-sharp minor

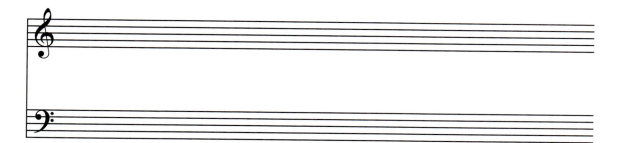

g-sharp minor

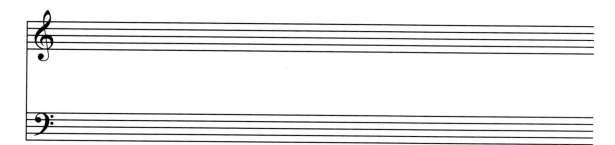

d-sharp minor

a-sharp minor

d minor

g minor

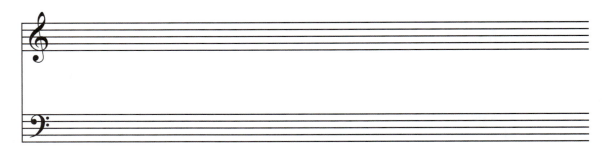

c minor

f minor

b-flat minor

a-flat minor

Exercise 9.5

Write Variation on a Russian Folk Song beginning on a G. Include the time signature, bar lines, and accidentals.

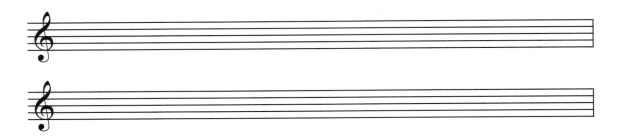

Write Variation on a Russian Folk Song beginning on A. Include the time signature, bar lines, and accidentals.

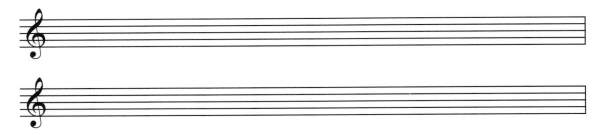

Write Variation on a Russian Folk Song beginning on F. Include the time signature, bar lines, and accidentals.

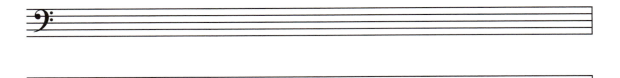

Write Variation on a Russian Folk Song beginning on B. Include the time signature, bar lines, and accidentals.

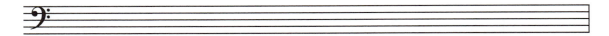

9.4 Exercise: Minor Key Signatures

Exercise 9.6

Write the key signature for each of the following minor scales.

1. e minor

2. b minor

3. f-sharp minor

4. g-sharp minor

5. b-flat minor

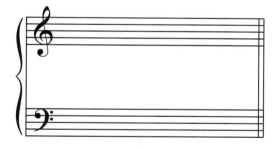

6. a-flat minor

7. c-sharp minor

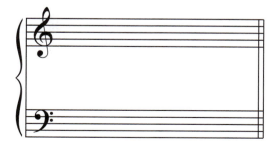

8. c minor

9.5 Exercises: Writing Natural Minor Scales and Melodies with a Key Signature

Exercise 9.7

Write the following natural minor scales in treble and bass clef using whole notes and accidentals ascending and descending. Include the solfège syllables and scale degrees, mark the half steps and determine the accidentals.

a minor

e minor

b minor

f-sharp minor

c-sharp minor

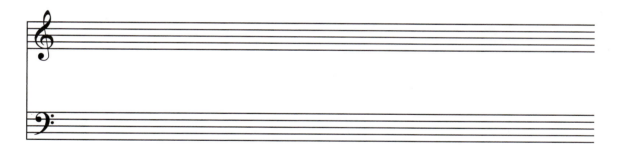

g-sharp minor

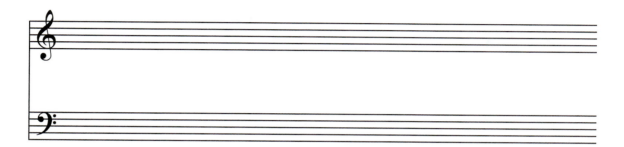

d-sharp minor

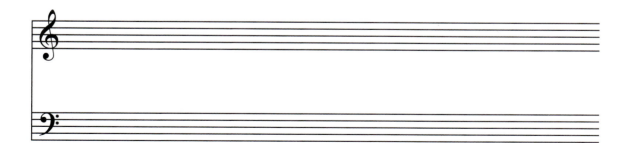

a-sharp minor

d minor

g minor

c minor

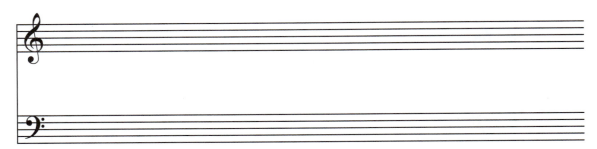

f- minor

b-flat minor

a-flat minor

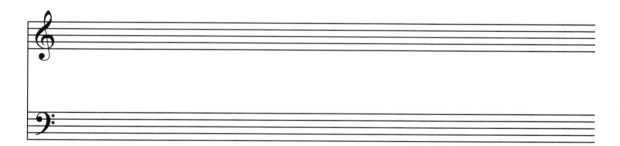

Exercise 9.8

Write Variation on a Russian Folk Song beginning on a G. Include the time signature, bar lines, and accidentals.

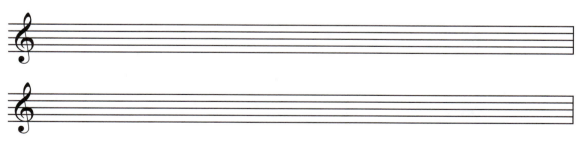

Write Variation on a Russian Folk Song beginning on A. Include the time signature, bar lines, and accidentals.

Write Variation on a Russian Folk Song beginning on F. Include the time signature, bar lines, and accidentals.

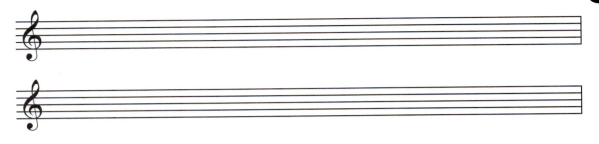

Write Variation on a Russian Folk Song beginning on B. Include the time signature, bar lines, and accidentals.

Exercise 9.9

Write a natural minor scale starting on A on the first staff. Label the scale beneath the staff. Write the parallel major of the a minor scale on the second staff. Label the scale beneath the staff. On the third staff write the relative minor of the A major scale. Label the scale beneath the staff.

Exercise 9.10

Use key signatures for this exercise. Write a natural minor scale starting on D on the first staff. Label the scale beneath the staff. Write the relative major of the d minor scale on the second staff. Label the scale beneath the staff. On the third staff write the relative minor of the D major scale. Label the scale beneath the staff.

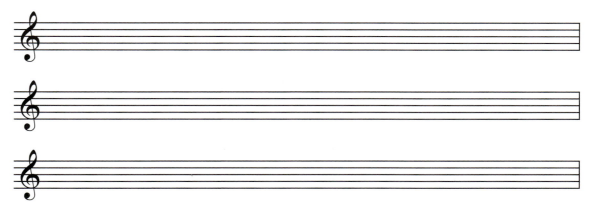

9.6 Exercises: Relative and Parallel Key Relationships

Exercise 9.11

What is the relative minor scale of the following major keys?

1. D major	2. A major	3. A-flat major
4. B-flat major	5. E-flat major	6. B major

Exercise 9.12

What is the relative major of the following minor keys?

1. d minor	2. g minor	3. e minor
4. c minor	5. b minor	6. c-sharp minor

Exercise 9.13

What is the parallel minor key signature of the following major keys?

1. D major	2. A major	3. A-flat major
4. B-flat major	5. E-flat major	6. B major

Exercise 9.14

What is the parallel major key signature of the following minor keys?

1. d minor	2. g minor	3. e minor
4. c minor	5. b minor	6. c-sharp minor

Exercise 9.15

Rewrite the melody Variation on a Russian Folk Song in the parallel major key of d minor.

9.7   Exercises: Harmonic Minor Scales and Melodies

Exercise 9.16

Write the solfège syllables beneath the notation of "Ah Poor Bird."

Exercise 9.17

Add the correct solfège syllables for the harmonic minor scale to the following chart.

Solfège Syllable	Corresponding Number
	1
	7
	6
	5
	4
	3
	2
	1

9.8 Exercises: Determining the Intervals Between the Notes of the Harmonic Minor Scale

Exercise 9.18

Complete the chart by writing in the solfège syllables for all intervals of a second for the harmonic minor scale.

Whole Steps Major 2	Half Steps Minor 2	Augmented Seconds

Exercise 9.19

Complete the chart by filling in the missing information for the harmonic minor scale.

Scale Degree	Solfège Syllables	Size	Number of Half Steps Contained in an Interval	Name of Interval	Abbreviation
$\hat{1}$–$\hat{2}$			2		
$\hat{1}$–$\hat{3}$					
$\hat{1}$–$\hat{4}$			5		
$\hat{1}$–$\hat{5}$			7		P5
$\hat{1}$–$\hat{7}$			11		

9.9 Exercises: Writing Harmonic Minor Scales and Melodies on the Staff Using Accidentals

Exercise 9.20

Write the following harmonic minor scales in treble and bass clef using whole notes and accidentals ascending and descending. Include the solfège syllables and scale degrees, mark the half steps, and determine the accidentals.

a harmonic minor

e harmonic minor

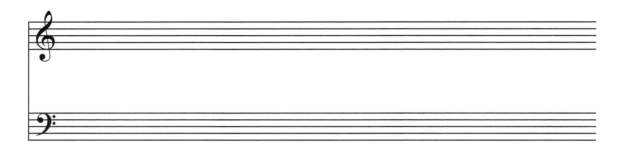

b harmonic minor

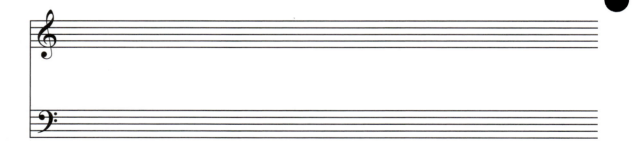

f-sharp harmonic minor

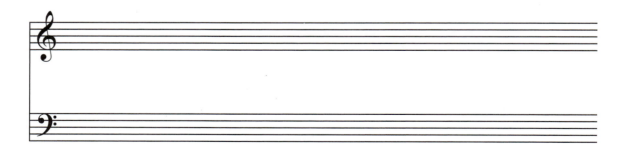

c-sharp harmonic minor

g-sharp harmonic minor

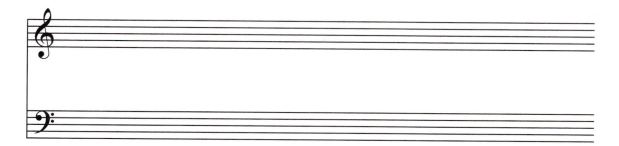

d-sharp harmonic minor

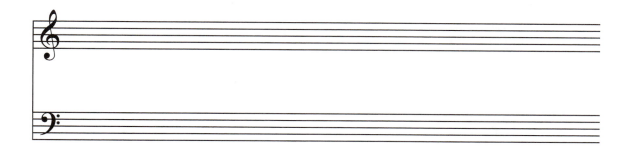

a-sharp harmonic minor

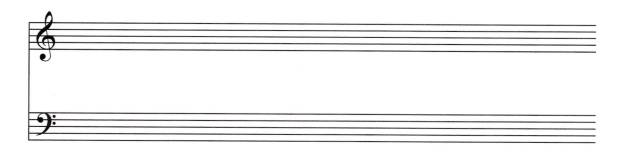

d harmonic minor

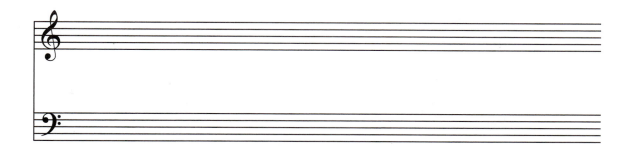

g harmonic minor

c harmonic minor

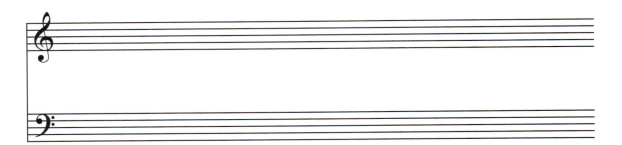

f harmonic minor

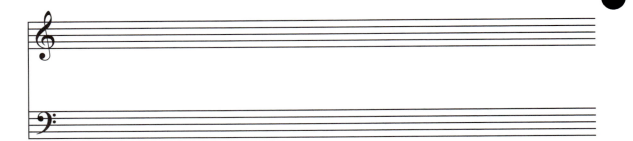

b-flat harmonic minor

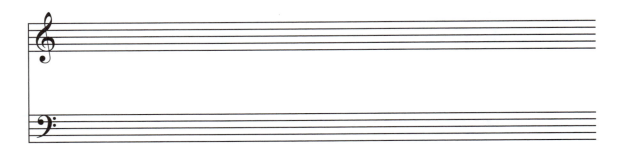

a-flat harmonic minor

Exercise 9.21

Write "Ah Poor Bird" beginning on a G. Include the time signature, bar lines, and accidentals.

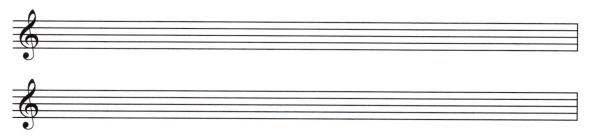

Write "Ah Poor Bird" beginning on C-sharp. Include the time signature, bar lines, and accidentals.

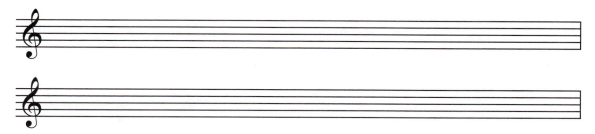

Write "Ah Poor Bird" beginning on C. Include the time signature, bar lines, and accidentals.

Write "Ah Poor Bird" beginning on B. Include the time signature, bar lines, and accidentals.

Exercise 9.22

1. What is the dominant note of b harmonic minor? _____

2. What is the leading tone of c harmonic minor? _____

3. What is the mediant of b-flat harmonic minor? _____

4. What is the subdominant of a harmonic minor? _____

5. What is the submediant of c-sharp harmonic minor? _____

6. What is the tonic note of e-flat harmonic minor? _____

9.10 Exercises: Melodic Minor Scales and Melodies

Exercise 9.23

Write the solfège syllables beneath "Louisiana Marching Song."

Exercise 9.24

Write "White Choral Bells" in the parallel minor key on the staves provided on p. 379.

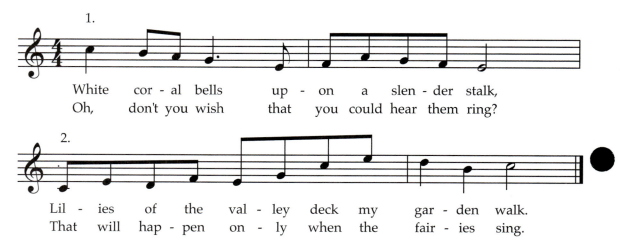

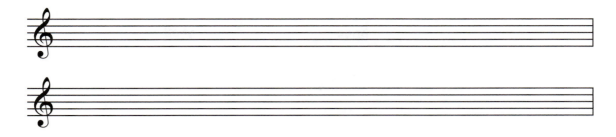

Exercise 9.25

Write the proper key signature for each of the following minor scales. Then write the scale in the form indicated.

d minor (natural)

1.

g minor (harmonic)

2.

b minor (melodic)

3.

c minor (harmonic)

4.

a minor (melodic)

5.

f-sharp minor (natural)

9.11   Exercise: Determining the Intervals Between the Notes of the Melodic Minor Scale

Exercise 9.26

Complete the chart by filling in the solfège syllables for all intervals of a second for the melodic minor scale.

Whole Steps	Half Steps
Major 2	Minor 2

Complete the chart by filling in the missing information for the melodic minor scale. Consider only the ascending form of the scale.

Scale Degree	Solfège Syllables	Size	Number of Half Steps Contained in an Interval	Name of Interval	Abbreviation
$\hat{1}$–$\hat{2}$			2		M2
$\hat{1}$–$\hat{3}$					
$\hat{1}$–$\hat{4}$					
$\hat{1}$–$\hat{5}$					P5
$\hat{1}$–$\hat{6}$					
$\hat{1}$–$\hat{7}$					
$\hat{1}$–$\hat{8}$			12		

9.12   Exercises: Writing Melodic Minor Scales and Melodies on the Staff Using Accidentals

Exercise 9.27

Write the following melodic minor scales in treble and bass clef using whole notes and accidentals ascending and descending. Include the solfège syllables and scale degrees, mark the half steps, and determine the accidentals.

a melodic minor

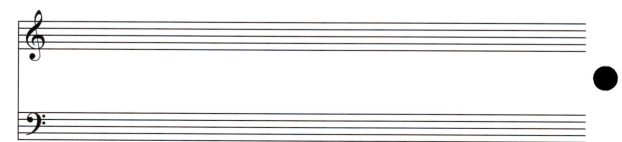

e melodic minor

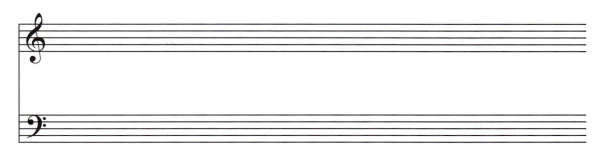

b melodic minor

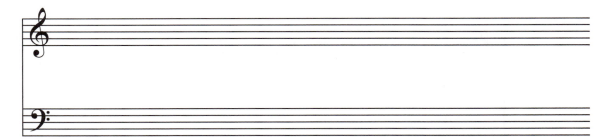

f-sharp melodic minor

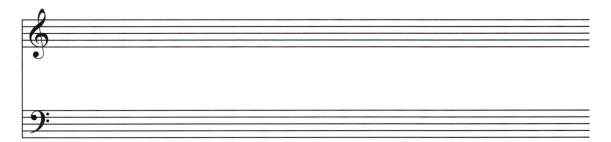

c-sharp melodic minor

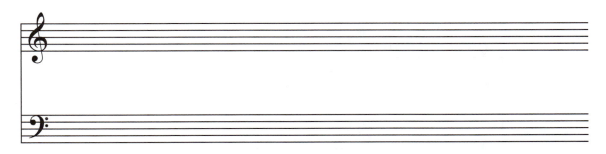

g-sharp melodic minor

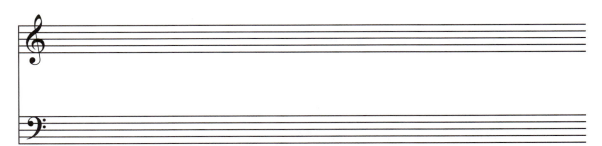

d-sharp melodic minor

a-sharp melodic minor

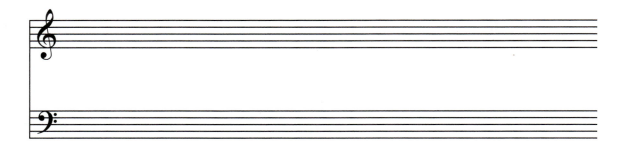

d melodic minor

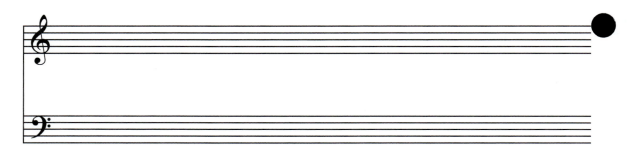

g melodic minor

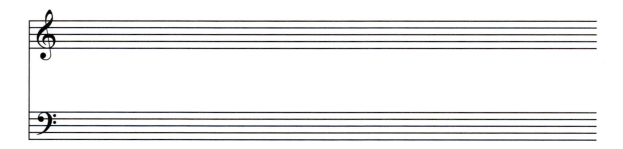

c melodic minor

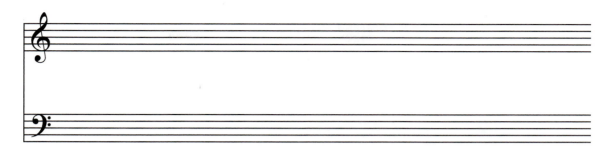

f melodic minor

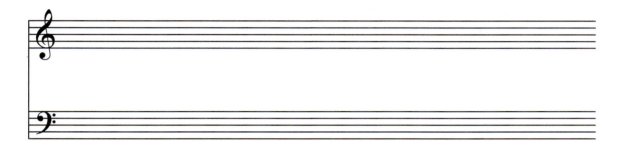

b-flat melodic minor

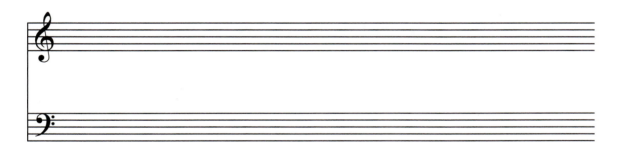

a-flat melodic minor

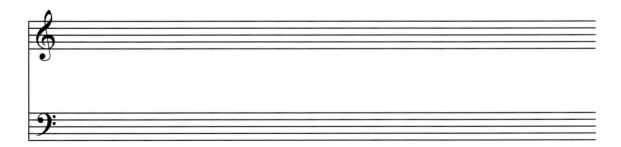

Exercise 9.28

Write "Louisiana Marching Song" in d melodic minor. Include the time signature, bar lines, and accidentals.

Write the "Louisiana Marching Song" in c melodic minor. Include the time signature, bar lines, and accidentals.

Write the "Louisiana Marching Song" in e melodic minor. Include the time signature, bar lines, and accidentals.

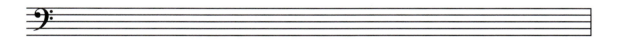

Write the "Louisiana Marching Song" in b melodic minor. Include the time signature, bar lines, and accidentals.

Exercise 9.29

1. What is the dominant note of a melodic minor? _____

2. What is the leading tone of c-sharp melodic minor? _____

3. What is the mediant of e-flat melodic minor? _____

4. What is the subdominant of g melodic minor?   _____

5. What is the submediant of b melodic minor?   _____

6. What is the supertonic note of c melodic minor?   _____

9.13 Exercise: Identifying the Key of a Composition

Music Theory Exercise 9.30

Identify the key and solfège inventory of each of the following compositions.

Shalom Chavarim   **Traditional Israel Song**

Brandenburg Concerto   **Johann Sebastian Bach (1685–1750)**

Organ Fugue   **Johann Sebastian Bach (1685–1750)**

Minuet   **Henry Purcell (1659–1695)**

Chapter **10**

Constructing and Labeling Triads

CHAPTER OVERVIEW

When three or more pitches are produced at the same time the resulting sound is called a chord. In this chapter you will learn how to construct and analyze chords. Triads, three-note chords, as well as four-note chords are the building blocks of music. Harmony occurs when a series of chords move horizontally in time. This chapter also addresses how to identify triads using two systems of analysis: roman numeral analysis and figured bass.

Listen as your instructor plays the following piece of music. What is the connection between the melody and accompanying chords?

Variation on a Lullaby   **Johannes Brahms (1833–1897)**

10.1   Major, Minor, Diminished, and Augmented Triads

A **triad** is a three-tone chord built on intervals of a third. Triads are composed of three notes: the root of the triad, the third of the triad, and the fifth of the triad. The following figure shows that triads are built on two superimposed thirds.

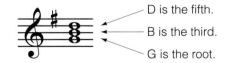

Triads may be classified as major, minor, diminished, or augmented.

Major Triads

Sing, Memorize, and Analyze

Internalizing Music

25

French Canon

1. Listen to the French Canon on Track 25. Perform and memorize the song.

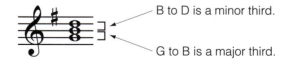

1.   2.   3.   4.

He   Dieu   qu'el - le   m'a_____   he   tra - hi,

qui   ma   tol - lu   mon_____   a - mis.

Analyzing What You Hear

1. Sing the canon from memory in four parts. Listen as the instructor plays the first note of each measure harmonically (all notes sounding together) and melodically (notes played one after another).
2. How many different notes do you hear?
3. What are the solfège syllables for these notes?
4. Listen as your instructor plays notes harmonically or melodically. Describe the notes of the triads with solfège syllables.
5. Name the interval between each note of the triad.
6. As a class, sing the triad in three parts.

Music Theory

A **major triad** consists of two superimposed thirds—a major third between the root and the third degree, a minor third between the third and the fifth degree—and a perfect fifth between the root and fifth degree of the triad. In root position, the third of the triad is a note positioned a third above the root, and the fifth of a triad is a note positioned a fifth above the root.

B to D is a minor third.

G to B is a major third.

The root determines the name of the triad.

C   F   G
major triad   major triad   major triad

Minor Triads

Sing, Memorize, and Analyze

Internalizing Music

Listen to "Hey Ho Nobody Home" on Track 26. Perform and memorize the song.

26

Hey Ho Nobody Home

Hey   Ho   No-bo-dy home,   meat nor drink nor   mo-ney have I none,

Yet,   I will be mer - ry, ve-ry mer-ry, Hey Ho   No-bo-dy home.

Analyzing What You Hear

1. Sing "Hey Ho" In Canon. Listen as the instructor plays all the notes on the first beat of each measure harmonically and melodically.
2. How many different notes do you hear?
3. Can you describe the notes of the triads with solfège? What is the interval between each note of the triad?
4. As a class, sing the triad.

We use the harmonic minor scale for deriving chords and triads because this form of the scale is used so frequently in harmony. Remember that the leading tone (7) of the harmonic minor scale is raised a half step; you will need to put an accidental in front of the leading tone, as it does not appear in the key signature.

Music Theory

A **minor triad** consists of two superimposed thirds: a minor third between the root and the third degree and a major third between the third and the fifth degree. There is a perfect fifth between the root and the fifth degree of the triad.

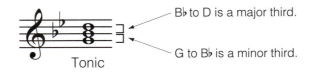

B♭ to D is a major third.

G to B♭ is a minor third.

Tonic

The root determines the name of the triad.

g minor   c minor

Scales and Triads

The following figure indicates that the intervals of a major triad are the same as the tonic, third, and fifth of a major scale

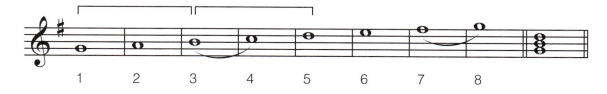

```
1   2   3   4   5   6   7   8
```

The following figure indicates that the intervals of a minor triad are the same as the tonic, third, and fifth of a minor scale.

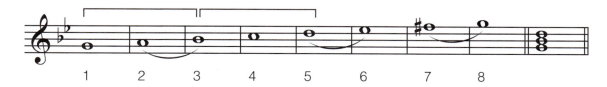

```
1   2   3   4   5   6   7   8
```

Diminished Triads

Sing, Memorize, and Analyze

Internalizing Music

Sing the following melody several times on Track 27.

27

The Sailor's Alphabet   **Folk Song**

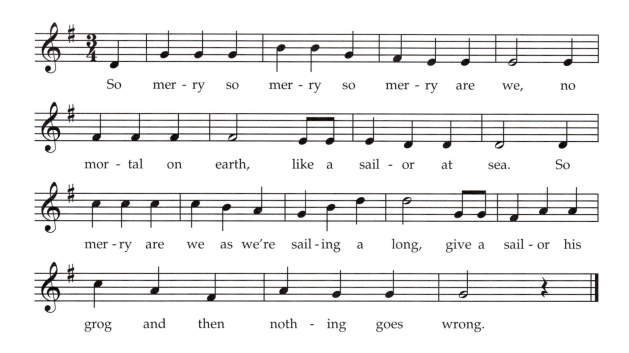

So mer-ry so mer-ry so mer-ry are we, no

mor-tal on earth, like a sail-or at sea. So

mer-ry are we as we're sail-ing a long, give a sail-or his

grog and then noth-ing goes wrong.

Analyzing What You Hear

1. Listen as your instructor plays the notes of the first measure of the last line harmonically and melodically.
2. Determine the solfège syllables for this triad.
3. As a class, sing the three notes of this triad.

| Music Theory | **Diminished triads** consist of three notes in the following configuration: a minor third between the root and the third of the triad, a minor third between the third and fifth, and a diminished fifth between the root and the fifth of the triad. Therefore, in root position, the diminished triad consists of two superimposed minor thirds, the minor third formed by the lower two notes and the minor third formed by the upper two notes. The following are examples of diminished triads. |

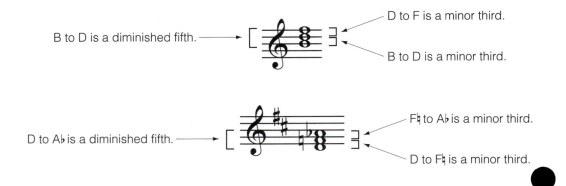

B to D is a diminished fifth. ⟶   D to F is a minor third.

B to D is a minor third.

D to A♭ is a diminished fifth. ⟶   F♮ to A♭ is a minor third.

D to F♮ is a minor third.

Augmented Triads

Sing, Memorize, and Analyze

Internalizing Music

Listen as your instructor plays this piece of music on Track 34.

Little Study   Robert Schumann (1810–1856)

Leise und sehr egal zu spielen

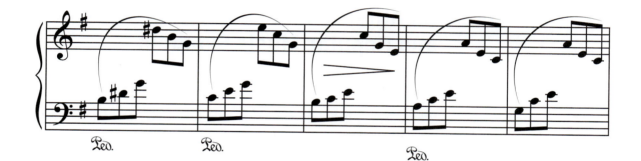

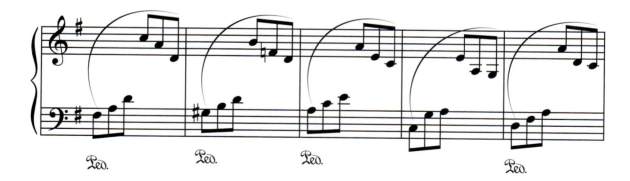

Analyzing What You Hear

1. Listen as your instructor plays the notes of the first measure of the last line harmonically and melodically.
2. Determine the solfège syllables for this triad.
3. As a class, sing the three notes of this triad.

| Music Theory | **Augmented triads** consist of a major third between the root and the third of the triad, a major third between the third and the fifth, and an augmented fifth between the root and the fifth of the triad. In root position, the augmented triad consists of two superimposed thirds, the third formed by the lower two notes and the third formed by the upper two notes. The lower third is a major interval and the upper third is a major interval. The following figure is an example of an augmented triad. |

D to A♯ is an augmented fifth. ⟶

F♯ to A♯ is a major third.

D to F♯ is a major third.

10.2   Identifying Triads Using Pitch Names and Popular Music Symbols

Pitch Name Identification for Triads

When using pitch name identification for triads, letter names are used to indicate the quality. An uppercase letter name identifies a major triad. A lowercase letter with the letter "m" indicates a minor triad. An uppercase letter with a "+" or with "aug" indicates an augmented triad, and a lowercase letter with an "o" or with "dim" indicates a diminished triad.

Introduction to Popular Music Symbols

In popular music, folk, and jazz, chords are indicated using the following symbols. Popular chord symbol nomenclature has not been standardized. A major triad is indicated by a capital letter. This letter indicates the root of the chord. The following two chords are G major and B-flat major.

A minor triad is indicated by a capital letter followed by a lowercase "m." The following two chords are g minor and a minor.

Diminished triads in popular music are indicated by adding "dim" or "o" to the root name. For example:

Augmented triads in popular music are indicated by adding "aug" or a plus sign (+) to the root name. For example:

Lead Sheets

Lead sheets are used in several styles of music including popular, jazz, and folk music. We have included the lead sheet for the folk song "Scarborough Fair." There are three components to a lead sheet: the first is a melody line, the second is lyrics written beneath the melody line, and the third is chord names written above the melody line. It is up to the performer to determine how to play these chords. There are several ways to accompany a melody when reading from a lead sheet.

Scarborough Fair

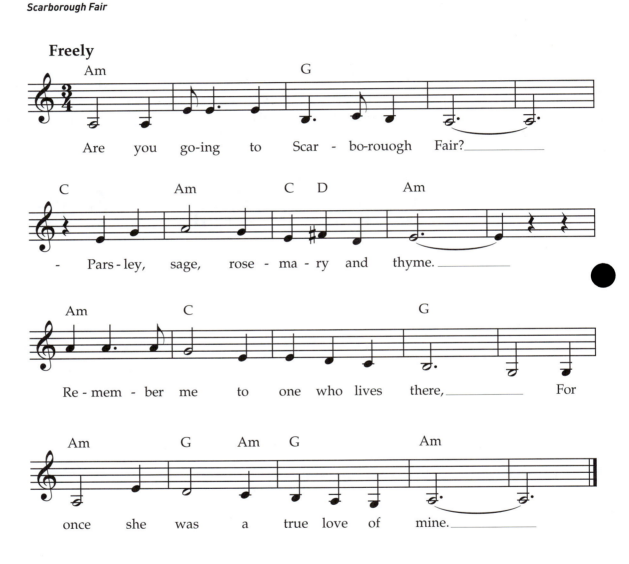

10.3 Close and Open Positions of a Triad

When triads appear as two superimposed thirds and are written within the range of an octave, they are said to be in close or simple position.

When the notes of the triad are not following in thirds, extend beyond the range of an octave, and are spaced more than a third apart, they are in open position.

In this open-position triad there is a skip between G and D. Using triads in open and close position provides different musical colors. Note that the pitches are the same as in close position but the spacing has changed. "Voicing" is the term we use to refer to the different color of chords in close or open position.

10.4 Labeling Triads Using Roman Numeral Analysis and Figured Bass

Triads can be constructed on any scale degree of major or minor scales. We label chords according to the scale degree of the chord in root position. This is referred to as **roman numeral analysis**. Roman numeral analysis helps identify both the scale degree and the quality of the triad. Uppercase roman numerals identify major triads; lowercase roman numerals identify minor triads. Lowercase roman numerals with a small circle identify diminished triads. Uppercase roman numerals with a plus sign identify augmented triads.

Using Roman Numerals to Label Major Scale Triads

The following are root-position triads built on each scale degree of a major scale:

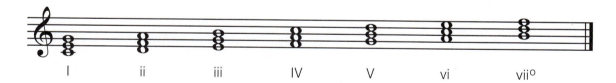

In a major scale:

> Chord I is a major, tonic triad.
> Chord ii is a minor, supertonic triad.
> Chord iii is a minor, mediant triad.
> Chord IV is a major, subdominant triad.
> Chord V is a major, dominant triad.
> Chord vi is a minor, submediant triad.
> Chord vii° is a diminished, leading tone triad.

Using Roman Numerals to Label Minor Scale Triads

Because there are three forms of the minor scale, naming triads can be more complicated. In minor keys, harmony is usually built on the harmonic form of the minor scale. We will limit this discussion to identifying the root-position triads built on each scale degree of the harmonic minor scale:

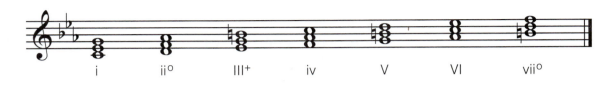

In a harmonic minor scale:

> Chord i is a minor, tonic triad.
> Chord ii° is a diminished, supertonic triad.
> Chord III⁺ is an augmented, mediant triad.
> Chord iv is a minor, subdominant triad.
> Chord V is a major, dominant triad.
> Chord VI is a major, submediant triad.
> Chord vii° is a diminished, leading tone triad.

Triads ii° and vii° in a minor key are diminished triads. Diminished triads are written with lowercase and include a superscript circle after the roman numeral. Look at triad III in the minor key. The III chord in minor is composed of two superimposed major thirds and is an augmented triad.

Figured Bass

During the Baroque period (1600–1750), it was commonplace for composers to write the keyboard part for an orchestral or small-ensemble composition using only a bass line with numbers written below the notation. These numbers indicated the intervals to be played above the bass notes. This is called **figured bass**. Figured bass was used in nearly all genres of music during the Baroque period but is seldom used in music today. Figured bass provides the harmonic structure of a composition so that the performer can create an accompaniment. It can be combined with roman numerals to provide a complete functional analysis of triads.

The following musical example shows a melody and the figured bass to be used to accompany the composition.

All triads in root position are referred to as $\frac{5}{3}$ triads because the triad consists of notes written a fifth and a third above the bass. When accidentals occur, they are also reflected in the figured bass notation. For the purposes of figured bass, $\frac{5}{3}$ is never written but always understood.

Root-position triads built on each scale degree of a C Major scale:

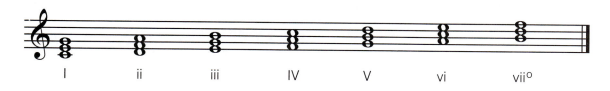

Root-position triads built on each scale degree of c harmonic minor scale:

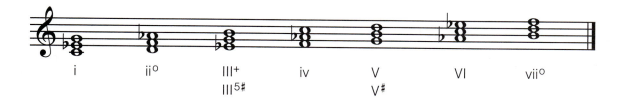

Note: The 5♯ in chord three indicates that the fifth note above the bass is raised. The sharp after chord five indicates that the third note above the bass is raised.

10. 5   Inversions of Triads

Like intervals, triads can also be inverted. When a note other than the root of a triad appears as the lowest note, the triad is inverted.

First-Inversion Triads Within a Major Tonality

First-inversion triads will have the third of the chord as the lowest note of the triad. For example, a major tonic triad in root position is *d–m–s* and in first inversion is *m–s–d'*. Because *m* to *s* is a third and *m* to *d* is a sixth, the figured bass for a first-inversion triad is referred to with the numbers $\frac{6}{3}$. In practice we only need to put a 6 under the note for a first-inversion chord.

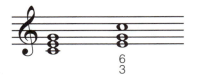

First-Inversion Triads Within a Minor Tonality

A minor tonic triad in root position is *1–3–5* and in first inversion is *3–5–1*. In the first inversion, the lowest interval is a third and the distance from the lowest note to the highest is a sixth, so the figured bass for a first-inversion triad will be $\frac{6}{3}$.

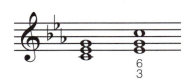

Second-Inversion Triads Within a Major Tonality

Second-inversion triads are written with the fifth of the chord as the lowest note of the triad. For example, a major tonic triad in root position is *d–m–s*, in first inversion is *m–s–d'*, and in second inversion is *s–d'–m'*. Since *s–d* is a fourth and *s–m'* is a sixth, the figured bass for a second-inversion triad will be $\frac{6}{4}$.

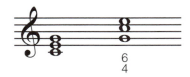

Second-Inversion Triads Within a Minor Tonality

A minor tonic triad in root position is 1–3–5 and in second inversion is 5–3–1. In the second inversion the lowest interval is a perfect fourth and the distance from the lowest note to the highest is a minor sixth. The figured bass for a second-inversion triad in minor is $\frac{6}{4}$.

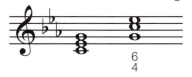

10.6   The Dominant Seventh Chord

Sing, Memorize, and Analyze

Internalizing Music

Sing the following four-part canon. The entrances occur at the beginning of each phrase (Track 28).

Canon   **Cherubini**

Analyzing What You Hear

1. Listen as the instructor plays the notes on the sixth beat (microbeat) of measure three of all the phrases and resolve this chord to a tonic triad.
2. Identify the number of different notes in the penultimate chord.
3. Using your ear, identify the notes with solfège syllables.
4. As a class, sing the chord in four parts.

Music Theory

A chord consists of three or more tones. We can construct a seventh chord by adding another note a third above the fifth of a triad. The dominant seventh chord is a four-note chord built on the fifth degree of a scale. The dominant seventh chord has the same structure in a major and in a minor tonality. In root position, a dominant seventh chord is a major chord with a minor seventh interval between the root and the seventh. This is also called a major-minor seventh chord. We use a superscript seven (7) following the roman numeral to indicate that the interval of a seventh has been added above the root of a triad.

In both a major and a minor tonality, a root-position dominant seventh chord consists of the fifth, seventh, second, and fourth scale degrees.

The dominant seventh chord requires resolution. In a dominant seventh chord there are two tendency tones that need to be resolved. The fourth scale degree resolves to the third scale degree and the seventh scale degree resolves to the first scale degree. The dominant seventh can replace the dominant triad in any of the previous chord progressions.

Seventh chords can be constructed on all scale degrees of the major and minor scales. There are five main types of seventh chords:

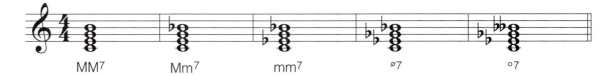

MM⁷   Mm⁷   mm⁷   ø7   °7

Inversions of a Dominant Seventh Chord

The dominant seventh chord can also be inverted. Because there are four notes in a seventh chord it will have three inversions. Here are the inversions of the dominant seventh chords with figured bass symbols:

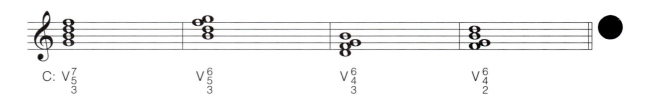

C: V$_{5\atop3}^{7}$ V$_{5\atop3}^{6}$ V$_{4\atop3}^{6}$ V$_{4\atop2}^{6}$

Key Terms and Concepts

Triads	Diminished Triad	Figured Bass
Major Triad	Augmented Triad	Chord Inversions
Minor Triad	Roman Numeral Analysis	

How to Practice

Here are some useful suggestions for practicing melody in a variety of ways. Remember to keep practicing in small groups with your peers.

Skill Development and Ear Training Exercises for Triads	Listen as the instructor plays a pitch from the keyboard and names the note. Students sing a major triad from that pitch using solfège syllables and letter names.
	Practice singing the intervals of different types of triads:
29–33	The instructor plays a pitch from the keyboard and names the note, then asks students to sing a major, minor, diminished, or augmented triad. Listen to Tracks 29–33, Vocal Exercises 1–5.
Performing	Sing all of the melodies in the chapter with solfège and scale degree numbers.
	Sing triads beginning on each degree of the major scale with solfège syllables, letter names, and scale degree numbers.
Sight Singing	Look at the meter and key. Choose a suitable tempo. What is the form? Sing or speak the rhythm patterns of the focus songs while tapping the beat. Identify any chords that may appear melodically in the sight-reading example. Sing with solfège syllables.
Dictation	Instructor hums or plays a series of triads from a given note. • Students must sing back with neutral syllables and solfège. • Students sing the triads with syllables. • Students notate the triads in a given key.

Using the Musical Skills CD

Access Chapter 10 on the skills CD to reinforce your knowledge of triads. You will be provided with the opportunity to practice the notation of triads and dominant seventh chords.

MUSIC THEORY EXERCISES

10.1 Exercises: Major, Minor, Diminished, and Augmented Triads

Exercise 10.1

Identify the root of the following triads and label each triad as major, minor, augmented, or diminished.

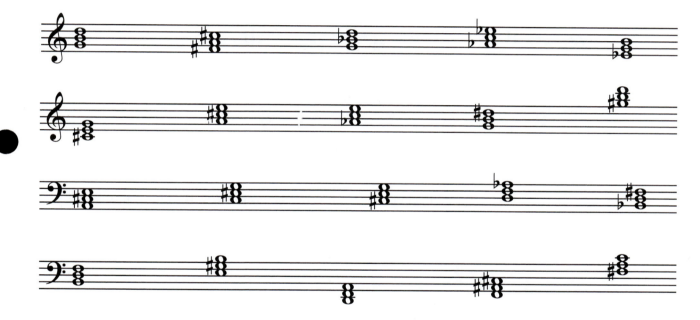

Exercise 10.2

Identify the root of the following triads and label each triad as major, minor, augmented, or diminished.

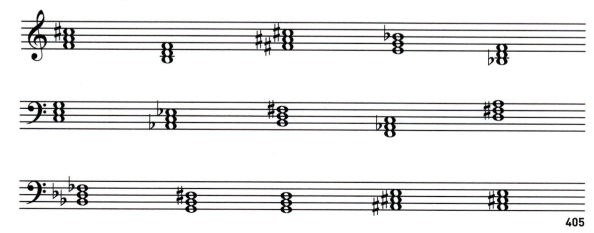

Exercise 10.3

Change each given major triad into a minor triad. Remember to lower the third of a major triad to derive a minor triad.

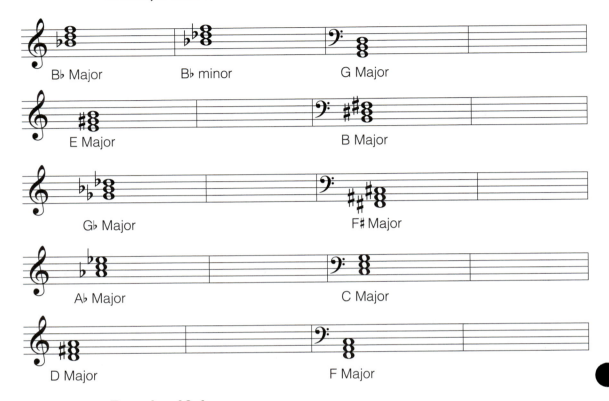

Exercise 10.4

Play the following chords on the keyboard. Name the chord inversions as you play.

10.2 Exercises: Identifying Triads Using Pitch Names and Popular Music Symbols

Exercise 10.5

Write the major and minor triads requested below each popular-music chord symbol.

1. E   2. B♭   3. Am   4. C   5. Dm   6. E♭m   7. G

8. D   9. Fm   10. Gm   11. Bm   12. A♭m   13. G♭   14. B

15. A♭   16. Cm   17. A   18. F   19. B♭m   20. D♭   21. Em

Exercise 10.6

Write the popular chord symbols for each of the following chords in the space above the chord.

1. Gm   2.   3.   4.   5.

6.   7.   8.   9.   10.

11.   12.   13.   14.   15.

Exercise 10.7

Write the popular chord symbols for each of the following chords in the space above the chord.

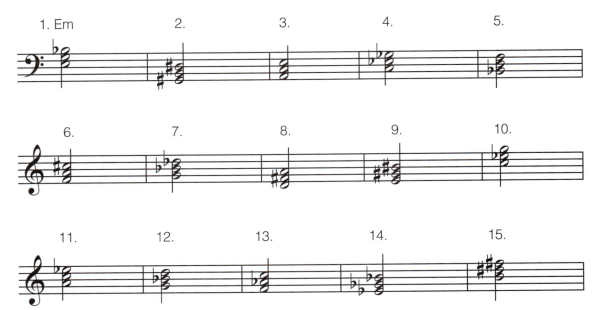

1. Em   2.   3.   4.   5.

6.   7.   8.   9.   10.

11.   12.   13.   14.   15.

Exercise 10.8

Write the major, minor, augmented, or diminished triads requested below each popular chord symbol.

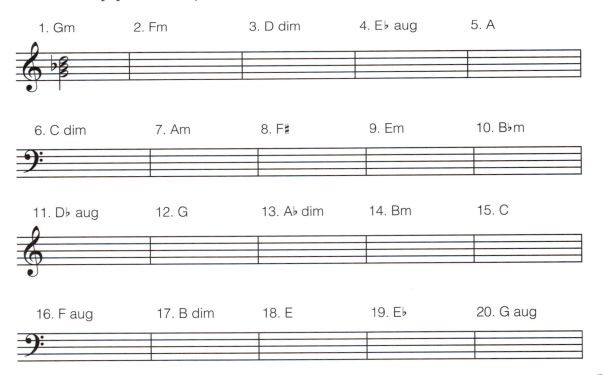

1. Gm   2. Fm   3. D dim   4. E♭ aug   5. A

6. C dim   7. Am   8. F♯   9. Em   10. B♭m

11. D♭ aug   12. G   13. A♭ dim   14. Bm   15. C

16. F aug   17. B dim   18. E   19. E♭   20. G aug

10.3   Exercises: Close and Open Position

Exercise 10.9

Rewrite the following triads in close position:

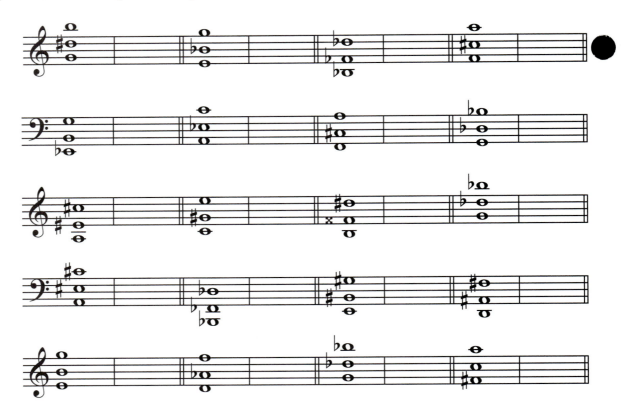

Exercise 10.10

Rewrite the following triads in open position:

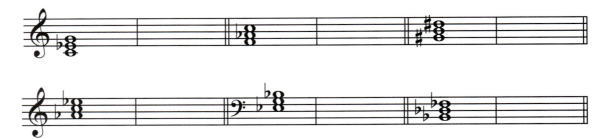

10.4   Exercises: Roman Numeral Analysis and Figured Bass

Exercise 10.11

Write the key signature and chords and identify the quality of each chord with a roman numeral.

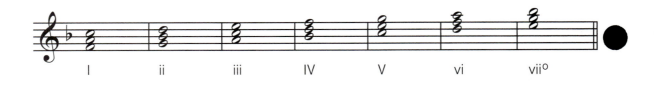

I   ii   iii   IV   V   vi   vii°

1. A Major

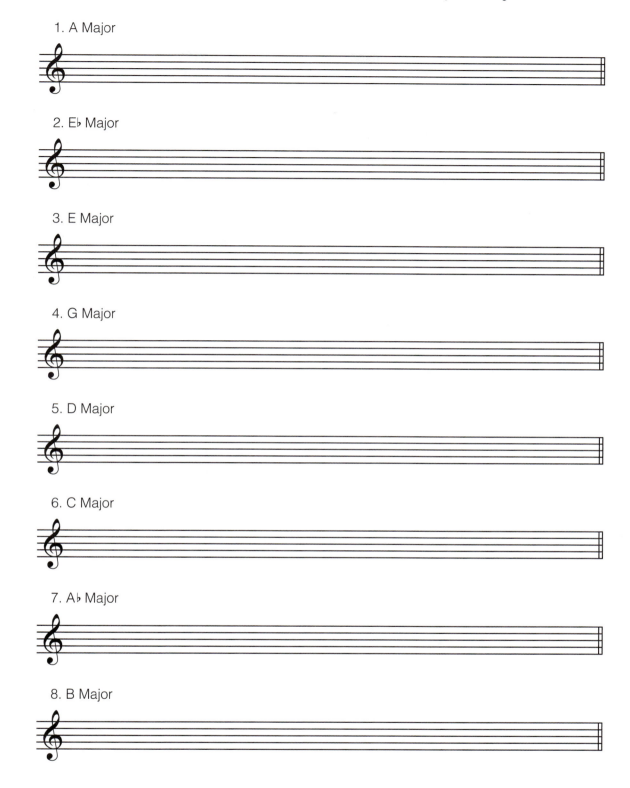

2. E♭ Major

3. E Major

4. G Major

5. D Major

6. C Major

7. A♭ Major

8. B Major

Exercise 10.12

The given key signature is for a major key in each of the following lines of music. Identify the key of each line and then identify each chord with a roman numeral.

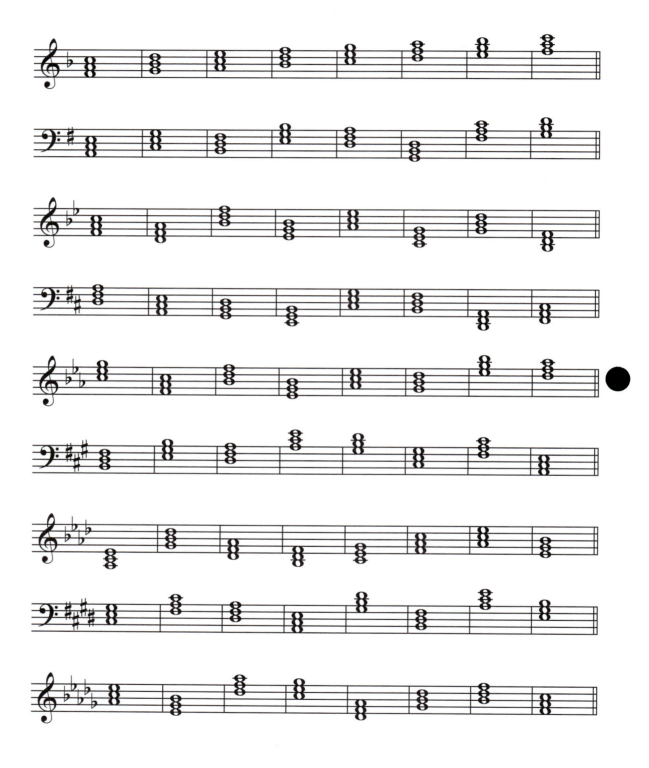

Exercise 10.13

Using the staff below, write each chord found in "The First Noel." Identify the chords with roman numerals and figured bass symbols.

The First Noel

10.5 Exercises: Triad Inversion

Exercise 10.14

Write the first and second inversions of these triads. Name each triad. An example is provided.

Example: F Major

Exercise 10.15

Write the triads that represent the roman numerals in each given key. Write these triads in both first and second inversion.

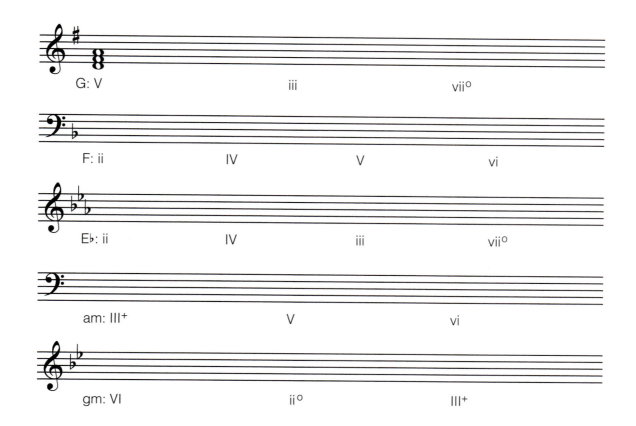

10.6 Exercises: The Dominant Seventh Chord

Exercise 10.16

Write seventh chords above each note; do not use accidentals. This exercise is to give you practice writing the consecutive thirds that form seventh chords.

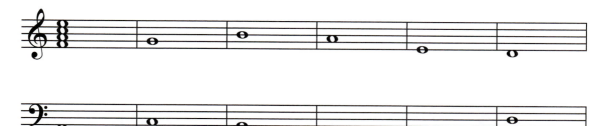

Exercise 10.17

Write the following dominant seventh chords.

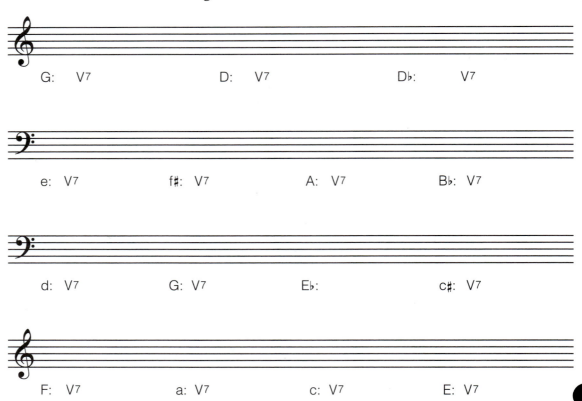

G: V7   D: V7   D♭:   V7

e: V7   f♯:   V7   A: V7   B♭:   V7

d: V7   G: V7   E♭:   c♯:   V7

F: V7   a: V7   c: V7   E: V7

Exercise 10.18

Write all the chords contained in "Go Down, Moses" on the staff provided. Identify each chord with a roman numeral.

Go Down, Moses   **Traditional African American Spiritual**

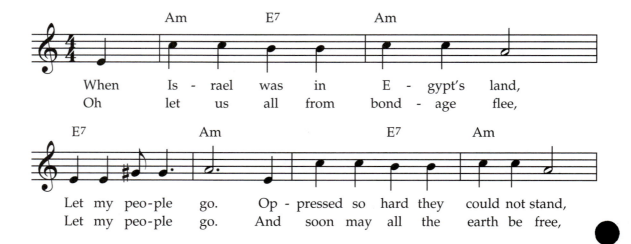

When   Is - rael   was   in   E - gypt's   land,
Oh   let   us   all   from   bond - age   flee,

Let my peo-ple   go.   Op - pressed so   hard they   could not stand,
Let my peo-ple   go.   And   soon may   all   the   earth be free,

Exercise 10.19

Identify the chords on the first beat of each measure in the following Beethoven sonatina with roman numerals and figured bass.

Sonatina in F Major, Movement 1   **Ludwig van Beethoven (1770–1827)**

Exercise 10.20

Identify the chords in the following Beethoven sonatina with roman numerals and figured bass. Your instructor will show you how to reduce the accompaniment pattern to block chords.

Sonatina in G Major, Movement 1   **Ludwig van Beethoven (1770–1827)**

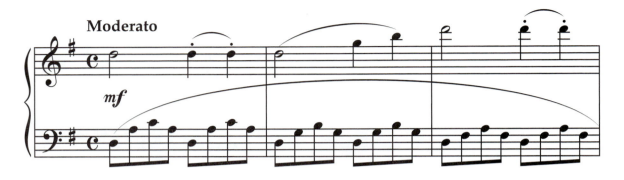

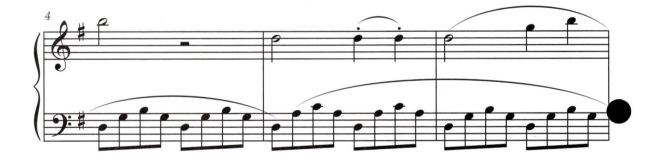

Chapter 11

An Introduction to Basic Chord Progressions

CHAPTER OVERVIEW

A **chord progression** refers to the succession of chords in a piece of music. In this chapter we will learn how to harmonize simple folk melodies using three chords, the tonic, subdominant, and dominant, known as *primary chords*. All notes of the diatonic scale can be harmonized using these three chords. You will learn how to write and play these chords so that your accompaniments sound fluid and connected. You will also learn how to recognize points of rest in music, called *cadences*, and how to harmonize these points of rest with appropriate chords. At the end of the chapter you will learn about secondary triads: triads that add harmonic variety to compositions. These are chords built on the supertonic, mediant, submediant, and leading tone degrees of the scale.

11.1 Tonic and Dominant Functions in a Major Key

Harmonic functions help guide our choice of chords for harmonizing a melody. All chords belong to one of three harmonic functions: tonic, subdominant (or predominant), and dominant.

Sing, Memorize, and Analyze
35

Internalizing Music

1. Sing "Paw Paw Patch" and memorize the melody (Track 35).

2. As the instructor or another student plays "Paw Paw Patch," clap the melodic contour of the accompaniment or bass line.

3. Clap the melodic contour of the bass line as you sing the melody with solfège syllables.

4. Pair off in the class.

5. Face your partner as student A sings the melody and claps the melodic contour and student B sings the lower accompanying part with solfège syllables and claps the melodic contour.

6. Switch parts.

Paw Paw Patch   **American Folk Song**

Analyzing What You Hear

1. How many different notes did you sing in the lower part?
2. Are the beginning and ending notes the same?
3. Sing the bass part as your instructor plays the melody.
4. Sing the melody with solfège syllables.
5. How many different solfège syllables do you sing in the first two measures of the melody? Name them.
6. How many different solfège syllables do you sing in measures three and four of the melody? Name them.
7. Consider the first four measures of the song. When you sing *d* in the bass part, what three different notes do you sing in the melody?
8. Consider the first four measures of the song. When you sing *s* in the bass part, what three different notes do you sing in the melody?

Constructing a Melodic Representation from Memory

Notate "Paw Paw Patch" in F major. Write the melody in the treble clef and the accompanying bass notes in the bass clef.

Music Theory	We can harmonize "Paw Paw Patch" with the solfège syllables *d* and *s,*. These notes also represent the harmonic functions of tonic and dominant. We can represent the tonic function with a T and the dominant function with a D.

d	*s,*	*d*
Tonic	Dominant	Tonic
T	D	T

Paw Paw Patch   **American Folk Song**

Listening 🎧

As you listen to these examples, try to identify the tonic and dominant functions.

"Sehnsucht nach dem Frühling," K. 596, by Wolfgang Amadeus Mozart (1756–1791).

"Skip to My Lou" from the album *Leadbelly, the Complete Recorded Works*, Vol. 2, 1940–1943.

"I's the B'y" as found on the CD *Classic Canadian Songs*.

11.2   Tonic and Dominant Chord Progressions

Sing, Memorize, and Analyze

💿 36

Internalizing Music

Listen as your instructor plays the following example (Track 36).

Sonatina in C, Movement 2   **Wolfgang Amadeus Mozart (1756–1791)**

Analyzing What You Hear

1. How many different notes fall on the beats in the bass part? Name them with solfège syllables.

2. Sing the bass part as your instructor plays the melody.

3. Sing the melody with solfège syllables.

4. How many different solfège syllables do you sing in the first two measures of the melody? Name them.

5. How many different solfège syllables do you sing in measure four of the melody? Name them.

6. Consider the first two measures. When you sing *d* in the bass part, what three different notes do you sing in the melody?

7. Consider the fourth measure. When you sing *s* in the bass part, what three different notes do you sing in the melody?

8. Sing the harmonic functions of this Mozart work as your instructor plays the melody on the keyboard. What roman numerals would you use to analyze the chords?

In Unit 11.1 we discovered how to harmonize a simple melody with tonic and dominant functions that are represented by the tonic and dominant notes of a scale. We can build chords on these two functions of tonic and dominant to produce a harmonic progression. Both chords I and V are primary triads. Chord I has a tonic function and chord V has a dominant function. In the key of C major, chord I is a C major chord, and chord V is a G major chord that moves to chord I.

Triads can be voiced in different ways. In keyboard or choral compositions we use four voices: soprano, alto, tenor, and bass. In choral compositions the notes of the triad are spaced among the four voices.

Johann Sebastian Bach (1685–1750)

In this text we are introducing you to chord progressions written in **keyboard style**. In keyboard style, notice that the soprano, alto, and tenor voices are played by the right hand while the bass voice is played by the left hand. The following chord progression, written in keyboard style.

Tonic and Dominant Chord Progressions in a Major Key

Since triads have only three notes, we need to double a note of the triad. We double the bass note of the tonic and dominant triads to strengthen the harmonic function of these chords. In root-position chords the bass note and root are the same.

The following chord progression is an example of a progression moving by a fifth. Chord progressions that move by a fifth that involve root-position triads need to keep common tones in the same voice part and move all other voice parts by a step to ensure smooth part writing, or voice leading. The term "voice leading" refers to how notes move from one chord to the next. Good voice leading means moving the smallest amount from one chord tone to the next. In a tonic to dominant progression, "*s*" is the common tone. When linking the tonic and dominant triads, remember to double the bass note, or root of the chord.

I–V–I Progression in Major

37-39

d	*t,*	*d*
s	*s*	*s*
m	*r*	*m*
d	*s*	*d*
I	**V**	**I**
T	**D**	**T**

m	*r*	*m*
d	*t*	*d*
s	*s*	*s*
d	*s*	*d*
I	**V**	**I**
T	**D**	**T**

s	*s*	*s*
m	*r*	*m*
d	*t*	*d*
d	*s*	*d*
I	**V**	**I**
T	**D**	**T**

This chord progression is one of the most common in music literature. Because of the instability of tones in the dominant chord, there is a strong gravitational attraction to notes of the tonic triad. We can say that the dominant chord creates tension and that the tonic chord provides a resolution to this tension.

11.3   Tonic and Dominant Functions in Minor

Ah Poor Bird

40

Sing, Memorize, and Analyze

40

Internalizing Music

1. Sing "Ah Poor Bird" and memorize the melody (Track 40).
2. As the instructor or another student plays "Ah Poor Bird," clap the melodic contour of the accompaniment or bass line.
3. Clap the melodic contour of the bass line as you sing the melody with solfège.
4. Pair off in the class.
5. Face your partner as student A sings the melody and claps the melodic contour and student B sings the lower accompanying part with solfège and claps the melodic contour.
6. Switch parts.

Analyzing What You Hear

1. Consider the notes that make up the pattern in the bass part. The notes of the bass part occur in four-beat patterns. How many different notes occur within the four-beat pattern? Name the notes with solfège syllables.
2. Are the beginning and ending notes of the accompaniment of "Ah Poor Bird" the same?
3. Sing the bass part as your instructor plays the melody.
4. Sing the melody with solfège syllables.
5. Sing the harmonic functions of "Ah Poor Bird" as your instructor plays the melody on the keyboard. What roman numerals would you use to analyze the chords in this song?

Constructing a Melodic Representation from Memory

Get a piece of staff paper. Write "Ah Poor Bird" in d minor. Write the melody in the treble clef and the accompanying bass notes in the bass clef.

Music Theory

La Minor

The bass line for "Ah Poor Bird" is composed of the notes *l,* and *m,* (we use a subscript to indicate that the notes are lower than *d*); these notes of the bass line are the tonic and dominant notes in a minor key. They also represent tonic and dominant functions.

l,	*m,*	*l,*
Tonic	Dominant	Tonic
T	D	T

Ah Poor Bird

Music Theory	***Do Minor***

The bass line for "Ah Poor Bird" is composed of a *d* and *s,* accompaniment; these notes of the bass line are the tonic and dominant notes in a minor key.

d	*s,*	*d*
Tonic	Dominant	Tonic
T	D	T

Ah Poor Bird

11.4 Tonic and Dominant Chord Progressions in Minor

In Unit 11.3 we discovered that we can harmonize a melody with tonic and dominant functions.

When harmonizing minor melodies, we use the harmonic minor form of the minor scale. This means that the dominant chord is major. Both chord i and chord V are primary triads. Chord i has a tonic function and is minor and chord V has a dominant function and is major.

41-43

i–V–i Progression in Minor

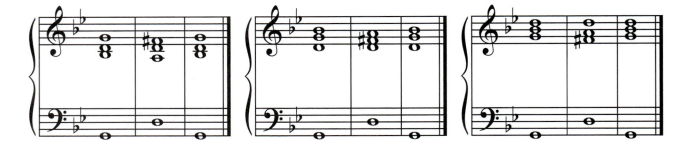

11.5 Tonic, Subdominant, and Dominant Functions in Major

White Sand and Gray Sand

Sing, Memorize, and Analyze

44

Internalizing Music

1. Sing "White Sand and Gray Sand" and memorize the melody (Track 44).
2. As the instructor or another student plays "White Sand and Gray Sand," clap the melodic contour of the accompaniment or bass line.
3. Clap the melodic contour of the bass line as you sing the melody with solfège.
4. Pair off in the class.
5. Face your partner as student A sings the melody and claps the melodic contour and student B sings the lower accompanying part with solfège and claps the melodic contour.
6. Switch parts.

Analyzing What You Hear

1. Consider the bass part. The notes occur in four-beat patterns. How many different notes occur within the four-beat pattern? Name the notes with solfège syllables.
2. Are the beginning and ending notes of the accompaniment of "White Sand and Gray Sand" the same?
3. Sing the bass part as your instructor plays the melody.
4. Sing the melody with solfège syllables.
5. Divide the class. Group A sings the melody with solfège syllables. Group B sings the bass part with solfège syllables. Switch parts.

Constructing a Melodic Representation from Memory

Get a piece of staff paper. Write "White Sand and Gray Sand" in G major. Write the melody in the treble clef and the accompanying bass notes in the bass clef.

Music Theory

The bass line for "White Sand and Gray Sand" can be harmonized by three different solfège notes: *d*, *f*, and *s*. These solfège syllables represent the tonic, subdominant, and dominant functions: *d* is the tonic, *s*, is the dominant, and *f*, is the subdominant.

d	*f,*	*s,*	*d*
Tonic	Subdominant	Dominant	Tonic
T	S	D	T

White Sand And Gray Sand

Listening 🎧   As you listen to these examples, try to identify tonic, subdominant, and dominant functions.

Violin Concerto in D, Movement 1 (principal theme), by Ludwig van Beethoven (1770–1827).

"Music Alone Shall Live," on the album *Psimple Psaltery Tunes*.

11.6 Primary Triads: Tonic, Subdominant, and Dominant Chord Progression in a Major Key

The tonic, subdominant, and dominant chords are referred to as the **primary chords**. In root position, the subdominant chord has its root doubled to strengthen the subdominant function. Voice leading in close position follows the same principles as the progression from tonic to dominant: the common tone is kept and the upper parts move by step.

I–IV–V – I Chord Progression in Major

45-47

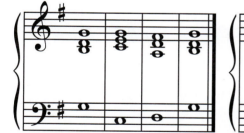

d	d	t	d
s	l	s	s
m	f	r	m
d	f,	s,	d
I	**IV**	**V**	**I**
T	**S**	**D**	**T**

m	f	r	m
d	d	t	d
s	l	s	s
d	f,	s,	d
I	**IV**	**V**	**I**
T	**S**	**D**	**T**

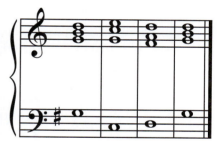

s	l	s	s
m	f	r	m
d	d	t	d
d	f,	s,	d
I	**IV**	**V**	**I**
T	**S**	**D**	**T**

11.7   Tonic, Subdominant, and Dominant Functions in Minor

Willum
48

Sing, Memorize, and Analyze	**Internalizing Music**

1. Sing "Willum" and memorize the melody.

2. As the instructor or another student plays "Willum," clap the melodic contour of the accompaniment or bass line.

3. Clap the melodic contour of the bass line as you sing the melody with solfège syllables.

4. Pair off in the class.

5. Face your partner as student A sings the melody and claps the melodic contour and student B sings the lower accompanying part with solfège and claps the melodic contour.

6. Switch parts.

Analyzing What You Hear

1. Consider the bass part. The notes occur in four-beat patterns. How many different notes occur within the four-beat pattern? Name the notes with solfège syllables.

2. Are the beginning and ending notes of the accompaniment of "Willum" the same?

3. Sing the bass part as your instructor plays the melody.

4. Sing the melody with solfège syllables.

5. Divide the class. Group A sings the melody with solfège syllables. Group B sings the bass part with solfège syllables. Switch parts.

Constructing a Melodic Representation from Memory

Get a piece of staff paper. Write "Willum" in d minor. Write the melody in the treble clef and the accompanying bass notes in the bass clef.

Music Theory	**La Minor**

The bass line for "Willum" is composed of the solfège syllables *l,*, *r,*, and *m,*. These solfège syllables are the tonic, subdominant, and dominant notes and represent the tonic, subdominant, and dominant functions.

l,	*r,*	*m,*	*l*
Tonic	Subdominant	Dominant	Tonic
T	S	D	T

Do Minor

The bass line for "Willum" is composed of the solfège syllables *d,*, *f,*, and *s,*. These solfège syllables are the tonic, subdominant and dominant notes.

d	*f,*	*s,*	*d*
Tonic	Subdominant	Dominant	Tonic
T	S	D	T

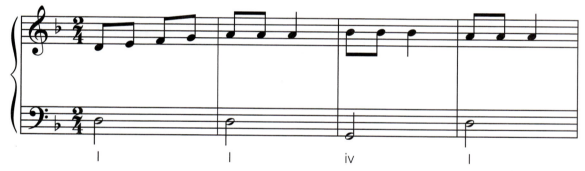

11.8 Primary Triads: Tonic, Subdominant, and Dominant Chord Progression in a Minor Key

i – iv – V – i Progression in Minor

49-51

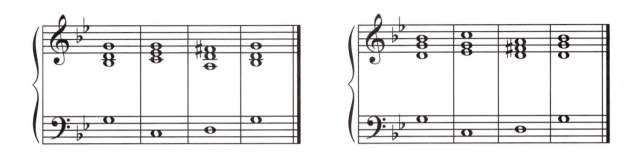

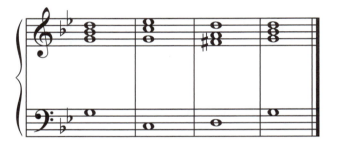

Scale Degrees and Primary Chords

The primary chords contain all of the seven tones of the scale in both major and minor keys. Thus any melody can be harmonized with these three chords. The tonic chord contains scale degrees 1, 3, and 5. The subdominant chord contains scale degrees 4, 6, and 1. The dominant chord contains scale degrees 5, 7, and 2.

11.9 Cadences

A **cadence** is a melodic or harmonic motion conventionally associated with the ending of a phrase, section, movement, or composition. It emphasizes arrival on the interval or chord most fundamental to the tonality of a passage.

A cadence is a point of rest or closure in a musical phrase; therefore, every phrase of a piece ends with a cadence. Rhythm, melodic line, and a harmonic progression combine to create a cadence. Cadences are normally composed of two chords. There are four different types of cadences that occur in music: authentic, half, plagal, and deceptive.

Note the second and third chords in measure two of the Bach chorale. Chord V moving to chord I is commonly referred to as an **authentic**, or full, cadence.

Chorale

Johann Sebastian Bach (1685–1750)

52

A **half cadence** is any chord followed by chord V. Chord IV going to chord V is a half cadence. Also, a half cadence is a point of rest at the end of a phrase leaving the piece of music unfinished. A half cadence normally consists of the dominant chord preceded by any other chord (most commonly I or IV). This cadence is used in every style of music, including classical and jazz.

In the following sonatina, the first phrase ends with a half cadence (measure four) and the second phrase ends with an authentic cadence.

Sonatina in C major, Op. 55, No.1, Movement 2   Friedrich Kuhlau (1786–1832)

53

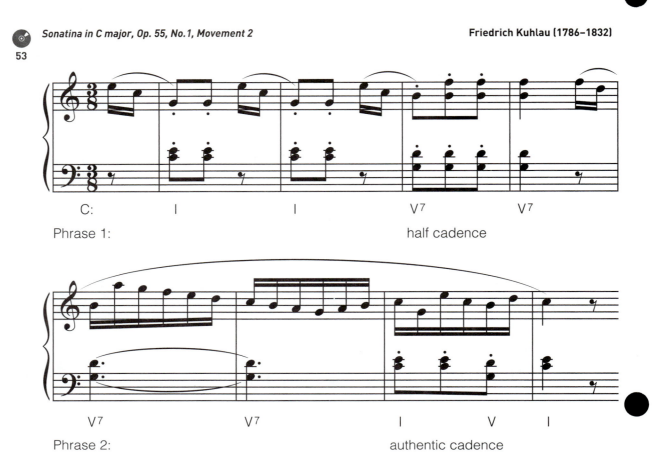

A **plagal cadence** consists of a tonic chord preceded by a subdominant chord. This is traditionally known as the "amen cadence." A plagal cadence is chord IV going to chord I. In comparison with the authentic cadence, it is not as strong.

Response   Marc'Antonio Ingegneri (c. 1547–1592)

54

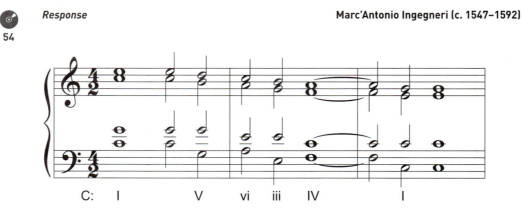

The **deceptive cadence** consists of the submediant chord preceded by the dominant chord. When we hear the dominant chord at the end of a phrase, we expect it to resolve to the tonic chord, but instead we hear the submediant chord.

The Marriage of Figaro (excerpt)   Wolfgang Amadeus Mozart (1756–1791)

11.10   An Introduction to Nonharmonic Tones, or Nonchord Tones

All melodies are composed of chord tones—notes belonging to a chord—and other notes that are not related to a chord and are commonly referred to as *nonchord tones*, or *nonharmonic tones*. In other words, not all pitches in a melody are chord tones. There are several types of nonharmonic tones. The note preceding the nonharmonic tone and the note to which it resolves are normally chord tones. In the following examples, we have provided the triads in the bass clef for you to play with the notes of the melody.

Passing Tone
56

Passing tones (PT) normally connect two chord tones a third apart. The passing tone may be accented or unaccented and part of an ascending or descending pattern. In the following example, B is not a chord tone—it does not belong to the A major chord. C-sharp and A are chord tones. Note that the B moves by step to the chord tone A. B is called a passing tone.

Appoggiatura
57

In the following example, D is not a chord tone—it does not belong to the A major chord. C-sharp is a chord tone. Note that the D moves by step to the chord tone C-sharp. In this example, the note D is an **appoggiatura**. The appoggiatura (APP) is approached by a leap and descends by a step.

Neighbor Tone
58

The **neighbor tone** (NT) is approached by a step and returns by a step and may occur on a strong or weak beat. In the following example, G-sharp is not a chord tone—it does not belong to the A major chord. A is a chord tone. Note that the G-sharp moves by step to the chord tone A. G-sharp is called a lower neighbor tone. If we substituted a B for the G-sharp, we would have an upper neighbor tone.

11.11 Chord Progressions Involving Secondary Triads

The Supertonic Triad

Sing, Memorize, and Analyze

59

Internalizing Music

Listen as your instructor plays the following musical excerpt.

Symphony No. 92, ("Oxford"), Movement 1   **Joseph Haydn (1732–1809)**

Analyzing What You Hear

1. After you have listened to this segment several times, sing the names of the harmonic functions you hear as your instructor plays the example.
2. Sing the bass line with solfège syllables.

Music Theory

The supertonic triad has a subdominant function (measure two of the above example), or predominant function. It usually precedes dominant-function chords. We can note that it occurs before chord V in measure three. The supertonic triad is a minor triad in major keys and a diminished triad in minor keys. The chord often appears in first inversion. Where possible, the third of the chord should be doubled to strengthen the subdominant function. The following is an example of a tonic, subdominant, dominant, tonic progression where the supertonic chord appears in the first inversion.

🔘 **Major**
60-61

d	r	t	d		m	f	r	m
s	l	s	s		d	r	t	d
m	f	r	m		s	l	s	s
d	f,	s,	d		d	f,	s,	d
I	**II⁶**	**V**	**I**		**I**	**II⁶**	**V**	**I**
T	**S**	**D**	**T**		**T**	**S**	**D**	**T**

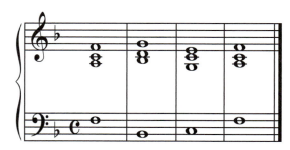
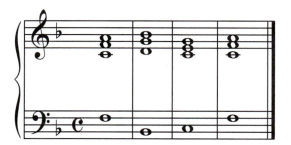

 Minor
62-63

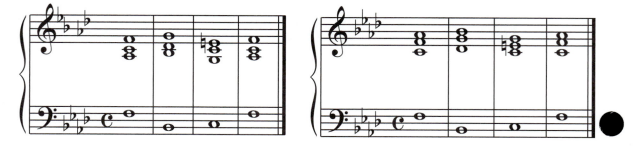

We now have an example of an exception to keeping the common tone. If we did keep the common tone, we would have the following chord progression:

d	r	r	m
s	l	t	d
m	f	s	s
d	f,	s,	d
I	**II⁶**	**V**	**I**

Notice that we have a parallel octave between the tenor and bass in the ii⁶ and chord V. In voice leading, we avoid parallel octaves and fifths as this lessens the richness of the harmony. We would have two voices moving in parallel motion with the same pitches, creating parallel octave motion.

The Submediant Chord

Sing, Memorize, and Analyze

64

Internalizing Music

Listen as your instructor plays the following musical excerpt.

The Marriage of Figaro, Excerpt   **Wolfgang Amadeus Mozart (1756–1791)**

Analyzing What You Hear

1. After you have listened to this segment several times, sing the names of the harmonic functions you hear as your instructor plays the example.
2. Sing the bass line with solfège syllables.
3. Analyze each chord using solfège syllables and provide a roman numeral analysis.

| Music Theory | The submediant triad is built on the sixth degree of the scale and consists of scale degrees 6, 1, and 3. When the submediant triad follows chord V in a cadence, it assumes a tonic function. Therefore the third of the chord should be doubled to strengthen the tonic function. The submediant chord is also commonly used to fill the musical space between the opening tonic chord and the subdominant or dominant chord. |

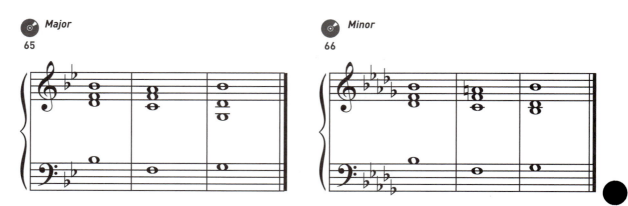

Major
65

Minor
66

11.12   Chord Progressions Involving the Tonic Six-Four Chord as a Cadential Chord

Sing, Memorize, and Analyze

Internalizing Music

Listen as your instructor plays the following musical excerpt.

67

Sonatina in G Major, Movement Two   **Ludwig van Beethoven (1770–1827)**

Analyzing What You Hear

1. Sing the melody with solfège syllables.
2. After you have listened to this segment several times, sing the names of the harmonic functions you hear as your instructor plays the example.
3. Sing the bass line with solfège syllables.
4. Analyze each chord using solfège syllables and provide a roman numeral analysis.

| Music Theory | The second inversion of the tonic chord can only be used in certain cases. One example of this is when the chord precedes a dominant chord in a cadence. It normally occurs on a beat stronger than the dominant chord. When chord I $\frac{6}{4}$ moves to chord V, it has a dominant function. We generally double the bass note of the tonic $\frac{6}{4}$ when moving to chord V. This emphasizes the dominant function of the chord. |

Major

68-70

d'	d'	d'	t	d'
s	l	s	s	m
m	f	m	r	d
d	f,	s,	s,	l,
I	**IV**	**I$\frac{6}{4}$**	**V**	**VI**

m'	f'	m'	r	d
d	d	d	t	d
s	l	s	s	m
d	f,	s,	s,	l,
I	**IV**	**I$\frac{6}{4}$**	**V**	**VI**

s	l	s	s	m
m	f	m	r	d
d	d	d	t	d
d	f,	s,	s,	l,
I	**IV**	**I$\frac{6}{4}$**	**V**	**VI**

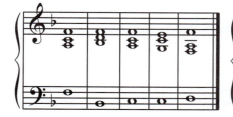

Minor

71-73

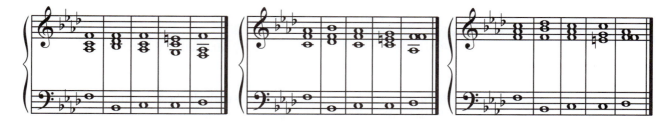

The above are exercises to practice typical chord progressions involving the tonic six-four chord.

11.13   Twelve-Bar Blues Progression

The twelve-bar blues chord progression is the basis of jazz, pop, and rock songs such as "One O'Clock Jump," "Night Train," Glenn Miller's "In the Mood," and The Beatles' "Why Don't We Do It in the Road?" The twelve-bar blues progression is based on the tonic, subdominant, and dominant chords. This chord progression occurs over three phrases:

Phrase 1:	I	I	I	I
Phrase 2:	IV	IV	I	I
Phrase 3:	V	V	I	I

Your instructor will play for you examples of the twelve-bar blues progression. Try to point to the chords as you listen to the examples several times.

Key Terms and Concepts

Chord Progression	Authentic Cadence	Appoggiatura
Harmonic Functions	Half Cadence	Neighbor Tone
Keyboard Style	Plagal Cadence	Twelve-Bar Blues
Primary Chords	Deceptive Cadence	Progression
Cadence	Passing Tone	

How to Practice

Here are some useful suggestions for practicing melody in a variety of ways. Remember to keep practicing in small groups with your peers.

Skill Development and Ear Training Exercises for Chord Progressions	Listen as the instructor plays a cadence on the keyboard and names the note. Students sing the bass notes and name the type of chord progression or cadence. The instructor plays a pitch from the keyboard and asks students to sing a specific chord progression.
Performing	Sing all of the chord progressions in the chapter with solfège and scale degree numbers.
Sight Singing	Sing "Paw Paw Patch" with solfège syllables. Sing "Paw Paw Patch" with numbers. Sing "Paw Paw Patch" with solfège and accompany with harmonic functions. For the I–V–I chord progression in major and minor: 1. Sing each chord vertically from the lowest note to the highest. In other words, sing the note in the bass voice, then sing the next note up from the bass, which is the tenor, followed by the alto, and finally the soprano. 2. Sing the soprano line and play the bass line on the piano in different keys. 3. Sing the chord progression in four parts with other class members. 4. We can use the tonic-dominant chord progression to harmonize "Paw Paw Patch." Which notes are harmonized by the tonic and dominant chords? 5. Sing the chord progression in four parts with other class members.

For the I–IV–V–I chord progression in major:
1. Sing each chord vertically from the lowest note to the highest. Sing the soprano line and play the bass line on the piano in different keys.
2. Sing the chord progression in four parts with other class members.
3. We can use the primary chords to harmonize "White Sands and Gray Sands." Chord I is used for the tonic function, chord IV for a subdominant function, and chord V for a dominant function. Sing "White Sands and Gray Sands" and accompany using the chords and voicing provided in this unit.

For the i–iv–V–i chord progression:
1. Sing each chord vertically from the lowest note to the highest. Sing the soprano line and play the bass line on the piano in different keys.
2. Sing the chord progression in four parts with other class members.
3. We can use the primary chords to harmonize "Willum." Chord i is used for the tonic function, chord iv for a subdominant function, and chord V for a dominant function. Sing "Willum" and accompany using the chords and voicing provided in this unit.

For the tonic, dominant, and submediant chord progressions:
1. Sing each chord vertically from the lowest note to the highest. Sing the soprano line and play the bass line on the piano in different keys.
2. Sing the chord progression in four parts with other class members.

Dictation

Instructor hums or plays a series of chords. Students must sing back with neutral syllables and solfège.

Students sing the chord progression with syllables and notate the chord progression in a given key.

Using the Musical Skills CD

Access Chapter 11 on the skills CD to reinforce your knowledge of chord progressions. You will be provided with the opportunity to practice the notation of chord progressions in major and minor.

MUSIC THEORY EXERCISES

11.1 Exercises: Tonic and Dominant Functions in a Major Key

Exercise 11.1

Name the major key and write the tonic and dominant notes of that key on the staff.

Eb Major: Tonic   Dominant

1._____

2._____

3._____

4._____

5._____

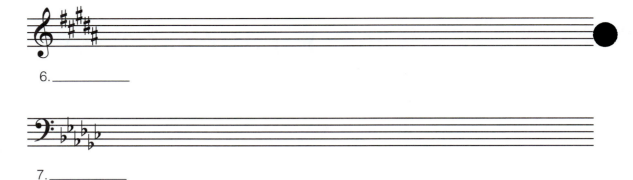

6.————————

7.————————

Writing an Accompaniment Using Tonic and Dominant Notes

Exercise 11.2

Write the harmonic accompaniment made up of the tonic and dominant notes for the following melodies. Please observe the correspondences between the bass note and the melody notes.

Procedure:
1. Sing each melody with solfège syllables.
2. While you sing each melody, try to accompany it with notes that represent the tonic and dominant functions on the piano.
3. Sing the notes that represent the harmonic functions and play the melody on the piano.
4. Write in the bass notes.
5. For now, let your ear decide (along with the help of your instructor) what notes can be accompanied by tonic and dominant functions.

Kitty Put the Kettle On

Love Somebody

London Bridge

Paw Paw Patch

Skip to My Lou

Skip to My Lou   *(continued)*

I's the B'y

Newfoundland Folk Song

Bonjour Pierrot

French Folk Song

Derry Ding Dong Dason

English Canon

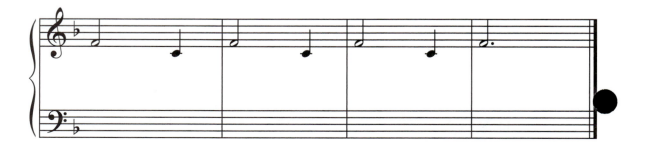

11.2   Exercises: Tonic and Dominant Chord Progressions

Exercise 11.3

Write the following progressions on the staff in G major, F major, B-flat major, and D major. Use treble and bass cleff. Put the top three voices in the treble clef.

d	t,	d
s	s	s
m	r	m
d	s	d
I	**V**	**I**
T	**D**	**T**

m	r	m
d	t	d
s	s	s
d	s	d
I	**V**	**I**
T	**D**	**T**

s	s	s
m	r	m
d	t	d
d	s	d
I	**V**	**I**
T	**D**	**T**

Exercise 11.4

Identify the common tones in these exercises by drawing horizontal lines between them. Write the name of each chord above the staff.

F major example:

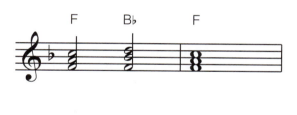

Exercise 11.5

Circle the common tone in each of the following chord progressions.

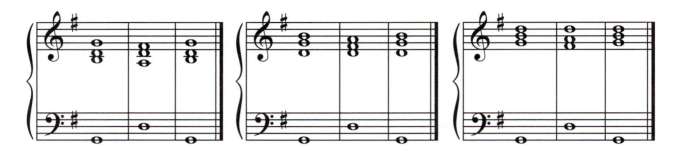

Exercise 11.6

1. Write a tonic-dominant-tonic chord progression in the key of F major. Include roman numerals beneath the chords.

2. Write a tonic-dominant-tonic chord progression in the key of B-flat major. Include roman numerals beneath the chords.

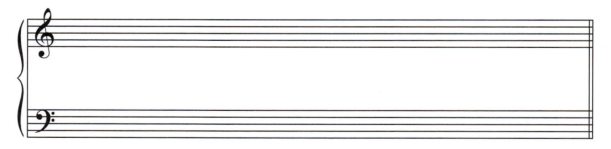

3. Write a tonic-dominant-tonic chord progression in the key of D major. Include roman numerals beneath the chords.

11.3   Exercises: Tonic and Dominant Functions in Minor

Exercise 11.7

Name the minor key and write the tonic and dominant notes on the staff.

C minor: Tonic   Dominant

1._____

2._____

3._____

4._____

5._____

6._____

7._____

Exercise 11.8

Write the harmonic accompaniment on the bass staff for each of the following melodies. Observe the correspondence between the bass notes and melody notes.

Procedure:

1. Sing each melody with solfège syllables.
2. While you sing each melody, try to accompany it with tonic and dominant functions on the piano.
3. Sing the functions and play the melody.
4. Write in the bass notes.

I's the B'y (minor)

I's the B'y (minor)   *(continued)*

Love Somebody (minor)

Exercise 11.9

Using your own staff paper, compose an eight-measure melody in G major that fits the following harmonic functions. Select a time signature and a clef. Use only the notes of the tonic, subdominant, and dominant triads.

Tonic | Dominant | Tonic | Dominant |

Tonic | Subdominant | Dominant | Tonic | |

11.4   Exercises: Tonic and Dominant Chord Progressions in Minor

Exercise 11.10

1. Add solfège to the following chord progressions.
2. Indicate the common tone.
3. Using your own staff paper, write these progressions in the keys of D, F, C, and F-sharp minor.

i–V–i Progression in Minor

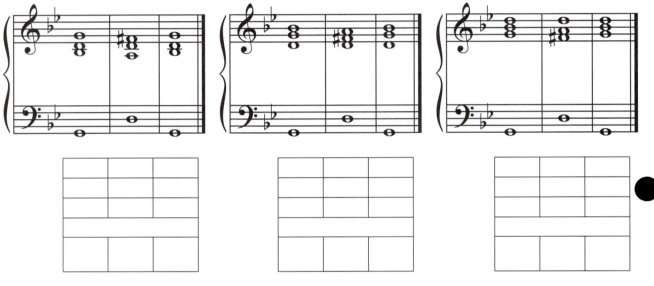

Exercise 11.11

1. Write a tonic-dominant-tonic chord progression in the key of d minor.
2. Include roman numerals beneath each chord.

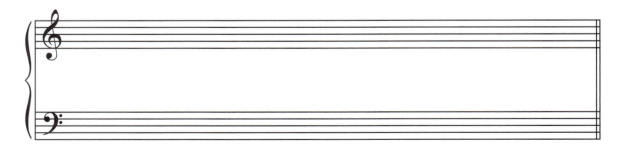

3. Write a tonic-dominant-tonic chord progression in the key of b minor.
4. Include roman numerals beneath each chord.

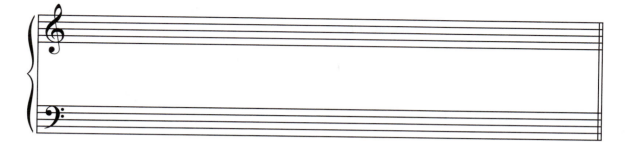

5. Write a tonic-dominant-tonic chord progression in the key of c minor.
6. Include roman numerals beneath each chord.

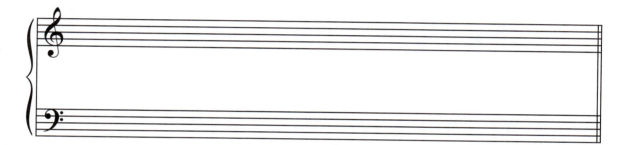

Exercise 11.12

1. Compose an eight-measure melody in g minor that fits the following harmonic functions. Select a time signature and a clef.
2. Try to use only the notes of the tonic, subdominant, and dominant triads.

Tonic		Dominant		Tonic		Dominant	
Tonic		Subdominant		Dominant		Tonic	||

11.5   Exercise: Tonic, Subdominant, and Dominant Functions in Major

Exercise 11.13

Write the harmonic accompaniment on the bass staff for each of the following melodies using the tonic, subdominant, and dominant notes.

Let's Go A-Huntin'   **Texas Folk Song**

Music Alone Shall Live

11.6   Exercises: Primary Triads: Tonic, Subdominant, and Dominant Chords in Root Position in a Major Key

Exercise 11.14

Name the major key for each of the following key signatures and write the tonic, subdominant, and dominant on the staff.

G Major: Tonic   Subdominant   Dominant

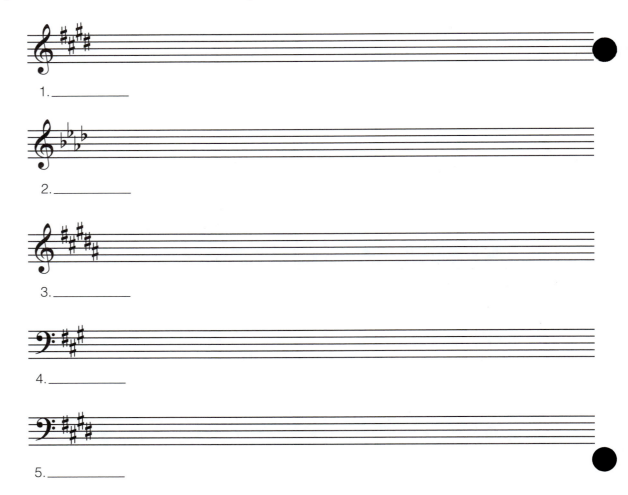

1._____

2._____

3._____

4._____

5._____

Exercise 11.15

1. Write the primary triads (I, IV, V) in each of the following major keys. Remember to write the proper key signature for each example.
2. Label each chord with the appropriate roman numeral.

E♭ major

1. D♭ major   2. F major

3. D major   4. C major

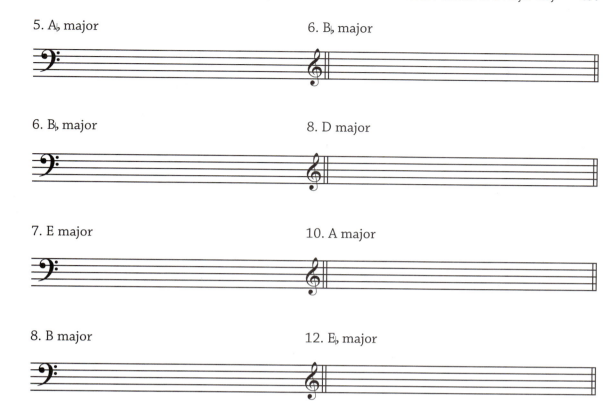

5. A♭ major

6. B♭ major

6. B♭ major

8. D major

7. E major

10. A major

8. B major

12. E♭ major

Exercise 11.16

Add the solfège syllables to the following chord progressions. Identify the common tones.

Exercise 11.17

Using your own staff paper, write the following chord progressions in G, F, B-flat, and A major.

d	d	t	d
s	l	s	s
m	f	r	m
d	f,	s,	d
I	**IV**	**V**	**I**
T	**S**	**D**	**T**

m	f	r	m
d	d	t	d
s	l	s	s
d	f,	s,	d
I	**IV**	**V**	**I**
T	**S**	**D**	**T**

s	l	s	s
m	f	r	m
d	d	t	d
d	f,	s,	d
I	**IV**	**V**	**I**
T	**S**	**D**	**T**

Exercise 11.18

Analyze the following chord progressions using roman numerals.

Cantate Domino   Guiseppe Ottavio Pitoni (1657–1743)

11.7 Exercises: Tonic, Subdominant, and Dominant Functions in Minor

Exercise 11.19

Write the harmonic accompaniment on the bass staff for each of the following melodies using tonic, subdominant, and dominant notes.

Procedure:
1. Sing each melody with solfège syllables.
2. While you sing each melody, try to accompany it with tonic and dominant functions on the piano.
3. Sing the functions and play the melody.
4. Write in the bass notes.

Music Alone Shall Live *German Round*

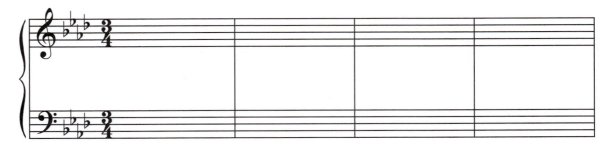

Exercise 11.20

Transpose "Music Alone Shall Live" to f minor. Be certain to add the harmonic accompaniment.

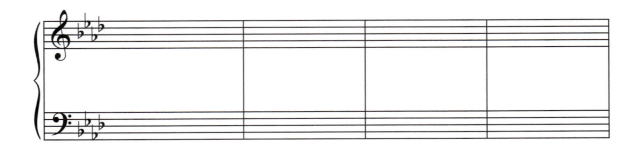

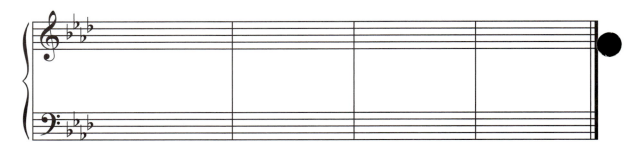

11.8 Exercises: Primary Triads: Tonic, Subdominant, and Dominant Chords in Root Position in a Minor Key

Exercise 11.21

Name the minor key for each of the following key signatures and write the tonic, subdominant, and dominant chords on the staff.

Example:

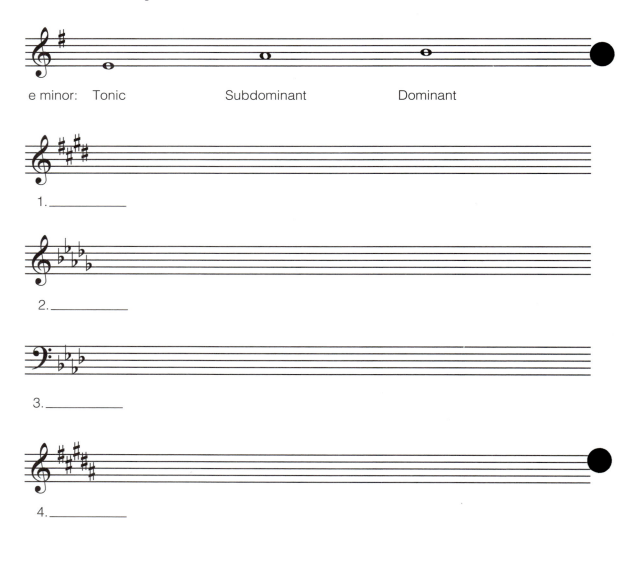

e minor: Tonic   Subdominant   Dominant

1._____

2._____

3._____

4._____

Exercise 11.22

1. Write the primary triads (i, iv, V) in each of the following minor keys.
2. Use the harmonic minor form of the scale for each key and remember to write the proper key signature. Label each chord with the appropriate roman numeral.

Example: d minor

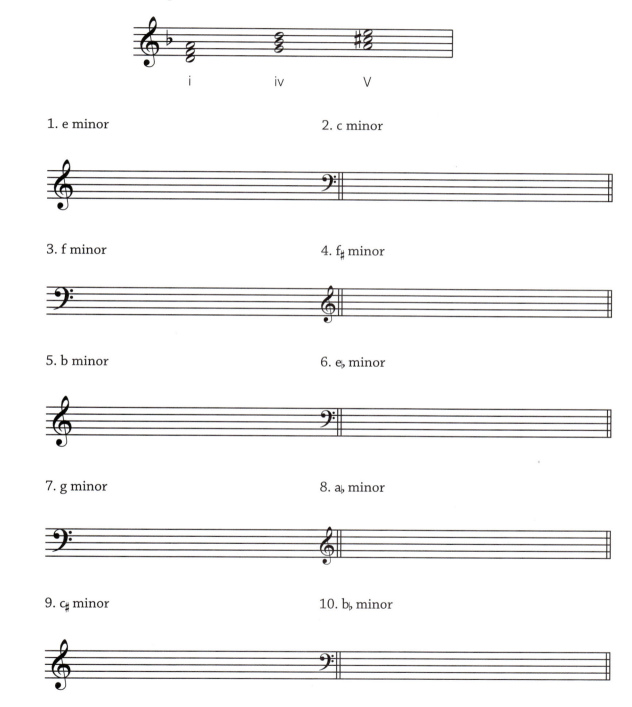

1. e minor   2. c minor

3. f minor   4. f♯ minor

5. b minor   6. e♭ minor

7. g minor   8. a♭ minor

9. c♯ minor   10. b♭ minor

11. a minor   12. e minor

Exercise 11.23

1. Write a tonic-subdominant-dominant-tonic chord progression in the key of g
   minor. Include roman numerals.

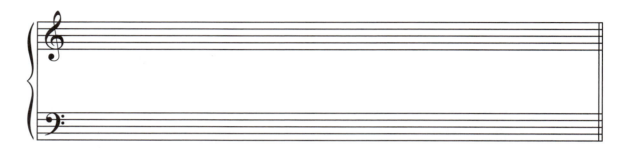

2. Write a tonic-subdominant-dominant-tonic chord progression in the key of d
   minor. Include roman numerals.

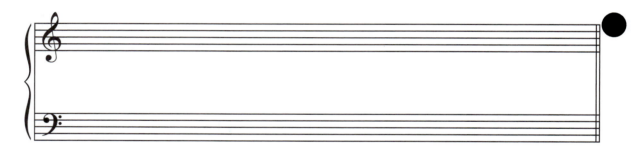

3. Write a tonic-subdominant-dominant-tonic chord progression in the key of e
   minor. Include roman numerals.

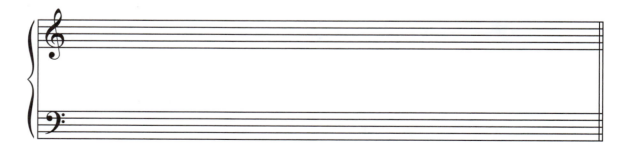

Exercise 11.24

1. Write a tonic-subdominant-dominant-tonic chord progression in the key of c minor. Include roman numerals.

2. Write a tonic-subdominant-dominant-tonic chord progression in the key of b minor. Include roman numerals.

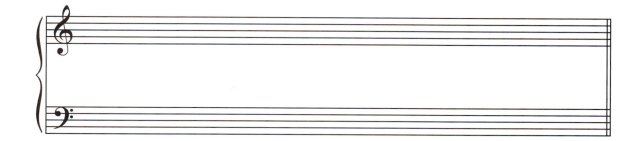

3. Write a tonic-subdominant-dominant-tonic chord progression in the key of g minor. Include roman numerals.

Exercise 11.25

1. Compose an eight-measure melody in g minor following the harmonic functions listed below.
2. Select a time signature. Try to use only the notes of the tonic, subdominant, and dominant triads.

Tonic	Dominant	Tonic	Dominant	
Tonic	Subdominant	Dominant	Tonic	‖

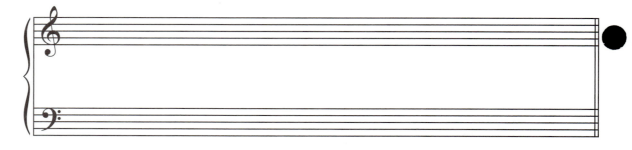

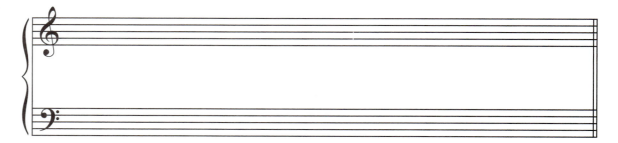

11.9   Exercises: Cadences

Exercise 11.26

Identify the cadences at the end of each phrase of "The First Noel."

The First Noel

Exercise 11-27

Identify the cadences at the end of each phrase of the Haydn sonata.

Sonata in D Major, Movement 3   **Joseph Haydn (1732–1809)**

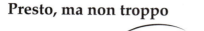

11.10 Exercises: An Introduction to Nonharmonic Tones, or Nonchord Tones

Exercise 11.28

Circle and name the nonharmonic tones in "Simple Gifts."

Simple Gifts

Exercise 11.29

Circle and name the nonharmonic tones in "Silent Night."

Silent Night

11.11 Exercises: Chord Progressions Involving Secondary Triads

Exercise 11.30

Analyze the phrases, cadences, and chords in the excerpt from Mozart's *Magic Flute*.

The Magic Flute (excerpt)   **Wolfgang Amadeus Mozart (1756–1791)**

Exercise 11.31

Analyze the chords, then circle and identify the nonharmonic tones.

Enchanting Bells   **Wolfgang Amadeus Mozart (1756–1791)**

Exercise 11.32

Identify the chords, cadences, and nonharmonic tones.

Bird in the Pine Tree (excerpt)   **Johannes Brahms (1833–1897)**

Chapter 12

Composing a Song

CHAPTER OVERVIEW

This chapter provides us with the opportunity to compose a piece of music building on all of the musical knowledge and skills we have developed in the previous chapters. We will investigate how to create several possible word rhythms based on a given text. Once we have decided on the meter for a given text and how we can create word rhythms to reflect the accents of the words, we can decide on the time signature. Next we will learn how to set word rhythms to music. We need to decide on the tonality and compose a melody to fit the character of our text. We can harmonize this melody with some of the basic chord patterns learned in Chapter 11.

12.1 Choosing the Lyrics

A song is a short vocal composition. It may be for one or more voices, accompanied or unaccompanied, sacred or secular, and is usually self-contained. There are several types of songs (folk song, part song, art song), but the term is generally taken to denote a secular piece of music. Songs may be unaccompanied or harmonized.

Begin the process of composing a song by choosing a text. Some composers use existing poems or lyrics for their music composition. Others compose a melody first and add the text later. George Gershwin composed many melodies to lyrics composed by his brother Ira. It is important to recognize that the style, rhythms, meter, form, and tonality for your song will be influenced by your choice of text.

Following are the texts of several songs that have been recorded by various artists. Each song contains several different verses, or stanzas. Look for recordings (many examples are available on YouTube) of the following songs and note the different stylistic approaches to the settings of the text.

Liza Jane   Traditional American Folk Song

Come my love and go with me, Little 'Liza Jane,
Come my love and go with me, Little 'Liza Jane.
O, Eliza, Little 'Liza Jane.
O, Eliza, Little 'Liza Jane.

I've got a house in Baltimore, Little 'Liza Jane
Street car runs right by my door, Little 'Liza Jane.
O, Eliza, Little 'Liza Jane.
O, Eliza, Little 'Liza Jane.

Scarborough Fair   Traditional English Folk Song

Are you going to Scarborough Fair?
Parsley, sage, rosemary, and thyme.
Remember me to one who lives there,
For once she was a true love of mine.

Tell her to make me a cambric shirt.
Parsley, sage, rosemary, and thyme.
Without no seams nor needle work,
Then she'll be a true love of mine.

Barbara Allen   Traditional English Folk Song

In Scarlet Town where I was born,
There was a fair maid dwelling,
Made ev'ry youth cry "Well a day!"
Her name was Barbara Allen

All in the merry month of May,
When green buds they were swelling,
Young Jimmy Grove on his deathbed lay,
For love of Barbara Allen.

Composition Activity 12.1

Read through the text of each of these folk songs and summarize what you believe the text is trying to express.

Liza Jane

Scarborough Fair

Barbara Allen

Composition Activity 12.2

Choose or write your own text. State the mood, effect, or image you're trying to create with your text.

12.2   Creating the Rhythmic Notation for Your Lyrics

Once you have either written your lyrics or chosen an existing text to use, say the lyrics out loud and accompany yourself by keeping the beat. Try to determine the metric accent; then determine if there are words that require a particular emphasis. Accenting words (verbal accents) in a text can convey various meanings. Look at the lyrics for "Liza Jane," "Scarborough Fair," and "Barbara Allen." Try reciting the text and accenting various words. Can accenting different words change the meaning of the text? Remember, your text can begin with an upbeat.

Review what you have learned about rhythms and meters in Chapters 1, 3, and 10. Consider our three songs, "Liza Jane," "Scarborough Fair," and "Barbara Allen." Clap the rhythm of each song as you say the lyrics.

Liza Jane

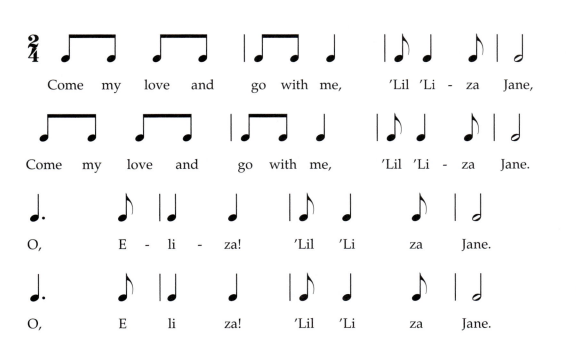

Scarborough Fair

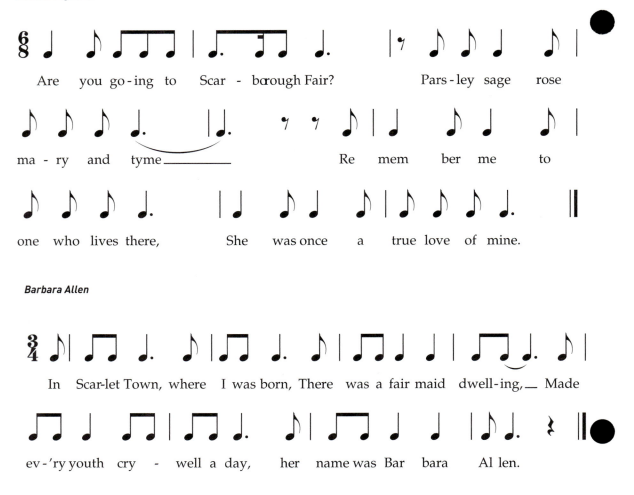

Are   you   go-ing to   Scar - borough Fair?   Pars-ley sage   rose

ma - ry   and   tyme_____   Re   mem   ber   me   to

one   who lives there,   She   was once   a   true love of mine.

Barbara Allen

In   Scar-let Town, where   I was born, There   was a fair maid   dwell-ing,__ Made

ev -'ry youth   cry - well a day,   her   name was Bar   bara   Al len.

What do you notice about the connection between the lyrics, meter, and rhythm? There are many different rhythmic possibilities for each of the above songs.

Composition Activity 12.3

Create another set of rhythmic notations for these texts.

Composition Activity 12.4

Create several rhythmic notations for your text.

12.3   Composing a Melody

Look at the text and decide whether to compose your melody in a major or minor tonality. Remember that for a major tonality you can use the major scale, the major pentatonic scale, or the major modes, Lydian and Mixolydian (see appendix). For a minor tonality you can use the three forms of the minor scale, the minor modes such as Phrygian or Dorian, or the minor pentatonic scale. Once you have determined the tonality of your composition, you can decide what key to write your composition in.

Remember to create phrasings in your song that will allow singers to breathe. It is important to remember that you are writing for voice and for now you should write your song in the range of an octave beginning around middle C.

Composition Activity 12.5

Analyze the key and tonality for each of the following compositions. Try writing these melodies in other tonalities and keys.

Barbara Allen

Liza Jane

Scarborough Fair

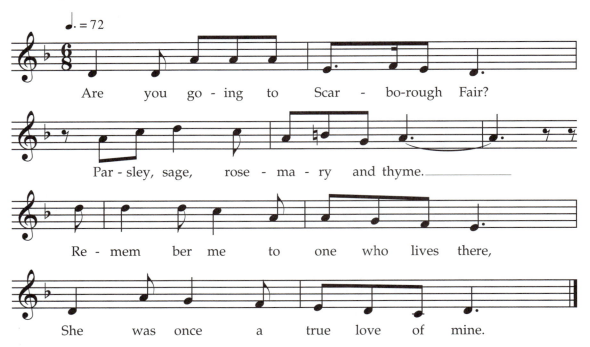

Are you go-ing to Scar - bo-rough Fair?

Par - sley, sage, rose - ma - ry and thyme.____

Re - mem ber me to one who lives there,

She was once a true love of mine.

Composition Activity 12.6

Decide on the tonality and key for your music composition. Compose a melody for your text. You might have to rework your melody several times to find the right one.

12.4 Unifying Your Composition

Rhythmic and/or melodic motives help you unify your composition. As you begin for experiment with creating the rhythmic notation for your text, look at how the rhythmic and melodic motives in "Liza Jane" play a role in the composition.

Liza Jane

Sing "Liza Jane" with rhythm syllables and solfège syllables.

The folk song is written in $\frac{2}{4}$ meter and has sixteen measures. When we arrange the pitches of "Liza Jane" in ascending order, we discover that there are five adjacent pitches. We can label these pitches with solfège syllables d – r – m – – s – l. We refer to this collection of notes as a major pentatonic scale or d pentatonic scale. The final note of the song "Liza Jane" is *d*.

A macroanalysis of the song indicates that there are two sections in the melody: section A and section B.

Each section may be perceived as two phrases. Therefore, the song has four phrases: a, a', b, b'.

The building blocks of these four phrases may be further broken down (micro-analysis) into motives. These motives built of pitch and rhythmic patterns are two measures long.

In the above example, the motives are:

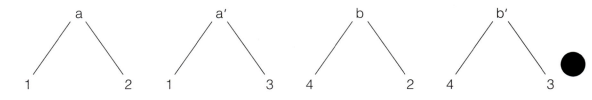

Each motive plays a role in defining the form of the complete folk song.

Note the contrast between the motives. Motive 1 is the beginning motive for phrases a and a′. Motive 4 is the beginning motive for phrases b and b′. Motive 2 turns phrase a into an open structure or a question, while motive 3 provides closure to both phrase a′ and phrase b′.

Motives 2 and 3 have the same rhythmic pattern.

The structure of the folk song provides an indication as to how the dynamics of the song should be performed. Motive 2 should be sung as a question, while motive 3 should be sung as an answer. Therefore, when performing this folk song, use suitable dynamics to bring out the structure of the melody.

Structural Hierarchy Summary of "Liza Jane"

In the above example, the motives are:

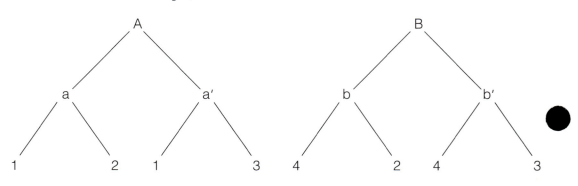

Composition Activity 12.7

Analyze the rhythmic structure of "Scarborough Fair" and "Barbara Allen."

Composition Activity 12.8

Create additional rhythmic and melodic notations for your chosen text, incorporating some repeating rhythmic motives.

Composition Activity 12.9

The form of "Au Claire de la Lune" is AABA. In this piece of music, each phrase is four measures long. The B section provides variety to the A section. AABA is a common form.

Create another version of the melody using a different form.

When this form is used in rock, popular music, and jazz, each phrase is normally eight measures in length, and is referred to as a 32-bar song form. Listen to the following recordings: "Frosty the Snowman," "Meet the Flintstones," "Somewhere Over the Rainbow," and "I Got Rhythm." Identify the form.

Composition Activity 12.10

Determine the form of "Greensleeves." Notice that the second phrase of this song is a variation of the first. We may indicate the form of phrase 1 and phrase 2 as a a'. When two phrases are related to each other, phrase 1 is called the *consequent* and phrase 2 is called the *antecedent*, and they may be referred to as a *period*. Because both phrases here use the same melodic and rhythmic material, this can be referred to as a *parallel period*. Two phrases that form a period but do not use the same musical material may be referred to as a *contrasting period*.

Greensleeves

A - las my love, ___ you do me wrong ___ to cast me off dis-

cour - teous-ly, And I have lov - ed you so long, ___ De -

light - ing in ___ your com-pa-ny. Green-sleeves ___ was all my joy, ___

Green - sleeves ___ was my de-light, Green - sleeves was my

heart of gold ___ And who but my la - dy Green - sleeves.

12.5   Harmonizing Your Composition

Your next task is to harmonize the melody you have composed; begin by using primary and secondary triads. Chords that are built on the supertonic, mediant, submediant, and leading tone degrees of the scale are called secondary chords or triads. The following figures illustrate secondary chords in a major and minor key.

Secondary triads in C major

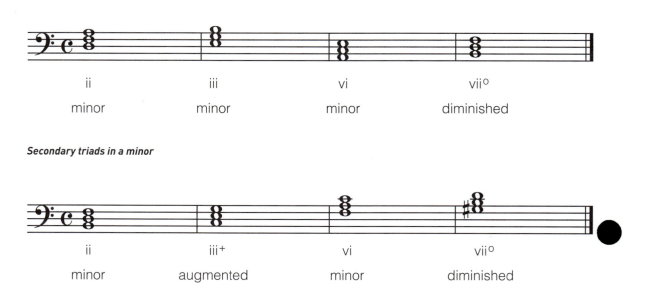

ii	iii	vi	vii°
minor	minor	minor	diminished

Secondary triads in a minor

ii	iii+	vi	vii°
minor	augmented	minor	diminished

The following figure illustrates the connection between primary and secondary triads. Sing the primary chords followed by the secondary chords and observe the notes that each chord shares with another chord.

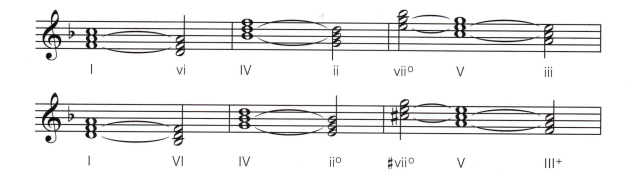

Secondary chords provide additional variety in harmonizations. For example: tonic-function chords include chord I and chord VI; subdominant-function chords include chord ii and chord IV; and dominant-function chords include V, V⁷, viii°, and iii.

Consider an example of a harmonization for "Barbara Allen" using primary chords and one using both primary and secondary chords. Sing and play through each example. Notice the musical effect of using a combination of primary and secondary chords.

"Barbara Allen" harmonized with primary chords:

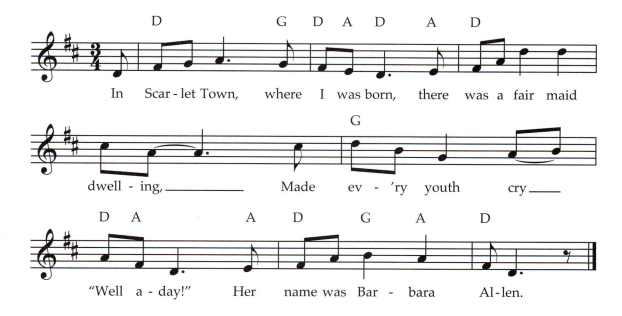

"Barbara Allen" harmonized with both primary chords and secondary chords:

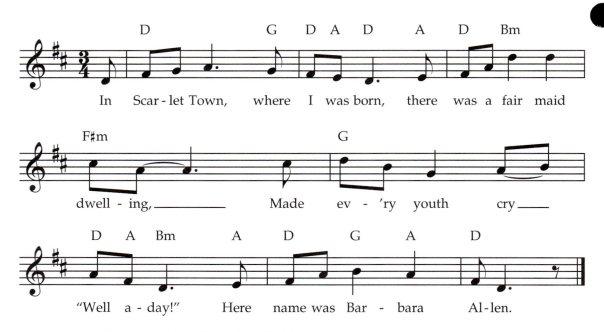

Composition Activity 12.11

Determine the harmonic functions for your composition. You can harmonize your melody using primary chords. Remember that your melody is composed of harmonic notes (notes belonging to a chord) and nonharmonic notes (notes that do not belong to a triad). It is also important to figure out the harmonic rhythm, the rate at which chords change in a piece of music. The harmonic rhythm will depend on the tempo of your composition.

Determine the phrases and then the cadences in your melody. Remember that the authentic cadence and plagal cadence sound finished while deceptive and half cadences are not as final sounding. Once you have harmonized your melody with primary chords try substituting some secondary chords in place of some primary chords. This will add interest and variety to your composition.

12.6 Determining an Appropriate Piano Accompaniment for Your Composition

Once you have determined the primary and secondary triads to be used in your music composition, your next task is to decide on an appropriate piano accompaniment. The following are examples of piano accompaniments. Composers generally use a variation of these when harmonizing melodies.

Accompanying with Block Chords

In this style of piano accompaniment, triads are arranged in block chords. Sometimes there are more than four notes in the chords, with several chord tones doubled. The following are examples of the different types of block-chord accompaniments.

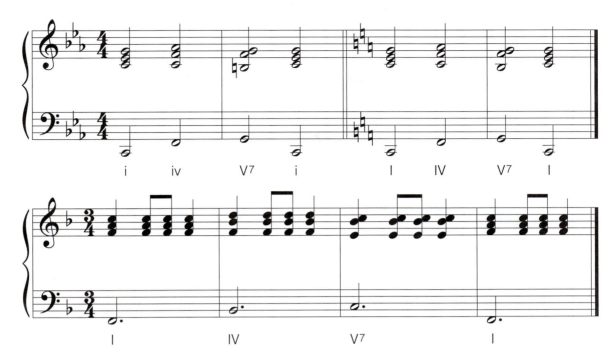

i   iv   V^7 i   I   IV   V^7 I

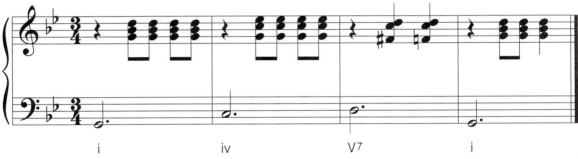

I   IV   V^7 I

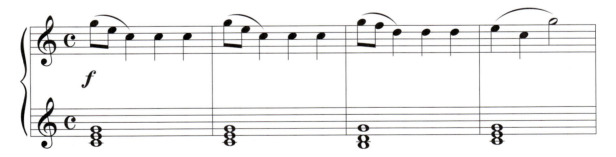

i   iv   V^7 i

The following dance by Czerny illustrates a block-chord accompaniment.

Dance, Op. 823, No. 11   **Carl Czerny (1791–1857)**

Accompanying with Arpeggiations, or Broken-Chord Patterns

In this style of accompaniment, each triad is broken into a pattern of melodic notes that is repeated throughout the duration of the music. Arpeggiations can be played by either the left hand or the right hand. Both classical and popular music composers use this type of accompaniment. The following are examples of chord accompaniments using arpeggios.

Once you've gained experience using block chords and arpeggiations as accompaniments, experiment with other styles of accompaniment.

The following waltz by Diabelli uses an arpeggiation-style accompaniment.

Waltz

Anton Diabelli (1781–1858)

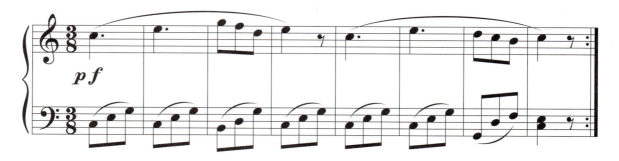

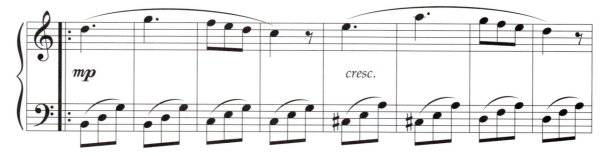

Music Composition Exercise 12.13

The chords for "Good-By Old Paint" are provided in the following musical example. Create a keyboard accompaniment to the song.

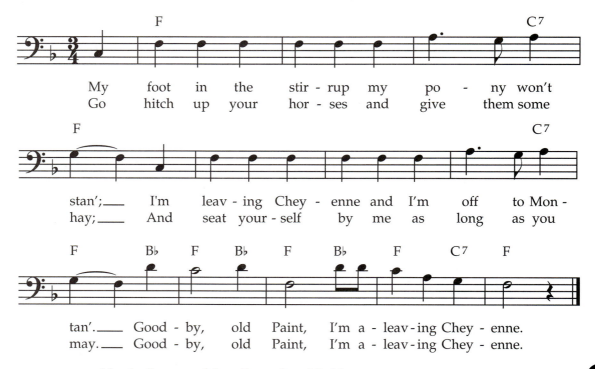

My foot in the stir - rup my po - ny won't
Go hitch up your hor - ses and give them some

stan';___ I'm leav - ing Chey - enne and I'm off to Mon -
hay;___ And seat your - self by me as long as you

tan'.___ Good - by, old Paint, I'm a - leav-ing Chey - enne.
may.___ Good - by, old Paint, I'm a - leav-ing Chey - enne.

Music Composition Exercise 12.14

The chords for "When the Saints Come Marching In" are provided in the following musical example. Create a keyboard accompaniment to the song.

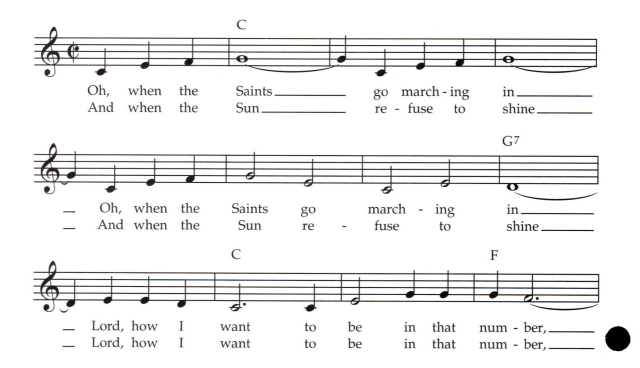

Oh, when the Saints___ go march - ing in___
And when the Sun___ re - fuse to shine___

___ Oh, when the Saints go march - ing in___
___ And when the Sun re - fuse to shine___

___ Lord, how I want to be in that num - ber,___
___ Lord, how I want to be in that num - ber,___

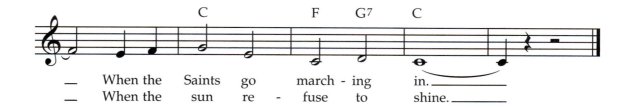

When the Saints go march - ing in._____
When the sun re - fuse to shine._____

Music Composition Exercise 12.15

Create a keyboard accompaniment for your own composition.

Glossary of Musical Terms

ACCIDENTAL Any sign that alters a note within a measure, that does not appear in the key signature. Once an accidental is marked, the note continues to be altered for the duration of the measure.

ANACRUSIS "An unstressed note or group of notes at the beginning of a phrase of music forming an upbeat" (*Oxford Dictionary of Musical Terms* p. 8).

ASYMMETRIC METER A meter that contains an uneven number of beats per measure. For example, $\frac{5}{4}$, $\frac{7}{4}$, $\frac{5}{8}$, and $\frac{7}{8}$.

AUGMENTED INTERVAL A perfect interval increased by a half step.

AUGMENTED TRIAD Consists of a major third between the root and the third of the triad, a major third between the third and the fifth, and an augmented fifth between the root and the fifth of the triad. In root position, the augmented triad consists of two superimposed thirds, the third formed by the lower two notes and the third formed by the upper two notes. The lower third is a major interval and the upper third is a major interval. An uppercase letter with a "+" or with "aug" indicates an augmented triad.

BAR LINE A vertical line always before a strong beat, used to mark off each measure with the exception of the first measure in a piece.

BASS CLEF, OR F CLEF Identifies the fourth line as F. This F is five notes below middle C on the piano. The bass clef normally indicates playing the keyboard with the left hand.

BEAT Basis for rhythm; a regular series of pulsations that divides a period of time into equal parts.

CHORD Three or more pitches produced at the same time; considered the building block of harmony in tonal music.

CHROMATIC HALF STEP A note that is a half step away but uses the same letter name; for example, C to C-sharp or A to A-flat.

CIRCLE OF FIFTHS "A graphic representation in the shape of a circle of keynotes with their signatures. C is at the top of the circle, from where the notes progress clockwise in ascending fifths. (Sharp keys move around the circle in a clockwise direction and flat keys in a counterclockwise direction.) At the bottom of the circle of fifths, the note F-sharp is called also by its enharmonic name G-flat and the same happens with the next note C-sharp/D-flat; the notes on the return to C are then called by their flat names" (*Oxford Dictionary of Musical Terms* p. 37).

COMPOUND INTERVAL An interval larger than an octave.

COMPOUND METER A meter in which the basic pulse is divided into three equal parts.

CONSONANCE "The quality inherent in an interval or chord which in a traditional tonal or modal context seems satisfactorily complete and stable in itself; opposite of dissonance" (*Oxford Dictionary of Musical Terms* p. 44).

DIMINISHED TRIAD Consists of a minor third between the root and the third of the triad, a minor third between the third and the fifth, and a diminished fifth between the root and the fifth of the triad. In root position, the diminished triad consists of two superimposed thirds, the third formed by the lower two notes and the third formed by the upper two notes. The lower third is a minor interval and the upper third is a minor interval. Indicated by adding "dim" or "°" to the root name, which is written in lowercase.

DISSONANCE "The quality of tension inherent in an interval or chord which in a traditional tonal or modal context involves a clash between adjacent notes of the scale and creates the expectation of resolution; opposite of consonance" (*Oxford Dictionary of Musical Terms* p. 37).

D.C. AL FINE *Da capo al fine* in Italian, meaning "from the head." This is an instruction provided at the end of the notation to go back to the beginning of a piece and play to the word *Fine* (end).

DIATONIC HALF STEP A note that is a half step away but uses a different letter name; for example, D to E-flat or E to F.

DOMINANT The fifth scale degree.

DOMINANT SEVENTH CHORD A four-note chord built on the fifth degree of a scale; it has the same structure in a major and in a minor tonality. In root position, a dominant seventh chord is a major chord with a minor seventh interval between the root and the seventh. This is called a Major-minor seventh chord. It is indicated with a ⁷ added to the chord name. In both a major and a minor tonality, a root-position dominant seventh chord consists of the fifth, seventh, second, and fourth scale degrees.

DOUBLE BAR LINE Indicates the end of a piece, of music or section. Two bar lines of equal width indicate the end of a large section of a piece, and one thin bar line followed by one thick bar line indicates the end of a piece of music.

DOUBLE FLAT (♭♭) Lowers the pitch by two half steps.

DOUBLE SHARP (𝄪) Raises the pitch by two half steps.

D.S. AL FINE *Dal segno al fine* in Italian, meaning that a passage is repeated not from the beginning of the composition but from the place marked by a *dal segno* sign. Return to the *dal segno* sign (𝄋) and perform to the end of the piece.

DUPLET   "A term used for two notes that are to be performed in the time of three. They are indicated by the figure '2' placed above or below the two notes" (*Oxford Dictionary of Musical Terms* p. 58). In compound meter the beat can be divided into two equal parts called a "duplet." Duplets appear as either two eighth notes with a "2" above, or two dotted eighth notes. We use the rhythm syllables *ta di*, borrowed from simple meter, to count a duplet.

DURATION   The length of time a sound lasts.

DYNAMICS   Refers to the varying degrees of loudness of a composition.

EIGHTH NOTE   A note made up of a note head, a stem, and a flag. The flag is always placed on the right of the stem.

ENHARMONIC SPELLING   Notating the same pitch with a different note name.

FIRST-INVERSION TRIAD   Will have the third of the chord in the bass.

FLAT SIGN (♭)   The musical symbol that indicates that a note has been lowered in pitch. On the keyboard, the black key immediately to the left and below a white key is named by adding a flat to the white-key name. Once a flat is indicated within a measure, it remains in effect for the remainder of the measure.

FORM   Describes the structure, architecture, or organization of a piece of music, indicated with letters.

FREQUENCY   "A ratio scale of measurement: each time pitch goes up by an octave, the frequency is doubled. The present international standard pitch A (above middle C) is equal to 440 Hz" (*Oxford Dictionary of Musical Terms* p. 140).

GRAND STAFF   The combination of the treble clef and the bass clef grouped together by a vertical line and a brace. Music for piano is written on the grand staff. Notes in the treble clef are generally played by the right hand and notes in the bass clef are generally played with the left hand. Middle C appears on a ledger line in the treble clef as well as in the bass clef.

HALF NOTE   A note made up of an empty note head and a stem.

HALF STEP   The smallest interval on the keyboard.

HARMONIC INTERVAL   Two pitches played simultaneously.

HARMONIC MINOR SCALE   A series of eight adjacent notes in which half steps occur between the second and third, fifth and sixth, and seventh and eighth degrees of the scale. All other steps are whole steps except for the one between degrees six and seven. When we write the pitches of "Ah Poor Bird" in ascending order and include *f*, we discover that these pitches labeled with solfège syllables are *d – r – me – f – s – le – t – d* or *l – t – d – r –m–f–si–la.–* respectively. We use the solfège syllable *si* to indicate that the seventh degree is raised a half step.

HARMONY   The simultaneous sounding of notes. "When a series of chords move horizontally in time" (*Oxford Dictionary of Musical Terms* p. 83).

HEXACHORD SCALE   A six-note section of a diatonic scale.

INTERVAL   The musical distance between two notes. The size of an interval is calculated by determining the distance between the first and the last pitch of an interval; adding the *quality* of the interval makes the designation more accurate and involves accidentals applied to pitches.

INVERSION   The reversal of the spatial relationship of the pitches; either moving the lower pitch of an interval up an octave or the upper pitch down an octave.

KEY   The relationship between notes in terms of a hierarchy of importance.

KEY SIGNATURE "A group of sharp or flat signs placed at the beginning of a composition (or after the clef) or during a composition (normally after a double bar) to indicate the key of the music that follows. By their positions on the staff the signs show which notes are to be consistently sharped or flattened throughout in all octaves, thus establishing the prevailing tonality of the music" (*Oxford Dictionary of Musical Terms* p. 95).

LEDGER LINES Short lines used to extend the staff above or below the five lines. The interchange of the line and space note names continues. Observe that notes can overlap between the clefs. Notes written as ledger lines in one clef can appear as notes on the staff in another clef. An octave sign (*8va...*) below a group of notes indicates that the notes are to be played one octave lower.

MAJOR HEXACHORD SCALE A series of six adjacent pitches or scale degrees, labeled $d - r - m - f - s - l$ or $1 - 2 - 3 - 4 - 5 - 6$.

MAJOR PENTACHORD SCALE A series of five adjacent tones ($d - r - m - f - s$) with a half step occurring between the third and fourth degrees.

MAJOR PENTATONIC SCALE Five pitches including a skip between the third and fourth degrees of the scale; if using solfège *m* skips to *s*. The solfège inventory of these pitches is $d - r - m - - s - l$, and the numbers are $1 - 2 - 3 - - 4 - 5$.

MAJOR SCALE A series of eight adjacent pitches using successive letter names; half steps occur between the third and fourth degrees and the seventh and first degrees of the scale. All other steps are whole steps. It is this pattern of half (m2) and whole steps (M2) that gives the major scale its particular configuration.

MAJOR TRIAD Consists of two superimposed thirds, a major third between the root and the third degree, and a minor third between the third and the fifth degree. There is a perfect fifth between the root and the fifth degree of the triad. In root position, the third of the triad is a note positioned a third above the root, and the fifth is a note positioned a fifth above the root.

MEDIANT Lies halfway between the tonic and dominant in a scale.

MELODIC INTERVAL Two pitches played one after the other.

MELODIC MINOR SCALE The melodic minor scale has an ascending form and a descending form. In the ascending form of the scale, the sixth and seventh degrees are raised; in the descending form these notes are lowered.

MELODY The result of the interaction of rhythm and pitch. "A succession of notes of varying pitch with an organized and recognized shape" (*Oxford Dictionary of Musical Terms* p. 109). It is composed of musical sounds that may be high or low.

MEASURES Mark each pattern of strong and weak beats. Also see **bar line**.

METER The regular grouping of beats that occur in patterns of strong (accented) and weak (unaccented). "The pattern of regular pulses (and the arrangement of their constituent parts) by which a piece of music is organized. One complete pattern is called a bar. The prevailing meter is identified at the beginning of a piece (and during it whenever it changes) by a time signature." (*Oxford Dictionary of Musical Terms* p. 110)

MINOR HEXACHORD SCALE Six adjacent pitches that are labeled with solfège syllables $l, - t, - d - r - m - f$ or numbers $1 - 2 - 3 - 4 - 5 - 6$.

MINOR PENTACHORD SCALE A series of five adjacent pitches with a half step occurring between the second and third degrees of the scale.

MINOR PENTATONIC SCALE Five pitches labeled with solfège syllables *l, – – d – r – m – – s.*

MINOR TRIAD Consists of a minor third between the root and the third degree; a major third between the third and fifth degrees; and a perfect fifth between the root and the fifth degree.

MOTIVE (MOTIF) "A short melodic or rhythmic idea, the smallest part of a theme or phrase to have a specific identity. A motif [motive] is the main building-block for themes and melodic lines, and brings unity and comprehensibility to a work through its repetition and varied occurrence" (*Oxford Dictionary of Musical Terms* p. 118).

NATURAL MINOR SCALE A series of eight adjacent pitches using successive letter names; half steps occur between the second and third degrees and fifth and sixth degrees of the scale. All other steps are whole steps. It is this pattern of half (m2) and whole steps (M2) that gives the minor scale its particular configuration. There are two different forms in addition to the natural minor melodic and harmonic.

NATURAL SIGN (♮) Used to cancel the preceding sharp or flat and remains in effect for the duration of the measure.

NOTATION A representation of the musical sounds we hear.

OCTAVE The relationship between two notes that are adjacent and have the same name; ex. from C to the next C on a keyboard is called an octave CDEFGABC

OCTAVE SIGN (8VA...) If placed above a group of notes, indicates that the notes are to be played one octave higher; if placed below indicates that the notes are to be played one octave lower.

PARALLEL MAJOR/MINOR When two keys share the same tonic note but different key signatures. For example, the relationship between the a minor and the A major scale.

PENTACHORD SCALE A five-note section of a diatonic scale.

PERFECT PITCH The ability to identify any note heard or to sing any note on demand without a pitch reference.

PHRASE "A musical unit defined by the interrelation of melody, rhythm, and harmony that ends with a cadence (a point of rest) of some kind...The length of a phrase varies, but is most frequently of four bars, often followed by an 'answering' phrase of the same length...The term 'phrasing' refers to the way in which a performer interprets both individual phrases and their combination in the piece as a whole." (*Oxford Dictionary of Musical Terms*, p. 139)

PHRASE MARK The arched line above a line of music that suggests a musical idea or the smallest complete musical idea. Marks the breath in a musical sentence.

PITCH "A characteristic of musical sound, which is the highness or lowness of a musical sound; a basic dimension of musical sounds, in which they are heard to be high or low" (*Oxford Dictionary of Musical Terms* p. 140).

QUARTER NOTE A note made up of a filled-in note head and a stem.

RELATIVE MAJOR/MINOR Both scales share the same pitch content or tone set and the same key signature. The relative minor scale begins on the sixth degree of the major scale, or three half steps (a minor third) below the tonic of the major scale. For example, a minor is the relative minor of C major.

RELATIVE PITCH   The ability to identify notes heard or to sing any note on demand when given the name of the starting pitch.

REPEAT SIGN   Always accompanied by double bar lines (||: :||). Appears at the beginning and end of a section of music that needs to be repeated. If the first measure of music is to be included in a repeat, then the repeat sign is omitted from the beginning of the composition.

REST   A symbol that represents the absence of sound. Rests may be counted silently using the rhythm syllables of the corresponding notes.

RHYTHM   "Perceptible organization of musical events in time" (*Oxford Dictionary of Musical Terms* p. 153). In other words, rhythms are different patterns of duration.

RHYTHM SYLLABLES   A system used to write rhythms that we hear in music. This book utilizes the *ta ka di mi* system with slight modifications; rhythm syllables relate to the number of sounds per beat.

RHYTHM NOTATION   A method for representing the number of actions in time that relate to the pulsation we call "beat"; represented by symbols referred to as "notes."

SCALE   "A sequence of notes ascending or descending stepwise" (*Oxford Dictionary of Musical Terms* p. 159).

SCALE DEGREE   The name that reflects a note's position in a scale.

SECOND-INVERSION TRIAD   Second-inversion triads will have the fifth in the bass.

SHARP SIGN (♯)   The musical symbol that indicates that a note has been raised in pitch. On the keyboard, the black key immediately to the right and above the white-key is named by adding a sharp to the white-key name. Once a sharp is indicated within a measure, it remains in effect for the remainder of the measure.

SIMPLE METER   A way to divide the pulse into two equal parts.

SOLFÈGE INVENTORY   A list of the solfège syllables written in ascending order.

SOLFÈGE SYLLABLES   A means for figuring out the relationships between the notes we hear.

STAFF   Made up of five lines and four spaces; the lines and spaces are always numbered from the bottom to the top.

SUBDOMINANT   The fourth scale degree; five notes, or degrees, below the tonic.

SYNCOPATION   "The displacement of the normal musical accent from a strong beat to a weak one" (*Oxford Dictionary of Musical Terms* p. 181); used extensively in jazz and rock music.

TEMPO   Refers to the speed of the beat.

TEXTURE   Refers to the number of individual instrumental or vocal parts a piece of music contains.

TIE   "A curved line in musical notation to join two successive notes of the same pitch, showing that they should form one sound lasting for the duration of their combined values" (*Oxford Dictionary of Musical Terms* p. 187).

TIMBRE   The tone quality of sound.

TONIC   Sometimes referred to as the "home note" or "keynote"; the most important note in a scale.

TREBLE CLEF, OR G CLEF   Identifies the second line on the staff as G, five notes above middle C. The treble clef normally indicates playing the keyboard with the right hand.

TRIAD A three-tone chord built in thirds composed of three notes: the root of the triad, the third of the triad, and the fifth of the triad; triads are composed of two superimposed thirds.

TRIAD INVERSION When a note other than the root of a triad appears in the bass, then the triad is inverted.

TRIPLET "Three notes performed in the time of two notes" (*Oxford Dictionary of Musical Terms* p. 394).

WHOLE NOTE A note made up of an empty note head.

WHOLE STEP The distance of two half steps on the keyboard.

Index

Audio CD Track List

Vocal	Piano
1 Are You Sleeping	34 Schumann: Little Study
2 Rocky Mountain	35 Paw Paw Patch
3 Beethoven: Violin Concerto, Theme	36 Mozart: Sonatina in C, Movement 2
4 Dinah	37 I–V–I Progression in Major
5 Ida Red	38 I–V–I Progression in Major
6 London Bridge	39 I–V–I Progression in Major
7 Birch Tree	40 Ah Poor Bird
8 Charlotte Town	41 i–V–i Progression in Minor
9 Canoe Song	42 i–V–i Progression in Minor
10 Hungarian Canon No. 1	43 i–V–i Progression in Minor
11 Twinkle, Twinkle, Little Star	44 White Sand and Gray Sand
12 Rocky Mountain	45 I–IV–V–I Progression in Major
13 Alleluia	46 I–IV–V–I Progression in Major
14 Row, Row, Row Your Boat	47 I–IV–V–I Progression in Major
15 Come, Let's Dance	48 Willum
16 Morning Is Come	49 i–iv–V–i Progression in Minor
17 Early to Bed	50 i–iv–V–i Progression in Minor
18 Little Partridge	51 i–iv–V–i Progression in Minor
19 Kis kece lányom	52 Bach: Chorale
20 Slovak Folk Song	53 Kuhlau: Sonatina in C Major Op. 55, No. 1, Movement 2
21 Gallows Pole	54 Ingegneri: Response
22 Variation on a Russian Folk Song	55 Mozart: The Marriage of Figaro (Excerpt)
23 Ah Poor Bird	56 Passing Tone
24 Louisiana Marching Song	57 Appoggiatura
25 French Canon	58 Neighbor Tone
26 Hey Ho Nobody Home	59 Haydn: Symphony No. 92 ("Oxford"), Movement 1
27 The Sailor's Alphabet	60 Supertonic Progression in Major
28 Cherubini: Canon	61 Supertonic Progression in Major
29 Vocal Exercise 1	62 Supertonic Progression in Minor
30 Vocal Exercise 2	63 Supertonic Progression in Minor
31 Vocal Exercise 3	64 Mozart: The Marriage of Figaro (Excerpt)
32 Vocal Exercise 4	65 Submediant Progression in Major
33 Vocal Exercise 5	66 Submediant Progression in Minor
	67 Beethoven: Sonatina in G Major, Movement 2
	68 Tonic Six-Four Progression in Major
	69 Tonic Six-Four Progression in Major
	70 Tonic Six-Four Progression in Major
	71 Tonic Six-Four Progression in Minor
	72 Tonic Six-Four Progression in Minor
	73 Tonic Six-Four Progression in Minor